RESIDENTIAL TREATMENT: A Tapestry of Many Therapies is a long awaited contribution to the difficult and misunderstood field of residential treatment as an effective form of out of home therapy for the severely disturbed child. Modeled o work of Forest Heights Lodge in Evergre hope and help to families and to professionals. Editor Vera Fahlberg, M.D., internationally respected pediatrician and psychotherapist who served for many years as medical director of Forest Heights Lodge, has interwoven the personal story of one family's experience with residential treatment with a clear description of the philolophy and program of the Lodge.

A variety of experts have offered their pre-publication praise for this book.

From Joseph H. Reid, retired Executive Director of the Child Welfare League of America, consultant on child welfare issues, and author, *Residential Treatment Centers for Emotionally Disturbed Children* . . .

This book is an essential tool for any parent seeking treatment for a severely disturbed child. It is equally valuable for any social worker, psychiatrist, or other professional charged with placing an emotionally disturbed child seeking to understand the basic principles of residential treatment.
Based on 35 years experience of one of the three or four best residential treatment centers in the United States, it can help the reader distinguish between good and poor programs and provides a sound model for those attempting to design new operations or improve old ones.

From Kathryn S. Donley, MSW, social welfare worker, supervisor and administrator focused mainly on issues of adoption and foster care now serving as trainer/consultant for the National Resource Center for Special Needs Adoption . . .

This book describes for the field the particular approach of Forest Heights Lodge and offers a few bonuses besides. I am delighted that specific suggestions are offered about how parents and professional helpers can approach making a decision about whether or not out-of-home care is necessary. For families struggling with a youngster whose history is fraught with traumatic separations, this decision is one of the most difficult they will ever make. This book provides parents (all kinds of parents—birth parents, adoptive parents, foster parents) and members of their extended families with an organized way to understand the need for residential treatment and what to look for as treatment unfolds. Information is empowering and this book is packed with information—not just about the program at Forest Heights Lodge—but about bewilderment and pain, recognition and investment, hard work and hope. Through it all runs a common sense thread (not "this is how it must be done" but "this is how we do it and why.") Very appealing approach.

From Edwin Millard, past president and life fellow of the American Association of Residential Centers, a director of residential treatment programs for 36 years and current Chief Executive Officer of Children's Home and Aid Society of Illinois . . .

RESIDENTIAL TREATMENT will be extremely important to education, mental health, and social service professionals making referrals to residential care and to parents. Too often referrals to residential treatment are made out of desperation when all else fails but with little understanding of why residential treatment may work. This book's greatest strength is in conveying to those who don't know what residential treatment is a clear understanding of this alternative.

From William W. Baak, M.D., senior staff consultant on Child and Family Psychiatry, Children's Hospital and Health Center of San Diego and clinical associate professor of Child Psychiatry at UCSD School of Medicine . . .

RESIDENTIAL TREATMENT: A Tapestry of Many Therapies is a story book, a textbook and a consumer's guide to residential treatment all in one. It is woven from the life history and the story of the treatment of a brave little boy, Kenny, and his parents, giving a dramatic sense of the sweat and dedication of an authentic staff, and is patterned by the wisdom of the visionary pioneers who founded Forest Heights Lodge.

Although highly instructive and guiding in principle, this is not a glib "how to do it" book, but rather one which describes what one should be trying to do with a program of milieu treatment. As life is not simple, parts of this book are not either. But the story, the teachings and the philosophy of treatment are presented in plain language, offering instruction to child therapists as well as to parents. This story of a treatment program offers a lively challenge to the current often short-sighted and therefore expensive doctrine of "brief intervention for everything."

From Bonnie Harlow, adoptive parent advocate and one of the founders of Dallas Council on Adoptable Children . . .

I am thrilled with the prospect of this manual! Parents are absolutely desperate for this kind of guide to help equip them for making decisions regarding out-of-home placement for their child. My years of experience with parents nationwide lead me to believe that most parents have no means for seeking help with these decisions. They either end up at the psychiatric hospital admissions out of sheer fear and frustration or the counselors they ask for help are themselves inadequately trained or experienced in placement needs and options and are therefore unable to help these parents.

From G.A. Orsund, MSW, director of the Myron Stratton Home . . .

This book is a very in-depth look at a residential treatment center which over the years has developed a highly effective treatment approach for severely emotionally disturbed children. The book will be a valuable resource for parents contemplating residential treatment, as well as trying to more fully understand their role in the treatment process. As well, educators, clinicians, administrators, and, importantly, child care workers, will appreciate the therapeutic value and effectiveness of such a carefully integrated and cohesive therapeutic millieu.

Kenny, his family, and many others have been fortunate to have discovered Forest Heights Lodge.

RESIDENTIAL TREATMENT
A TAPESTRY OF MANY THERAPIES

RESIDENTIAL TREATMENT

A TAPESTRY OF MANY THERAPIES

Contributing authors:
Russ Colburn, M.S.W.
Glen Lein
Vera Fahlberg, M.D.
John McGovern, M.S.W.
Ray Curtis, M.S.W.
Carol Benedict, M.Ed.
Linda Clefisch, M.S.W.
J. G. Benedict, Ph.D.
Bernie Mayer, M.S.W.
Reggie Gray, M.S.W.

Edited by Vera Fahlberg, M.D.

Perspectives Press
P.O. Box 90318
Indianapolis, IN 46290-0318

Perspectives Press
P.O. Box 90318
Indianapolis, IN 46290-0318

Manufactured in the United States of America
ISBN 0-944934-02-1

On the Cover:
From the workshop of Karel van Mander, Belgium (1579-1623), a tapestry titled *Anthony Catches a Salted Fish*, ca. 1640. The detail is from the waist area of the seated woman, lower right section of the tapestry.

Both photographs used by permission:
© 1990 Indianapolis Museum of Art, Gift of Mr. and Mrs. Herman C. Krannert.

Library of Congress Cataloging-in-Publication Data

Residential treatment : a tapestry of many therapies / edited by
  Vera Fahlberg.
    p.   cm.
    ISBN 0-944934-02-1 : $24.95
    1. Child psychotherapy--Residential treatment.   I. Fahlberg,
  Vera.
    (DNLM: 1. Affective Disorders--in infancy & childhood--case
  studies.   2. Affective Disorders--rehabilitation--case studies.
  3. Residential Treatment.   WS 350.2 R433)
  RJ504.5.R47   1990
  618.92'8914--dc20
  DNLM/DLC
  for Library of Congress   90-6790
                                                                        CIP

To the Lodge boys and their families

To Lodge staff, past and present

To the community of Evergreen

C O N T E N T S

Introduction   9

Chapter 1   21
    Selecting a Placement
Chapter 2   45
    Philosophy
Chapter 3   67
    Organizational and Staffing Structure
Chapter 4   91
    Before Admission
Chapter 5   127
    Milieu
Chapter 6   185
    Education
Chapter 7   213
    Working with Families
Chapter 8   245
    Individual and Group Therapy
Chapter 9   281
    Discharge Planning and Follow-Up

Glossary   307

Index   311

Introduction

A disturbed child
lives in a world which is not quite
the same as the one in which we live.
When we are sad, he is desperate.
When the usual reaction is anger, he is
lost in uncontrollable rage.
When we are happy and content, he is
explosively ecstatic.
When we fear, he disregards danger or has
fears so magnified that he withdraws
completely rather than face them.

Henry Swartwood
Founder, Forest Heights Lodge

Residential treatment centers are like rich tapestries. Each is a unique intricate interweaving of the various threads that comprise the component parts of treatment. This book is an attempt to provide mental health professionals and lay people alike with a further understanding of the various aspects that come together to form a comprehensive residential treatment center.

Residential treatment provides a variety of services under one roof. Individual therapy, family therapy, academic remediation, recreational therapy, and peer group socialization skills can all be provided in an environment which encourages the development of close interpersonal relationships which resemble family life. Although each of these services, except for the daily living environment, can be provided by various out-patient facilities, it is difficult to achieve the same level of effectiveness when services are offered by providers who work within differing philosophical and administrative frameworks. In residential care all of these services are provided in one facility, thereby maximizing the potential of milieu therapy, which is the heart of residential treatment.

The milieu is the daily environment of structure and interactions. The child is immersed in his surroundings. He responds on a continual basis. More importantly, it is the arena in which an ongoing effort toward making the child's life more gratifying can be made by all adults. Interactions surrounding simple daily tasks such as getting dressed, enjoying a meal, or playing a game all become part of the therapeutic arena with the potential for helping the child alter his perceptions of himself and his relationships. In a residential facility, the milieu is the setting in which trust between adults and children grows. It is this trust that will provide the foundation for change and growth. Milieu therapy is not a group of isolated concepts. It is here that the rich, colorful tapestry, this time created by the interweaving of the varied aspects of the group living process, becomes most apparent.

Although the milieu is the unique aspect of residential work, all other parts of the program are equally important. The way that the specific elements are interwoven gives residential treatment its advantage over similar services provided by a variety of different agencies. Attention to detail in the blending of the component strands enhances the overall result. In effect, the total becomes greater than the sum of the individual parts.

The first chapter looks at identifying those children who might benefit from placement in a residential treatment center and selecting a center. It is written primarily for those referring families for treatment and for parents. In the remainder of this book we will explore each of the component parts of residential treatment in detail. A center's philosophy is the background against which all the richly colored threads will be woven. It provides the substance to the overall fabric. The second chapter focuses on this. Administrative style and staff selection either lend strength to the philosophy or weaken it. Staff cannot do their work without a supportive administration that is built on a sound financial base. The third chapter addresses this area.

Direct patient services from the first pre-placement contact to post-discharge planning and supportive services provide the threads for the remainder of the book. The complex interweaving of these

strands leads to the individual character of each residential center.
Each facility has its own style, philosophy, and culture. However, by looking at one center in detail we hope that readers may gain ideas as to ways to create, enhance, implement, or assess other programs. A section at the end of each chapter provides readers with questions to guide them in gaining information about and assessing residential facilities.

By using our center, Forest Heights Lodge in Evergreen, Colorado, as an example, we will look at how these various strands come together to create a unique whole. A case example is used to translate theory to practice as we describe what happens in residential treatment from beginning to end. The case chosen is nearly ideal. We recognize this. We believe that only by completely understanding what one wants ideally to do can we realistically formulate good plans for alternate circumstances. Not all of the services provided for Kenny and his family are necessary, or possible, in all cases. On the other hand, some children may need some additional services not indicated in the case example. We have tried to use a variety of types of cases as individual examples in the various chapters. Our goal is to provide individualized services for each of our residents.

Forest Heights is located in the community of Evergreen, Colorado, thirty miles west of Denver in the foothills of the Rocky Mountains. Because the Lodge was started when Evergreen was just a quiet little village, it has been able to develop a singular relationship with the town as both have grown together. It is looked upon as an integral part of the community, with the children being accepted by the townspeople as a whole, by neighbors, and by the schools. The boys are visible about town, utilizing the recreational facilities, public schools, visiting the various shops, and attending local events such as the rodeo and Mountain Rendezvous.

Prior to founding Forest Heights in 1955, Hank and Claire Swartwood had been involved, with others, in establishing Secret Harbor Farm, a residential treatment center in the San Juan Islands in Puget Sound. Migrating to Colorado Springs with seven severely disturbed boys, for a time they operated Pikeview House. Forced to find a new location, they camped temporarily above Georgetown, Colorado, at 10,000 feet in the still wintry month of April. By fortuitous accident they located the present property and settled in Evergreen that spring.

The camping experience in the cold and snow helped to reinforce their belief that the most important ingredient in the successful treatment of emotionally disturbed children is the development of close interpersonal relationships. This concept remains the cornerstone of the Lodge's treatment philosophy today.

The Swartwoods provided the parenting and therapeutic milieu. Hank and Claire were with the boys twenty-four hours a day as

12   parents, teachers, therapists. Their only help were a part-time cleaning lady and a part-time psychiatric consultant. In addition to being the mother surrogate,[N] Claire provided the boys' education. Hank was not only responsible for being the father figure, he was also active in the community, from the beginning creating acceptance by neighbors and the community as a whole. Hank was an intelligent, philosophical, and charismatic man who had the intuitive ability to work with these children. Claire, on the other hand, provided the structure and attention to detail necessary for the successful daily functioning. Although neither of them was professionally trained, they had read extensively, so that they were able to incorporate not only their intuitive approach, but also a psychodynamic formulation into their therapy approach and they soon found themselves accepted by the professional community in Denver.

As they added more boys to the program they also started adding part time help, primarily graduate students at the University of Denver who functioned as relief child care workers. However, it was Hank and Claire who remained the primary therapeutic agents at the Lodge. Eventually their intense day-to-day involvement took its toll.

Hank developed health problems that made it impossible for them to continue. While a graduate student at the University of Denver, I had been a relief child care worker. When the Swartwoods realized that they must leave the Lodge, they asked me to come back as Director, a position I have held since May 1963. By that time there were 17 boys in residence. Because of how the program evolved and the physical configuration of the residence, the in-patient program continues to be for boys only.[N] However, the same philosophy, implemented in the same ways, could be applied to co-ed programs.

Because of our location, we are able not only to utilize the mountains for many activities such as skiing, hiking, camping, and fishing, but we are also able to take advantage of the cultural and recreational facilities available in Denver.

A private, non-profit facility, Forest Heights is governed by a fifteen member board of trustees, people from the community of Evergreen. An auxiliary, The Friends of Forest Heights Lodge, is also comprised primarily of Evergreen residents. In 1974 Forest Heights became accredited by the Joint Commission for Accreditation of Healthcare Organizations as a Psychiatric Facility for Children and Adolescents.[N]

Although there have been refinements and additions to the program, the philosophy that Hank and Claire developed remains the foundation of our treatment. The strong commitment to intense interpersonal relationships determines staffing patterns, efforts to keep consistency and continuity in staff, work with families, and administrative policies as well as guiding the nature of the relationships between staff members. It pervades the atmosphere at all levels.

Currently, 23 boys at a time reside in the residential program. The average length of stay for boys at Forest Heights is two years. In some cases the child stays longer, in others he is ready for discharge prior to two years. Rather than enlarge the residential program, Forest Heights has chosen to expand services by developing an out-patient clinic and a broad range of consultation and training services.[N] In addition to impacting the lives of many additional children and their families in this manner, staff members who do training are exposed to the ideas of others in the mental health field. These experiences stimulate growth and change in the Lodge program itself.

Many people contributed to this book. Key contributors for the basic material are listed at the beginning of each chapter. Special mention must be made of Vera Fahlberg, M.D., who was Medical Director of Forest Heights Lodge thoughout the entire conceptual process and early writing stages of this book. Not only is she a major contributor to the text, but I can safely say that this book might never have been completed without her comprehensive skills. After she left her position as Medical Director in 1987, she organized and re-wrote the manuscript extensively, producing the cohesive whole. She also created the case history which adds continuity and depth to the text.

To help readers better understand the roles of various staff members, a copy of the organizational chart is provided in Figure 1. A brief description of the various tasks done by various staff is provided in an addendum to Figure 1. This will help the reader identify people mentioned in Kenny's case. Because there has been a core group of administrative and clinical staff who have worked together for a number of years, current job descriptions have evolved rather than being described from the outset.

In writing this book we have chosen to use the male pronoun in describing children needing services. We do this not to be discriminatory or judgemental, only to simplify the presentation. We certainly realize that girls, too, need and deserve good services. At the end of each chapter there is a section of notes and elaborations relating to material presented in the chapter. Concepts that are included in the notes have an "N" notation within the text. There is also a glossary at the end of the volume which explains some of the terms used throughout the text.

We hope that this book will help both parents and professionals formulate the questions they need to ask and assist them in making observations during their search for an appropriate placement. We hope that it will help those in the field of residential treatment reassess and fine-tune their individual programs. The process of writing this has helped us do just that.

Russ Colburn, Executive Director

14

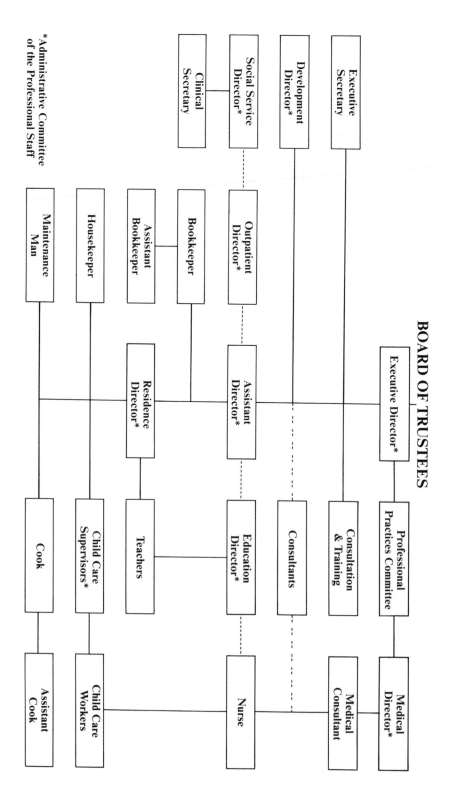

BOARD OF TRUSTEES

Executive Secretary

Development Director*

Social Service Director*

Clinical Secretary

Executive Director*

Professional Practices Committee

Consultation & Training

Consultants

Medical Director*

Medical Consultant

Outpatient Director*

Bookkeeper

Assistant Bookkeeper

Housekeeper

Maintenance Man

Assistant Director*

Residence Director*

Education Director*

Teachers

Child Care Supervisors*

Cook

Nurse

Child Care Workers

Assistant Cook

*Administrative Committee of the Professional Staff

Executive Director, Russ Colburn, MSW: responsibility for all aspects of the program; keeper of the philosophy; enforcer of parameters; final decision maker on all contended issues; responsibility for identifying long-term course of the Lodge; responsibility for implementing policies determined by board; responsibility, along with the Board, for insuring adequate funding; guarantor that all personnel are of high quality; coordinator of admission decisions with upcoming discharge planning; trainer/ consultant; advocate for children's services, working with community, state and national organizations.

Medical Director, Jules M. Kluger, M.D. Child Psychiatrist: overseer of all medical decisions; participant in treatment planning for all in-patients; responsibility for evaluating in-patients on an ongoing basis; therapist; responsibility for peer-review; source for translating psychoanalytic concepts into actions and activities for child care staff use with residents.[N]

Assistant Director, Glen Lien: overall responsibility for in-patient program; model for and trainer of child care workers; relief child care worker; anchor in the Lodge, with office there rather than in the administration building; participant with boys on a daily basis; planning coordinator and orchestrator of the milieu; responsibility for building and grounds; budget planner and overseer; liaison with families; morning meeting leader; resource person at Board meetings.

Residence Director, John McGovern, MBA, MSW: child care worker and supervisor; direct daily participant with boys; child care shift coordinator; liaison with families in conjunction with assistant director; therapist with individuals and groups; liaison with Friends of Forest Heights.

Social Services Director, Ray Curtis, MSW: responsibility for developing and writing policies and procedures; responsibility for clinical records and quality assurance; individual and family therapist; trainer/consultant; supervisor of graduate students.[N]

Education Director, Carol Benedict, M. Ed.: overall responsibility for school; selector and supervisor of other teachers; teacher; source for staff and parents in understanding how learning strengths and weaknesses affect all areas of the child's functioning; coordinator with assistant director of integrated functioning of school and milieu; responsibility for educational assessments; co-leader for activity group; trainer/consultant.

Out-patient Director, Linda Clefisch, MSW: out-patient therapist; responsibility for out-patient records; in-patient therapist; makes pre-admission home visits in most cases; initial liaison with families; liaison to therapists in home communities; arts and crafts coordinator and teacher; trainer/consultant.

Consulting Psychologist, J. G. Benedict, Ph.D: participant in treatment planning for all residents; responsibility for psychological testing; individual and family therapist; interpreter, translating theory into practice.

Consulting Psychiatrist, Joyce Borelli, M.D.: individual and family therapist; specialist on developmental issues.

Consulting Physician, Ronald Jendry, M.D.: responsibility for admission physicals; responsibility for ongoing medical care of residents; liaison with any medical specialists who are seeing residents.

Nurse, Kristin Rushford, R.N.: overseer of medical care of residents; responsibility for scheduling medical and dental appointments and accompanying boys to these appointments; supervisor of administering medications; supervisor of infection control.

Child Care Workers: re-parenters of the residents; providers of psychological nurturing, limit setting, role models; planners and implementers of a wide variety of activities with residents; teachers of self-care, social and daily living skills; participants in individual and family therapy sessions; participants in treatment planning for all children; persons most knowledgeable about each boy's behaviors; assistants in leading various therapy groups.

Child Care Shift Leaders, one worker on each shift: responsibility for overall supervision of milieu during his/her shift; responsibility for minute-by-minute happenings in milieu; coordinators for smooth shift transition.

Teachers: instructors of academic subjects, shop, and physical education; relief child care workers one night per week and during school vacations; active participants in milieu before and after school; participants in group outings such as camping and skiing; sharers of their special interests and talents with the boys.

Development and Public Relations, Maryanna Ware: public relations and publicity coordinator; special events coordinator, with Board members; responsibility for fundraising; newsletter editor; provides assistance to other staff in editing and proofreading their writings; copyeditor and editorial assistant for this book.

Administrative Committee (highlighted on Figure 1): meets weekly to coordinate program areas; decision makers on issues that need input from a variety of people; information sharers; admission and discharge planners; quality assurance monitors, including utilization review and patient care.

The Professional Practices Committee, comprised of well qualified volunteer professionals from the disciplines of child psychiatry, psychology, social work, and education, primarily from the Denver metropolitan area, meet with administrative and professional staff of the Lodge on a periodic basis. They are used both as a sounding board and in an advisory capacity if changes in the program are contemplated. In addition if the board has questions about the program or the professional staff, this committee is available to them for consultation.

Notes and Elaborations

pg. 12　Mother surrogate: someone who takes on the roles usually performed by mothers—a mother substitute.

pg. 12　When Forest Heights was started in 1952, few girls were being placed in residential care. It started as a facility serving only boys. Although there would be some advantages to opening the program to girls as well, after weighing all of the pros and cons we have decided to remain a resource for males only. It would be difficult to provide adequate physical facilities for both sexes within the one building in which all of our residents are housed.

pg. 12　Recognizing the need for in-patient treatment resources based on a different, less restrictive and less costly model than that used by psychiatric hospitals, in 1974 the Joint Commission for Accreditation of Healthcare Organizations developed a series of guidelines for services and an accreditation process which facilities may volunteer to participate in. Some health insurance plans will pay for placement in JCAHO accredited facilities.

pg. 13　In the late 1970's the board and administrative staff spent considerable time deciding on long range goals for FHL. A variety of options including starting a second facility for girls; adding further units in the present locale; adding a day treatment program, etc. were deliberated. However, it was finally decided that FHL would continue to provide only the one in-patient unit, but would expand by increasing out-patient services and developing a training and consultation program. Via the latter we have had an opportunity to impact children's services not only in terms of residential care, but also in the child welfare system and out-patient mental health services.

18   pg. 15   At the time Kenny was at the Lodge Vera Fahlberg, M.D., was Medical Director. As a full time employee with a pediatric background she had additional tasks including those currently done by the consulting pediatrician and nurse. She also saw outpatients and did training and consultation. Currently she does only training and consultation for the Lodge.

        pg. 15   Students from a variety of programs ranging from undergraduate social work, to graduate degrees in social work, psychology, and education, as well as psychiatric residents have done some of their practical experience at Forest Heights. In addition, we have had mental health and social service professionals from other countries spend anywhere from a few days to several months in training at the Lodge.

C O N T E N T S

Selecting a Placement

Kenny's Case   21
Beginning Steps   28
Who Needs Placement   29
What Kind of Placement   31
Types of Therapeutic Placements   35
Therapeutic Placement as an Assessment Tool   37
Looking for Places   38
Guide for Parents   41
Conclusion   41
Notes and Elaborations   43

Primary Contributor Vera Fahlberg, M.D.

Selecting a Placement

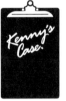

With a sigh of relief Martha replaced the telephone and poured another cup of tea. She had found excuse after excuse to postpone making the call until John, her husband, had become totally exasperated with her. She knew that if she delayed one more day, John would become really angry. Actually, she didn't know why. He could have made the call just as well. In fact, she knew that deep inside she had strong feelings about the fact that John always left such matters to her. Of course, she wouldn't confront him about this directly. Speaking up for herself was difficult for Martha.

As she drank her tea, she reviewed the telephone conversation. In spite of many rehearsals it had gone much differently than she had expected. Luckily it had not been nearly as difficult as she had imagined. The person who had answered the telephone had been friendly and reassuring. While she was talking with the secretary, the person in charge of admissions had walked in and was able to take Martha's call.

Martha had tried to explain the situation with her son, Kenny. Mr. Colburn seemed to understand. He had already reviewed the information sent by Dr. Jorgenson. He indicated that he thought Kenny might be appropriate for admission to Forest Heights Lodge. Mr. Colburn had then asked some further questions about Kenny's behaviors both at school and at home. Although he asked some questions about the family, he had not asked the kinds of questions asked by others in the past—questions which had made her feel both guilty and defensive. Oh, well, she supposed these would come later, when she and John went to Evergreen to visit.

Since Dr. Jorgenson had recommended that the Summers contact more than one residential treatment center, Mr. Colburn suggested that she and John come first without Kenny. Then, if everyone agreed that this might be an appropriate placement, another visit, this time with Kenny, would be scheduled. Martha liked this idea. It would give her a chance to see what the facility looked like and what type of boys were there before she tried to prepare Kenny for his visit. He knew they were considering residential treatment, but he always asked so many questions about new situations and became so hyperactive and angry if she couldn't answer them.

On the other hand, she wasn't certain how John would feel about making two trips to Colorado. It was a five hundred mile trip. That meant it would be costly both in terms of money and time. John always seemed to be so busy with his business. Taking time from work would probably bother him even more than the money. It was difficult for her to be certain about his reaction when it came to things relating to Kenny and his problems. One time John would show great concern and caring. The next he would seem frustrated that she had bothered him with the problems.

His reactions made it more difficult for her. Were they doing the right thing to even consider residential treatment? Dr. Jorgenson seemed to believe that it was absolutely necessary. She was less certain whether the doctor who had evaluated Kenny at the Medical Center felt the same way. Initially, when she and John had taken Kenny for the three week evaluation, this doctor had indicated that he didn't think that the problem was very serious. In fact, the young resident had seemed to imply that if only she could be more firm and consistent with Kenny there probably would be no problems. Well, he had learned what consistency and firmness accomplished with Kenny, hadn't he? She had to admit that she was nearly relieved when, after the evaluation, she had learned that Kenny had literally torn apart the ward. On one occasion it had taken three people to control him enough to give him a shot to calm him down. On the other hand, she did not like to think of Kenny having to be sedated so that adults could manage him. At any rate, the hospital staff had concurred that residential treatment was *probably* necessary.

Martha had sensed for a long time that Kenny had problems. Even as a baby he had seemed different. He was a fussier infant than her others had been. At first she had thought that maybe she just noticed it more because she was older. However, when she held Kenny and tried to rock him, something she had really enjoyed with her other children, he constantly squirmed and pulled away from her. In fact, if she really thought about it, maybe there had been indications of problems even before he was born. First of all she had been older, 39, when she got pregnant with Kenny. Then she had had many minor problems. She certainly had been tired a lot and somewhat depressed during the pregnancy.

She and John had originally planned to have three children. However, long before she became pregnant with Kenny they had reconciled themselves to having only two. When Kenny was born John Jr. was 14 and Sarah was 12. It wasn't as though they hadn't tried to have a third child earlier. In truth, it was the fact that they had tried and had been unsuccessful that made it such a surprise when she had, after all those years, become pregnant.

At first, she thought she was starting menopause early. Then when she had some spotting she was concerned that maybe she had cancer. Because of her fears she put off going to the doctor for several weeks. When the physician said he thought she was pregnant she didn't know whether to laugh or to cry. When the pregnancy test confirmed his suspicions, she continued to be ambivalent. Briefly, thoughts of abortion crossed her mind, but she knew she would never be able to follow through with this course of action. John had, surprisingly, been very excited about the prospect of a baby, verbalizing his desire to have another son.

At any rate, in spite of the early pregnancy problems, Kenny had been very active in the later months of pregnancy. In fact he was so active that it had been difficult for her to get much sleep. The delivery had gone well. The minute he was born Kenny had let it be known that he had a fine pair of lungs. For that matter, he had continued to this day to let them know that, whatever other problems he might have, there was nothing wrong with his vocal cords.

His course in the hospital immediately after birth seemed normal. They were discharged after the usual three days. Both J.J., as the family called John Jr., and Sarah doted over Kenny initially, although they too got tired of his fussing and crying. Martha, feeling that everyone else in the family needed their sleep because of work and school expectations, would stay up for hours at night trying to comfort Kenny, hoping that the fussing would stop and that he would fall asleep. But it seemed that nothing she tried worked. She realized that the more frustrated she got the more Kenny seemed to cry. When she consulted the pediatrician, he seemed to infer that if only she would relax everything would be fine. "You try and relax with a baby who fusses from 5:00 p.m. until 3:00 a.m.," she had wanted to say to him. But of course she said nothing and thought that probably he was right. It was her fault. In some way she was not measuring up as a mother.

Part of her believed that and part of her really did not accept it. The other children were doing pretty well. Well, she knew that they depended on her more than some of their friends seemed to depend on their parents. But then, she had always been home to do things for them and they had come to expect it. It was true that they weren't asked to do much around the house. Even when Kenny was a toddler and she was exhausted from running after him all day, she had hesitated to ask other family members to help at all. That had been the worst period of her life. Kenny had learned to walk early—at ten and a half months— and instead of walking, he was running constantly, usually away from her. She remembered his toddler years as ones when he was constantly on the go, into everything. She had not wanted to put so many things up where he couldn't reach them but had found it to be absolutely necessary. He was so curious about everything.

Even as a one year old he had been stubborn. Thinking back, Martha could remember frequent battles with Kenny when she had tried to dress him. He would not stay still and it had been so difficult to try and put clothes on him with him bouncing around. She had stuck him with the diaper pins more than once. With the others, if she had tried to distract them or had given them a toy to play with they would calm down, but not Kenny. Nothing had seemed to work at that stage.

At least it had not been difficult to wean him from the bottle. He had thrown it out of the crib one day when he was ten months old. After that he refused to take a bottle even if it was offered. Toilet training had been more difficult. For the longest time, Kenny refused to have his bowel movements in the potty chair. He would wait until she took him off the chair and then would promptly go. Sometimes he would have his bowel movement during nap time and more than once Martha had entered his room to find feces smeared all over the walls. Those were the times when she had spanked him harder than she had ever spanked either of the others. She still felt guilty about that. Eventually, Kenny had learned to use the toilet most of the time. There were intermittent problems with bedwetting until he was seven and, even now, at age nine, he sometimes soiled his underpants, but it was infrequent.

When Kenny was a toddler, Martha tried joining a Mother's Day Out group. The other mothers complained that Kenny was too difficult to keep track of and that he would hit and bite the other children "for no reason." In fact, there was nearly a year in there when she and John rarely went out at all because of problems getting a babysitter.

From the time Kenny started pre-school at age three it was apparent that there were going to be school problems. He wouldn't mind the teachers. He had difficulty getting along with the other children. They went through three pre-schools in a year's time before they found one which did not ask for his removal. The teachers at this pre-school had recognized there were problems but they were sympathetic. By the time he was four and a half they were recommending that he see a therapist. Up until that time John had certainly minimized Kenny's problems. He always left it to Martha to handle school contacts and to arrange for sitters. When the school recommended therapy, John was initially angry. He was certain there was really nothing wrong. "Kenny is just all boy," he would say. "I can't

Martha smiled, remembering when John first recognized how difficult it was to be with Kenny all day. Shortly after Kenny turned 5, Martha's father was very ill. It was summer and John had insisted that between the older two children and himself they could take care of Kenny while Martha was gone for a week. Well, it took only three days before John was on the phone to her complaining about Kenny's behavior. He had planned to do some work at home that week but had found it to be virtually impossible with Kenny constantly running through the house screaming.

Then there had been the incident with the neighbor's cat. They had found Kenny twirling it around by the tail, while laughing. That uproar had really interrupted John's work. He also had found that bedtimes didn't go smoothly. No matter who put Kenny to bed he would procrastinate on getting ready and then would come out repeatedly with excuses such as needing a drink or to go to the bathroom. John had tried being very firm and putting him back in bed. Kenny had "wailed" for four hours non-stop. For the first time, John seemed to have some understanding of what Martha was putting up with day in and day out and why she would lie down with Kenny when he went to bed until he fell asleep.

When Kenny was five, they had sought help from the local mental health clinic. One person was seeing Kenny in play therapy while another worked with Martha on behavior management techniques. Martha never was quite certain as to what went on during Kenny's contacts with his therapist. She asked repeatedly and always received vague answers. She knew that she certainly did not feel part of his therapy. She also knew that although the person she was working with had some good ideas, things that Martha knew would have worked with her other children, clearly this woman didn't really know or understand what it was like to live with Kenny.

During this period Kenny was in kindergarten and first grade. There were problems at school. The kindergarten teacher was in her second year of teaching. She seemed totally overwhelmed by Kenny. Because of his aggressive outbursts when he was frustrated, she didn't ask anything of him. She just tried to keep him happy. Although he seemed bright enough in many areas, Kenny was not learning his letters and numbers as the other children were. Martha recognized that this probably was because he never stayed in one place long enough to learn anything. He had few friends because of his aggressive outbursts with classmates. He and one other boy who was also identified as having emotional problems alternately were best friends and bitter enemies.

In first grade Kenny had an experienced teacher who set firm limits. Initially she had seemed certain that she and Kenny would get along fine and that the previous problems would not exist in her classroom. However, at the November parent-teacher conference, she indicated that there were severe problems. Kenny would not stay in his seat. He was always talking out in class. He teased others incessantly and if they tried, in any way, to stand up for themselves or teased him back he would physically explode, lashing out at them while crying, "Nothing is fair." In spite of his conduct he did seem to be learning. Reading was easier for him than math. This discrepancy became more pronounced as the school year progressed. Kenny became very frustrated with math even if the aide worked with him one on one. By mid-year, the teacher was able to predict that Kenny would disrupt the class when it was time for his group to have arithmetic. Nothing seemed to work for this problem. She tried sending him out in the hall; sending him to the office; keeping his desk close to hers; having him sit in the back of the room by himself; offering a star reward for acceptable behavior. Nothing worked.

Kenny had no friends. On the rare occasions that he was not confined to his classroom for lunch because of misbehaviors, he sat by himself in the cafeteria. When he did get to go out to recess he was constantly involved in hassles. He refused to wait his turn and would bully others. Again, if someone started bullying him, he would burst into tears.

With increasing school problems and no change in his behaviors at home, the family had decided that they should switch therapists. Martha had been doing a lot of reading about children with problems and was wondering if Kenny was hyperactive and if dietary changes or medication would help. She consulted with Kenny's pediatrician who referred her to a local developmental specialist.

This doctor, after taking a careful history and seeing Kenny for a physical examination suggested that he was indeed hyperactive and recommended that he be placed on Ritalin.[N] Martha and John were both hopeful that this approach would solve Kenny's problems and, in turn, theirs. At first, Kenny had seemed calmer and the teacher noted a positive change in his behavior at school. However, after a month or two all of the old behaviors had returned. During the remainder of his first grade year attempts were made to increase the dosage of Ritalin with the hope that it might again make a difference. Before this could be accomplished, school was out for the summer. John and Martha had never noted marked behavioral changes at home while he was on Ritalin so it was hard to tell if the changing doses were having any real impact.

When Kenny started second grade, the doctor again tried to find a dosage of Ritalin that would make a difference. When this didn't occur he tried Dexedrine. However, Kenny's sleep problems increased markedly with this medication, and his appetite, which had always been reasonably good, became very poor. He was losing weight. With

that, another control issue emerged between Martha and Kenny as she
tried to insure that he ate enough. If anything, his hyperactivity seemed
to escalate on the Dexedrine, so that by Christmas he was taken off
all medications.

Academically, he was falling further behind, but the teachers
and school principal were attributing this to his continuing behavioral
problems. They were discussing the possibility of placing him in
a special classroom for emotionally disturbed children. This
recommendation was quite frightening for John and Martha. They
could not see how having Kenny in a classroom with other problem
children, who would be even more likely to provoke his outbursts,
could possibly help. He already had difficulty making friends. It didn't
seem to them that placement with other "problem children" would help
his peer problems. They were also concerned that there would be so
many disruptions in such a classroom that the likelihood of any
academic learning would be low.

By March, Kenny was approaching his eighth birthday and
nothing was getting better. The older children were both in college.
Martha was becoming more and more depressed as she struggled
through week after week of problems with Kenny and conferences with
upset school personnel. Kenny was being shunned by more and more
of the children and adults in the neighborhood. He was never invited to
birthday parties or other neighborhood activities. Martha and John
themselves were being asked to fewer and fewer social events. When
they were invited, Martha was usually too tired to go. John seemed to be
busier than ever at work. With two children in college, it was understandable that he felt under pressure to work more. However, to
Martha, it seemed that the more hectic it was at home and the more that
she needed help, the more John increased his working hours.

One day, Martha had received a frantic telephone call from the
school demanding that she come and get Kenny *immediately.* He had
gotten angry at a little girl in his class and had tried to choke her. It took
both the teacher and aide to gain control of the situation. The other
children in the classroom were terrified. Kenny was to be suspended for
a week. When Martha picked Kenny up at school, he did not seem to
feel any guilt or remorse about the situation, but rather blamed the girl
because, "She started the whole thing."

When John had come home from work, he started lecturing
Kenny about his behavior. At the dinner table Martha broke into tears.
John became angry at her for this show of emotion in front of Kenny
and the latter started calling himself "dumb" and "stupid" for always
getting in trouble. For once, Kenny went to bed without a fuss.

John and Martha had stayed up late talking about the
problems. They again decided that they must seek outside help. A
friend had suggested a therapist in a town about thirty miles away. He
had a reputation for being very good with children, particularly with

acting out boys. They had hesitated to get involved with a therapist that far away, but this recent episode made them reconsider. Martha had called Dr. Jorgenson the following day and was lucky enough to be able to set up an appointment later that week. ∎

Beginning Steps

Parents or professionals responsible for a seriously disturbed child are confronted with a confusing variety of services. The decisions they make may well have a lifelong impact. They are not to be taken lightly. Indeed, such decisions are usually accompanied by considerable concern, thought, anxiety, and exploration of alternatives. The goal is to find that service which best fits all of the needs of the child. The process in itself may lead to increased stress and frustration on the part of all involved.

Residential treatment, providing a variety of services under one roof, is part of several different continuums of services. Clinical providers see it primarly as a mental health service option. Social Services personnel are more likely to view it as a type of out-of-home placement. Others, looking primarily at the child's academic and peer group dysfunction, may be thinking primarily in terms of the educational needs of the child as they consider alternatives. All three views have validity.

When is it really necessary for a child to receive mental health services in an out-of-home setting? What are the differences between various types of placements—therapeutic fostercare, group homes, residential treatment facilities, psychiatric hospitals? Which type of care best meets the needs of varying young people? How much will it cost and how can the costs be met? These questions are faced by parents, mental health professionals, and others involved in decision making for children and youth.

If children are to grow to be healthy adults their basic physical, intellectual, and psychological needs must all be met. For most children this is possible within their family environment. For some, out-of-home placement is necessary. The young person's problems may reflect individual vulnerabilities, family dynamics, past physical or psychological trauma, or any combination of these factors. Decisions about out-of-home care center around matching the child with a setting that can best meet his identified needs.

It is rare for a therapeutic placement to be considered prior to some type of out-patient intervention. If it becomes apparent that the child needs more intensive services, various placement alternatives are then explored. Even though the out-patient treatment has not been successful in avoiding placement, it should have yielded important information as to the nature and seriousness of the problems, the rate of

change possible, resistances to change, and the level of care needed to
facilitate the change process.

Who Needs Placement?

Both in terms of deciding who needs placement and what level of care is optimal, assessment of the child's functioning in the various aspects of his life—family, school, peer relationships, community, and personal functioning—needs to be undertaken. In making decisions on the youth's behalf, the following are questions to be jointly considered by parents and professionals.

Family Functioning:
How does this child respond to the family rules and routine requests? Does he need constant adult supervision? Does he act out even when directly supervised? Is this child's behavior consuming a disproportionate amount of the parental time, energy, and attention, thereby depleting adult availability for meeting the needs of the other family members? Have the parents curtailed their involvement in outside activities because of this child? (for example, have they stopped going to community or extended family functions because of this child's behaviors?) Has it become difficult or impossible for the parents to go out together without their children because it is impossible to provide adequate supervision for this child without a parent present? How does he relate to siblings? Has he acted out physically or sexually with siblings? Do the disciplinary techniques that work with other children seem to have no effect, or backfire, when used with this child? Are the parents in frequent disagreement about the nature or degree of the child's problems? Are parents, or siblings, feeling isolated from their friends because of this child's acting out behaviors?

Educational Functioning:
Three areas of school functioning should be considered—academic, peer relationships, and response to basic behavioral expectations. How is this child doing academically? Is work completed? Turned in? Is he passing or failing? If there are academic problems are they of recent onset or of long term duration? Has there been any educational testing done? How does this child learn best? (one-on-one? in a group? when material is presented visually or by auditory means?) Is this child a behavior problem at school? Has he been suspended, expelled, or attended many different schools? Do parents receive frequent calls from the school because of the child's behaviors? Is he frequently truant? Does he refuse to go to school? Does he act out in the classroom or on the playground? Is he a loner or is he involved with peers in the lunchroom and during recess or free time? Has he been in special education programs? If so, how has he responded to them academically and behaviorally?

Peer Relationships:

Does this child make friends easily, only with difficulty, or not at all? Can he sustain friendships? Does he differentiate between acquaintances and friends? Do the parents know who the child's friends are? Are his friends others who are frequently in trouble at school or with the law? How does this child behave when with friends? What group activities—sports, scouts, church groups, etc—has this child been involved in? How have things gone for him in these semi-structured activities? When observed with peers does he seem immature, isolated or rebellious in comparison with others his age?

Community Functioning:

Can this child be trusted to handle himself in the community—going to the store, riding his bike, going to a movie—without adult supervision? Do neighbors make positive observations or are there frequent complaints about him? Does he shoplift, steal, or break other laws?

Personal Functioning:

How does this child do in the self-care areas (i.e. dress, cleanliness, etc)? Are his emotions extreme—i.e. does anger automatically escalate to rage? Do events that would lead to mild unhappiness in most, lead to extreme sadness, apathy, or feelings of helplessness in this child? Does he use drugs or alcohol? What does he do for enjoyment? Is he cruel to animals? Is he truthful? If not, what does he lie about? Can you tell when he is lying? Has he ever set fires? Is he sexually active?

Additional Information:

How long has this child been perceived as having problems—by the parents? by others? What sorts of help have the parents sought for the child? for the family? for themselves? Has the child or the family been in therapy? If so, what type, how long, and with what results? How do the parents feel about the therapist's ability to understand and help both the child and them? If you are a parent, do you feel that the therapist viewed you only as part of the problem or were you viewed as part of the solution as well? If you are a professional, are the parents expecting someone to "fix" this child or do they see themselves as part of the solution? Has there been any educational or psychological testing? Do the parents know any other parents with a child like this? Have they gotten support from parent groups?[N]

The answers to the above questions should help both parents and professionals gain a clearer picture of the severity of the child's problems. Unexpected strengths, as well as difficulties, may be identified. If there are severe problems in three or more areas, with little or no improvement with out-patient therapy, then strong consideration of out-of-home placement should be given.

When a family is contemplating placement of their child, parents are under tremendous pressure. Frequently there have been conflicts between them as to the nature of the problems and what needs to be done. This is not unusual and is not a sign of family pathology in and of itself. By this time parents are usually questioning their own abilities—their ability to parent not only this child but any child; their ability to be objective; their ability to provide for their child's needs. Parents are going through a grief reaction, with all of its usual stages including shock, denial, anger, bargaining, and sadness.[N] Their expectations and visions of what parenting was going to be like certainly never included the current child and family problems.

Financial concerns usually add to the stress as they contemplate the alternatives. They may face criticism from extended family members, from school personnel, from friends or the community at large. Some may question if the child needs placement at all while others may question the likelihood of any treatment success. It is not uncommon for parents at this juncture to be angry (at the child, their spouse, themselves, the educational system etc.); depressed; frustrated with both the child and with professionals who don't seem to understand or be able to offer alternatives. Parents may feel hopeless and helpless. In the face of this multitude of difficult emotions the child may appear nonchalant and oblivious to his own problems.

This is a time when parents need, and deserve, tremendous amounts of help and emotional support as they make the necessary choices and decisions on their child's behalf. They often know no one who has experienced similar problems. Because of this, they may benefit greatly from participating in some type of parent support group, where others have had to cope with similar emotions and make comparable decisions.[N]

What Kind of Placement?

Once a child has been identified as needing placement, the next question to be answered is, "What kind of placement?" Review of the answers to the questions presented earlier can guide in selecting the type of placement that will best meet the child's needs and provide an environment conducive to growth and change.

A variety of therapeutic techniques exist. However, most are based on one of two basic strategies for facilitating psychological and behavioral changes. Both presuppose that external behaviors and internal perceptions, struggles, and needs influence each other.

External ⟷ Internal

32   A variety of modalities have evolved from the idea that changes in external behaviors and/or interactions will lead to internal changes. A second perspective implements the change process in the reverse manner. It focuses on internally changing perceptions and/or emotions so that behaviors or interactions will subsequently change. In general, behavioral or environmental interventions facilitate change using the external to internal direction while drug therapies and insight oriented psychotherapy work from internal to the external.

> **Example I:** Beth, age 15, does not trust male parental figures. During her pre-school years, she was severely physically abused by her father. She has developed a series of behaviors that emotionally, and sometimes physically, distance adult males. For example, she refuses to talk to her step-father and frequently leaves the room when he enters. The **external ⟶ internal** approach to treatment of this problem might include having an adult male become increasingly more involved with Beth the more that she tries to distance him. Her attempts at distancing adult males would be unsuccessful. Hopefully, she would then learn that she could be physically and emotionally close without harm coming to her. Taking the other approach, **(internal ⟶ external)** insight therapy might help Beth recognize that her behaviors made sense in her early life; they originated from her attempts to keep herself physically safe, a healthy goal. However, now that she is older she is capable of developing other, more mature, modes of assessing situations and relationships, thereby still keeping herself physically safe while behaving in different ways.

> **Example II:** Jeff, 8, has Attention Deficit Disorder. He is constantly "on the go." It is difficult for him to stay focused on his school work. He has trouble attending to what the teacher says, completing his work, and remembering to turn it in. He is starting to think of himself as "dumb." An **external ⟶ internal** approach might institute some form of reward system to reinforce positive behaviors on Jeff's part. For example he might receive stars, to be accumulated for a more concrete reward, for every 10 minute period that he stayed in his seat in the classroom. The objective would be that as he received positive feedback for acceptable behaviors it would become easier for him to maintain these behaviors on his own.

On the other hand, someone using the internal to external approach might decide that medication would help him focus on the task at hand, thereby helping him become more successful, and secondarily raising his self-esteem.

Although it is usually acknowledged that all children who need out of home care will benefit from changes in the environmental responses to the child's behaviors, it is also frequently obvious that there are underlying issues such as past physical or sexual abuse, or parental separations or losses that need to be addressed as well.

> Example III: Elaine, age 14, joined her adoptive family at age 8. She had been sexually abused in her family of origin prior to being placed in fostercare when she was 5. She had become strongly attached to the last of her three foster families. She had very strong feelings about leaving this family to join an adoptive family. Although there had been some problem behaviors throughout her early years with her current family, they have reached crisis proportions during the past year and a half. She has run away frequently; she has become sexually active; she has been experimenting with drugs and alcohol; her grades have dropped from B's and C's during grade school years to D's and F's. Family life with Elaine is filled with constant anxiety and frequent crises. She and her parents have been in therapy together. Both the therapist and Elaine's parents realize that her current behavioral problems stem from her past and recognize that she needs to re-explore her early life experiences through individual psychotherapy. However, Elaine keeps the focus on current events by creating one crisis after another. She needs placement in an environment which provides both the supervision and structure necessary to interrupt the cycle of recurrent crises (the **external ⟶ internal** approach) while simultaneously providing more formalized psychotherapy (**internal ⟶ external** approach) for addressing the underlying issues and feelings.

Some types of placement provide only one treatment approach; others are strong in one and weak in the other while still others provide both equally well. Elaine needs a program that provides both.

Most forms of out-of-home placement include day to day relearning experiences for the child. (See Philosophy, Chapter 2 for

34amplification) The emphasis is on creating an environment that allows the child to experience new forms of adult-child interactions and teaches new daily living and interactional skills. Attachment and behavioral models of treatment each provide for a strong emphasis on re-education experiences. The former focuses on identifying and meeting early needs via the development of strong interpersonal connections, while the latter targets problem behaviors that will be modified by changing the environmental response to them. In general, the younger the child, the more potent the effect of the re-learning experiences.

The second set of therapeutic techniques involves helping an individual mentally and intellectually re-explore previous life events and/or family interactions and helping him perceive these occurrences in a way that changes their current impact on him. These techniques can be utilized in individual, group, or family therapy. They are dependent upon the individual being treated having the intellectual capacity to recall events, recognize emotions and use abstract thinking to modify current reactions to past life events. Insight therapy, psychoanalysis, psychodrama, gestalt techniques, and certain forms of holding therapies are some of the modalities that treat problems primarily from the internal to external perspective. With the exception of certain identifiable psychiatric illnesses that respond to specific medications, most individuals might be successfully treated by several of the variety of techniques for changing their perceptions.

What those who are looking for placements want to be aware of is whether or not the treatment options mesh with the young person's strengths. Some forms of insight-oriented therapy are non-directive. The therapist waits for the person being treated to bring up traumatic events or feelings. Other insight-oriented therapeutic techniques take a much more active approach with the therapist not only introducing topics to be considered, but possibly even pressing the individual to consider difficult past life events. Which modalities will be most successful with which youngster depends upon a variety of factors, including the amount of resistance to change, the particular types of psychological defenses used, and learning strengths and weaknesses. For example, art therapy provides both a way to communicate psychological concepts and to explore past perceptions and emotions. It is an especially useful modality for someone who learns better by what he sees than what he hears; it would not be very useful for someone with severe problems in eye-hand coordination. In general, the older the young person and/or the more traumatic the past life events, the more important the **internal** ⟶ **external** strategies of therapy will be in overall treatment. However, as mentioned above, these strategies are dependent upon certain levels of intellectual functioning.

Parents and professionals who have been involved with the

child should be able to determine together what kind of environmental supervision and controls are necessary for a particular child to be safe and whether or not the young person has the intellectual capacity to make use of insight therapy. These are the factors that will influence the decisions about the type of placement. The least restrictive environment that meets the child's needs is the optimum placement. In general, the more severe the problems, the more protective the environment needs to be. Usually, the more protective the environment and inten sive the therapy the greater the financial cost.

Although it is clearly a waste of money and resources to place a child in a more restrictive placement than he needs, it is an equal waste of both resources and money to place him in a setting that cannot adequately meet his treatment needs.

Types of Therapeutic Placements

Although technically it is not a therapeutic placement, Custodial Care as an option should be mentioned. Custodial care meets the current basic needs of the individual without necessarily providing any form of remediation or enhancing skill acquisition. As such, custodial care is appropriate both for those without any treatment or remediation needs and for those with conditions for which there is no known successful treatment. In the past throughout the United States large numbers of children who did not have families to raise them grew up in institutions providing custodial care. As the emphasis has switched to permanency planning[N] and family placement alternatives, group care placements which provide only custodial care have diminished in number. However, such placements may still be appropriate when it is determined that an individual's current needs cannot be met in a family setting yet there is no known form of therapy which will change these needs. Examples might include cases of severe physical disabilities such as a patient in a coma; severe intellectual disabilities such as profound retardation; or severe psychological or behavioral disabilities. In the latter case custodial care may be supplied either to protect the individual from harming himself or to protect society from being harmed by him.

In Therapeutic Fostercare children live in foster families who usually have received training in working with emotionally disturbed children and their behaviors. A caseworker or therapist is commonly available to work closely with the therapeutic foster family to develop an environment which meets the child's current needs. Resistance to change may be less when the youngster is in a different family setting where the demands for emotional closeness may be different and where the adult expectations may be different. The strength of therapeutic fostercare is in the potential for providing an environment

36   for re-education on a daily basis with minimal overall restrictiveness. It provides for ongoing opportunities to interact with a normal community. The child must be able to successfully attend public school, and, in general, the child's behaviors must be able to be controlled within a family environment. The amount of individual therapy and type of work with both the child's legal and foster family varies considerably from program to program.

There are two types of <u>Group Homes.</u> Although they may make use of some relief help, the first type makes use of primarily one set of parenting figures, usually a married couple, who live in the same house as the children in their care. Both adults may be available on a 24 hour basis or one may work outside the home. The number of children in the home is usually eight or under. In the second type, the group home is not the primary residence of the adult caregivers. They work some type of shift. In both situations the residents are usually within a specified age range (i.e. adolescents) or have a similar underlying condition (i.e. a group home for developmentally delayed youngsters). Group homes may be administered either by public or private agencies. Again, the amount and type of individual and family work done is extremely variable and is rarely co-ordinated with the residential work. The young person's educational needs are met by the local school system. The cost and funding sources are similar to therapeutic fostercare.

Facilities that provide services such as psychiatric hospitalization or residential treatment may also provide the option of a <u>Day Treatment Program</u> as an alternative to out-of-home placement. They may or may not have their own educational program. They provide before and after school care in an environment aimed at providing re-learning experiences for the young person. In addition these facilities frequently provide both individual and/or family therapy along with a variety of parenting education programs. Such programs are usually more expensive than therapeutic fostercare, but less expensive than residential treatment. To be most successful the family and facility need to work together to transfer the expectations and behavioral controls from the program to the home setting where the child will be during evening hours, week-ends and vacation periods.

<u>Residential Treatment Centers</u> provide an opportunity to supply both the re-learning and the intrapsychic form of therapy in a co-ordinated program. They utilize fully the concept of milieu therapy, in which it is assumed that the many hours spent in daily living can be used to therapeutic benefit. Expertise of a variety of professions, including psychiatric, psychological, social work, educational, and medical can be coordinated in one program. In quality residential care the milieu is carefully organized to meet each child's needs for re-learning while simultaneously providing individual and family therapy that is well co-ordinated and integrated with the daily living program. Facilities with on-grounds school programs can treat those

children who are unable to successfully learn in a public school setting.
Twenty four hour care, seven days a week, is provided. Programs vary in terms of the population served, the types of problems they are most successful in treating, the services provided and the cost. Residential facilities may be either publicly or privately administered.

Psychiatric Hospitalization may take place on either a psychiatric ward of a general hospital or in a specialized psychiatric facility. In recent years a variety of in-patient adolescent psychiatric programs have evolved. This type of care is especially useful when there is need for an emergency placement such as a suicidal crisis; during psychotic episodes with hallucinations or delusions; or for drug or alchohol detoxification. They provide twenty four hour medical and nursing coverage in what is usually a quite restrictive environment. Intensive individual and family therapy may be provided. Primarily because of cost, but also because of the basic medical model, these faciliites are less appropriate for the long term treatment of long-standing emotional or behavioral problems.

In spite of attempting to give some idea of the different types of services provided in differing forms of out-of-home placement, it must be understood that there is tremendous variation in the actual services provided by varying programs. The boundaries between types of programs may seem clearer than they frequently are.

Therapeutic Placement as an Assessment Tool

Although it may be apparent to all that placement of a particular child it needed, the correct level of care might not be equally obvious. Placement itself may be used as an assessment tool. Let us use Elaine's case as an example once more. The question of type of placement centers around identifying how both types of therapy might be adequately provided. A case could be made for any of several options. No matter which placement alternative is initially selected for Elaine, it is important that there be a process for evaluating the appropriateness of the placement on an periodic basis.

Placement in a closed psychiatric unit with her therapist meeting with her daily would be one option. It is quite likely that the level of supervision and structure provided in a hospital setting would interrupt the frequent crises. Therapy sessions could then focus on past life events and their impact on her current behaviors. If successful, within a short period of time the internal changes would lead to behavioral changes sufficient that Elaine could return home to live while she continued with out-patient psychotherapy. On the other hand, it might become apparent during her hospital stay that her resistance to exploring past life events will necessitate long term placement in a highly controlled environment before enough internal

38 change will occur to modify her behavior. Referral for residential treatment might then be made.

An equal case might be made for placing Elaine in a closely supervised group home while having her continue with her therapist on an out-patient basis. This would usually be the least costly option. It might be successful. However, it might become apparent that the level of structure and supervision necessary to interrupt the crises cycle could not be supplied in a group home with public school attendance and referral to a residential treatment center might then be made.

An equal case might also be made for determining that the preferred placement would initially be in a residential treatment center, where supervision, structure, re-education and individual therapy were combined as part of the same program. Still, ongoing evaluation of the program's ability to adequately provide both aspects of therapy should occur.

In reality the decision will usually be based upon knowledge of the availabity of various programs and on funding sources.

Looking for Places

The availability and cost of programs, as well as help in meeting the costs, is extremely variable from one part of the country to another. Unfortunately, in general there are currently inadequate resources for emotionally disturbed children and adolescents and what resources are available are costly.

Placement options may be provided either by governmental or private agencies. Private sources of care may be either non-profit organizations or they may be profit making businesses. The balance between providing adequate services and fiscal responsibility is critical no matter who administers the programs.

Families must become strong advocates if they are to have any likelihood of finding a program that can meet their child's needs. As the persons who have spent the most time with him, parents usually have the most extensive knowledge of the particular child. However, at the same time, because of the their unique position in the child's life and his influence on theirs, it is difficult for parents to be totally objective. The placement search is most likely to be successful when parents collaborate with someone who can help assess both the child's needs and what various programs can supply. This person may be either a therapist who has already worked with the child or family, a placement consultant, or some other person who has had experience in various forms of out-of-home placement.

Many professionals who provide excellent out-patient therapy have had little experience in assessing or selecting out-of-home placements. They, like parents, may need help in locating what resources are available. They may need to seek help from local mental health facilities or private practitioners who do know the resources available within their community or state and who have had experience with them. Contacts in professional associations may provide information for the mental health personnel. In many urban areas there are independent educational counselors[N] who have extensive knowledge of both private schools and residential treatment centers throughout the country. Because they receive ongoing reports on children they have referred to treatment centers, they are in a position to evaluate the effectiveness of the programs. In addition to on-site visits, they also network with each other so that they have a constant flow of information about changes in programs. Members of parent support groups may provide parents with ideas about placement options. Most public Social Service Departments have a unit responsible for placing those children they are legally responsible for in therapeutic settings. Although a particular child and family may not be eligible for funding help from public agencies, these social workers may still be a source of information. At minimum they should be able to provide a listing of all facilities licensed by the state.

Information in succeeding chapters of this book should help parents and professionals alike in assessing the various placement alternatives available.

In general the more restrictive the environment, the more intensive and diversified the services offered, the more expensive the cost will be. Most families will need to spend considerable time obtaining detailed knowledge about their insurance benefits for mental health services. The percentage paid differs from plan to plan. Some policies provide good coverage; many provide poor. Some set a lifetime limit on mental health benefits. Some health care plans will pay for residential programs accredited as Psychiatric Facilities for Children and Adolescents by the JCAHO; others will not.[N] Some large employers administer their own health care plans. They sometimes provide flexibility in coverage. A few even have a list of residential facilities they will fund. Public welfare agencies may be able to assist in funding. Some children are eligible for Social Security and/or Medicaid benefits. Educational funding may be transferred from the home school district to the current supplier of educational services. Dependents of active or retired military personnel may be eligible for financial help via the Office of Civilian Health and Medical Program of Uniformed Services. (CHAMPUS)[N]

Therapeutic fostercare and group homes are usually the least expensive of out-of-home therapeutic alternatives. Public departments of social services or community mental health clinics may help fund these services. Health insurance may pay for the individual therapy, but would be unlikely to pay for placement costs.

Day treatment involves a variety of relatively expensive

services and usually costs more than either of the above alternatives. Health insurance may pay for some aspects of the program, but not others, such as the educational component.

Residential treatment is usually more expensive because of its twenty-four hour a day coverage and the variety of its services. It is quite common for families to combine a variety of funding options to facilitate payment. For example, educational costs might be paid by the home school district that was previously supplying special education services. Health insurance may pick up some of the therapeutic costs. The child might be eligible for disability benefits and the family picks up the remaining cost.

In general, psychiatric hospital programs are the most expensive form of out-of-home placement, usually running 3-4 times the cost of residential care per month. On the other hand they are the programs most likely to be covered by insurance. A major disadvantage is that lifetime psychiatric benefits can be consumed in a very short period of time. Because of the high cost, in general the period of hospitalization will be limited, usually 60-90 days. Most youth who can benefit from these services will need some sort of long term post-discharge follow-up. This should be considered as one decides how and where to spend the mental health care dollars that are available.

If any type of financial support is provided by either governmental or private agencies, parents should understand that these agencies may insist on taking a role in the decision making. This role may vary from nominal to extreme. Funding sources frequently demand input into the selection of services and the length of time they will pay for such services. In these situations the recommendations of funding sources and of providers of services may not necessarily agree. It is not unusual for public social service agencies to demand that they be accorded some form of legal custody of the child before agreeing to financially support a placement. This takes the parents out of the role of having the full legal power and responsibility for making the major decisions on their child's behalf.

Funding is a major factor in the decision making process. It is a rare family that is not faced with difficult financial decisions. The monetary outlay for the child with problems must always be balanced against the competing financial needs of other family members. Although parents may seek emotional support and advice from others, they are responsible for making the final decision as to what best meets their entire family's unique needs. Parents working with a supportive person who can help them locate and evaluate treatment options and resources will stand the greatest likelihood of success in the placement search.

A variety of decisions must be made before a child is placed in residential treatment. These include decisions about the necessity of placement, the type of placement, what will be provided in the way of treatment and how the family will finance the placement. The following questions provide a guide as options are explored and decisions are made.

1. Using the questions presented on pages 29-31, has it been determined that this young person needs some form of out of home placement?

2. What level of supervision and structure does this child need? What skills does he need to attain during placement? What behavioral controls does he need to develop?

3. Is this child also capable of making the use of therapy modalities based on the **internal → external** concept of change?

4. In looking at placement options, how do the chilld's needs for both types of therapy (re-learning and insight-oriented) mesh with the facility's treatment philosophy and program? How are the two types of therapeutic experiences coordinated?

5. What funding sources are available for providing for this child's mental health needs? What part will funding sources play in placement decisions both with respect to where a child might be placed and the length of time financial support for treatment will be provided?

Conclusion

A child's functioning at home, school, in the community and with peers needs to be fully assessed prior to any decisions about out of home placement. The youngster's needs then should be matched with a placement that can provide the treatment necessary to facilitate the change process. Parents will undoubtedly need help in locating facilties and funding sources. However, they have the most knowledge about the child and as the individuals who are legally responsible for the child's welfare they must be his primary advocate both during the search for services and throughout the entire treatment process.

Notes and Elaborations

pg. 26   The term *hyperactive* means more active than normal; however, it is frequently used as a label for a clinical condition more correctly called Attention Deficit Disorder which is characterized by hyperactivity, distractibility, impulsivity, and shortened attention span. It is usually considered to be due to some form of organic brain dysfunction, most likely of a neurochemical (the chemicals which are released by and control the functioning of the nervous system) nature.

  Ritalin, Cylert, and Dexidrine (particularly in days past, less frequently used now) are medications which may be prescribed for this condition. They seem to act by increasing the individual's attention span, which in turn positively impacts on the other symptoms.

pg. 30,   There are a wide variety of parent support groups. For example
31   there are support groups for parents of children with learning problems, with developmental delays, with drug or alcohol problems. There are adoptive parent groups, single parent groups, etc. Members meet other parents who are facing similar problems and decisions. Participants frequently share knowledge of community resources, professionals, and placement alternatives.

pg. 31   Humans are prone to grief reactions not only around real losses but also in reaction to the loss of a fantasy. Most parents have pleasurable fantasies of what family life with children will be like. When they are not realized, the grief for what never was may be just as painful as the grief following the loss of a real person. More about the grief process is included in the final chapter of this book.

pg. 35   Permanency planning is the concept that looks at long term planning for children. It usually is used in terms of looking at the long term legal options around deciding who will be the child's long term family of resource—will it be the birth family? will the child join an adoptive family? will there be a guardianship arrangement? etc.

pg. 39   Independent Educational Counselors Association
William B. Pierce, Executive Director
38 Cove Road
P.O. Box 125
Forestdale, MA 02644
617-477-2127

pg. 39   Joint Commission on Accreditation of Healthcare
          Organizations
          875 N. Michigan Avenue
          Chicago, IL 60611-1846
          312-642-6061
          1-800-621-8007

pg. 39   CHAMPUS
          Aurora, CO 80045 (no street address needed)

Other organizations that might be helpful to contact while searching
for appropriate placements include:

American Association of Children's Residential Centers
Claudia Waller, Executive Director
440 First Street NW, Suite 310
Washington D.C. 20001
202-638-1604

National Association of Psychiatric Treatment Centers for
  Children
Joy Midman, Executive Director
2000 L Street N.W. Suite 200
Washington D.C. 20036 202-955-3828

National Association of Homes for Children
Brenda Nordlinger, Executive Director
1701 K Street N.W. Suite 200
Washington D.C. 20006
202-223-3447

Child Welfare League of America
67 Irving Place
New York, NY 10003

C O N T E N T S

Philosophy

Kenny's Case   45
The Importance of a Philosophical Base   49
Characteristics of an Effective Philosophical Foundation   51
The Treatment Philosophy of Forest Heights Lodge   53
    The Crucial Role of Attachment   56
    Re-education Within a Developmental Framework 58
    The Role of the Family   60
Guide for Parents   62
Conclusion   62
Notes and Elaborations   63

Philosophy

Dr. Jorgenson had worked quite differently than the previous therapists. He insisted on meeting with both parents periodically. He shared many of his thoughts about Kenny and his problems. Martha was again quite hopeful that this time changes would occur. Indeed between the initial appointment in April and the end of the school year things did seem to improve. At least there were no further major explosions at school. Of course, both children and teachers seemed to be handling Kenny with "kid gloves." Dr. J. convinced Martha and John that placement in the special class might be the best alternative for school the following year. The adult-child ratio was much higher. It was a highly structured class and the teacher was trained to deal both with behavior problems and to teach children who had fallen behind academically.

Summertime, when Kenny was eight, had started out well enough. Both older children were home for the summer. Sarah had a job in the late afternoon and evenings. She was very good with Kenny. He seemed to respond more positively to her than to most others, and she had many ideas for activities with him. She wasn't even hesitant about taking him with her on errands and would frequently plan special outings with him. At times she tried to take neighbor children along, but few would agree to come even the first time. If they did come once they never accepted a subsequent invitation. When Sarah took others she noted that Kenny would become sullen and pouty initially. Eventually there would be some kind of verbal hassle between him and the others. He seemed to prefer to see this as his special time with his sister.

With John and J.J. both home in the evenings Martha felt that she had some support in handling Kenny. Dr. J. had insisted that John become more involved with Kenny. This seemed to help. When J.J. and Sarah came home from university for the summer Dr. Jorgenson had met with the entire family. However, J.J. resisted going to any further sessions. He saw Kenny as a "spoiled brat." He continually said, "You would never have let me get away with that. All he needs is a good spanking." In fact, on one occasion after J.J. had been babysitting, Martha noted bruises on Kenny's buttocks and upper legs. She didn't talk to J.J. about this, but she made certain he didn't babysit again unless Kenny was already in bed.

In late July, John, Martha, and Kenny had set off for a long planned trip to Disneyland. What a disaster that had been. The car travel alone was horrendous. Kenny was constantly asking, "When will we stop?" He bounced around in the back seat. In fact, he even reverted to rocking himself on occasion—something Martha had nearly forgotten that he had done both in the car and in bed as a pre-schooler. At least he didn't revert to banging his head as he had also done when he was younger.

At Disneyland, it was all she and John together could do to keep him in hand. Kenny was always running off so that much of the time was spent trying to find him. He was so careless about watching for vehicles that Martha was constantly afraid that he would be hurt. Her memories of the time that he was nearly hit by a car when he was in kindergarten came flooding back. He had pulled free of her as they left a store and dashed out into the street without looking. She could feel once more her heart in her throat as she thought that he had been hit. However, the car had stopped just short of Kenny. He had fallen but had not hurt himself and wondered what all of the fuss was about when the driver and his mother had both started yelling at him.

Prior to the trip to Disneyland, he had talked of all the rides he wanted to go on. He would get in line with great anticipation, but by the time they were first in line he was crying that he didn't want to go. One parent or the other would go with him and he would calm down some. Both parents tried to talk him out of going to the Haunted House but he insisted. The line was long and as they got closer Kenny became more and more restless and agitated but kept insisting that he wanted to go. However, once they got in the crowded elevator Kenny started shrieking. Nothing that either she or John said seemed to work. Everyone was looking at them with "that look" that Martha frequently got from others. The look that said, "What kind of mother are you? Such a spoiled brat!" More and more frequently Martha, herself, was wondering what kind of mother she was—certainly it seemed like she was the wrong mother for such a child as Kenny. Once the elevator stopped, Kenny wanted to continue with the ride. However, John insisted that they be allowed to leave the Haunted House. Then, as she could have predicted, Kenny started screaming because they had interrupted his "fun." "Nobody *ever* lets me have any fun. I hate you both. I wish I were dead." John told Kenny to stop the nonsense, but Martha was really worried about the last statement. Could his careless behavior and his frequent minor accidents reflect suicidal wishes on his part? It was so difficult to know what to do. One person would say, "Ignore his behavior." Another would say, "Clearly he needs more attention." No matter what they tried it didn't seem to be working.

John and Martha had interrupted the vacation and returned home early. It had not turned out at all the way they had planned. Martha had hoped that, with the extra attention from both parents on the trip, things would get better. Instead they had gotten worse.

When the Summers met the new teacher for the special classroom in September, again their hopes went up. She was an experienced teacher who combined a genuine warmth and liking for children with an ability to set limits and provide structure. She explained that a time out room would be used when Kenny, or others, needed it so that they would not get extra attention for negative behavior. At the same time, a behavior modification system with positive rewards would be used to encourage good behavior. It all sounded so surefire and systematic. Could it work? Maybe so. Martha certainly hoped it would. Again, for a while, things seemed to be going better. Martha and Kenny were meeting with Dr. Jorgenson once a week. John would join them for their meetings once a month and Dr. J. and Ms. Street, the teacher, were working closely together.

However, over Christmas vacation everything had seemed to start downhill again. Then in late January Ms. Street was ill and was hospitalized for several weeks. Altogether she was out of the classroom for two months. The new teacher just wasn't the same. All of the pupils were having more problems. Simultaneously, several would need to be in time-out. The substitute tried putting Kenny and another boy into the time-out room together on one occasion. What a mistake that was. They got into a real fight. One had a bloody nose. The other had a blackened eye. Both were again sent to the principal's office.

Everyone hoped that when Ms. Street returned in late March things would again calm down. That didn't happen. Kenny was spending an increasing amount of time in the time-out room. He was getting virtually no school work done and his behavior was such that positive rewards were becoming very rare for him. He was talking more and more about how "rotten" he was. In fact, he would periodically seem to withdraw into his own world for a day or two at a time. This behavior would alternate with frantically hyperactive outbursts.

Dr. J. recommended that a battery of psychological tests be completed on Kenny in late April. The psychologist noted Kenny to be very restless and to have a short attention span, being quite distractible both in terms of auditory and visual stimuli. She described him as, "An attractive child who was quite sullen, and who resisted reasonable requests to the point of becoming belligerently uncooperative during some tests. He occasionally allowed an open show of anger after failing on individual test items." At other times, he seemed to give purposely incorrect responses while insisting that he was doing his best. On tasks where he was more successful Kenny's attitude changed considerably. He was then less defensive and less irritable although he remained restless. His I.Q. score had been within the normal range, with a full scale score of 110, a verbal score of 107 and a performance score of 111. There was a marked scatter in his subtest scores.

On the Wide Range Achievement Test[N] scores, Kenny was noted to be functioning about a year behind grade level, with arithmetic being his lowest score (2.3 grade level) and reading his highest (2.8). Kenny's performance on the Bender-Gestalt[N] test revealed rather marked perceptual dysfunction with visual-motor immaturity and striking impulsivity. His productions were poorly organized and inaccurately completed frequently being rotated 90-180 degrees.

Projective testing[N] revealed him to be anxious and tense. He demonstrated fears of not measuring up. In general he saw mother figures as frail and uncertain, while father figures were perceived as distant and uncaring. Fear of the dark was a common underlying fear. There was evidence of Kenny's projecting his own anger onto others.

Following this testing, Dr. Jorgenson had suggested that residental treatment might be necessary. He had further suggested a more complete evaluation at the closest medical center, where Kenny could be a patient on the Observation and Evaluation ward for a period of three weeks.

So now here they were. Kenny had had his ninth birthday a month ago. He was home from the medical center with no changes in his behavior in spite of various medications being tried. And the family was strongly considering residential treatment. Martha was relieved that at least the financial concerns were not major in their case. J.J. had graduated from college and was living on his own in town in an apartment with two other young men and with a reasonably good beginning job. Sarah was to begin her senior year this fall. She was living at home this summer, to save money. She had two jobs and had received a scholarship to help offset her costs for next year. It looked like John's medical insurance would pick up much of the cost of treatment. School funds might be available to help offset the educational costs of treatment and there was a trust fund which could be tapped if absolutely necessary.

Martha knew they were much more fortunate than most when it came to the financial aspects of providing care. A woman in their church had an adolescent girl with severe problems. Although an appropriate placement had been located for her, no funding had been

available. The family's insurance wouldn't cover residential treatment.
Public agencies were hesitant to fund out-of-state placements. The
girl's problems had escalated. She repeatedly broke the law and was
now in a state institution for delinquents.

At times, Martha worried whether Kenny, too, as an adolescent, would be in trouble with the law. He had been so aggressive as a
young child. The problems had continued without respite. What hope
was there for the future? █

The Importance of a Philosophical Base

*"Cheshire Puss . . . Would you tell me, please, which
way I ought to go from here?"*
*"That depends a good deal on where you want to get
to" said the cat.*
"I don't much care where" said Alice.
*"Then it doesn't matter which way you go" said the
cat.*

Lewis Carroll
The Annotated Alice
Bromball House, 1960

A consistent philosophical approach provides the strong threads
through which the many different components of a residential
treatment program will be interwoven. Like Alice, we all need to have
some way of choosing which road to take. If the philosophical
approach is clear to all staff members, there will be a frame of reference
for answering the, "What do I do when...?" questions that come up
numerous times each day in the treatment of each resident. If all staff
members are supportive of the same philosophical approach, their
individual approaches to interactions will not seem fragmented or
conflictual.

It is through the power of the total environment within which a
child lives that the milieu treatment approach is effective. All elements
of the environment influence a child's growth and development. The
residential unit, the school, the recreational component, individual
and family therapy, the kitchen, the maintenance crew, administration,
and office staff are all part of the environment. If they do not pull
together, the power of residential treatment will be diminished by
inconsistencies and contradictions. The philosophy provides a
common bond of shared convictions between various staff
members.

Consider a 12 year old child who has a history of repeated out-of-home placements, poor peer skills, shallow relationships with
adults, self-destructive behaviors and low academic performance. One

philosophical approach might suggest that the essential treatment goal is to develop the social and academic skills that will allow this child to function in society. As a secondary gain to the achievement of these skills, the child will feel better about himself, will give up maladaptive behaviors, and will gradually begin to trust adults. Therefore, a treatment program based on this approach emphasizes skill development and uses its most powerful incentives to promote participation in academic and social learning programs. Staff are encouraged to emphasize the teacher-student aspect of relationships and to measure their success in terms of the skill achievement of the child.

A second approach might assume that disrupted relationships are the core issue. The primary focus of treatment will be on the establishment of trusting relationships. The establishment of this type of trust requires placing a great deal of emphasis on the development of nurturing relationships between staff and child.

A third outlook suggests that it is change in maladaptive patterns of behaviors that ought to occupy the center ring. Therefore, a program of behavior modification is instituted and the primary role of staff is to deliver reinforcers in accordance with a predetermined set of guidelines.[N]

Any of the three basic philosophical approaches to treatment might be successful with this 12 year old. However, it is unlikely that success will occur if different components of the facility use differing approaches to the problem. Suppose that the first approach is adopted by the treatment center's school, the second by the child care staff, and the third by the child's therapist. One morning the child throws a temper tantrum because of a child care worker's insistence on the completion of his daily chore. The child care worker therefore keeps the child in the living unit beyond the beginning of school in order to have the child resolve the incident and to demonstrate that such behaviors will not be allowed to sabotage their relationship. The child settles down, a positive interaction occurs and he goes to school.

The school staff, following a philosophical approach which focuses on skill development, insists that all the missed work must be completed, keeps the child after school, complains to the administration about the incorrect emphasis of the child care staff and manages to convey to the child that the most important problem was not the inappropriate interaction but the amount of school missed. Using a third approach to the problem, the therapist argues that both the individual time with the child care worker and the time after school with the teacher only reinforces the negative behaviors.

At the next case conference the focus is on the conflicting perceptions of the basic problem and little time is spent concentrating on the child per se. The emphasis is on discussion of the merits of varying philosophies. The same type of argument will soon erupt again in a slightly altered context. Such staff conflicts are damaging to the health of the child, the staff and the program.

This is likely to be the scenario when there is not a unifying philosophical framework within which all staff work. This does not mean that a broad variety of techniques cannot be used, but rather that they must all be subservient to the central theme of treatment as articulated by the organization's philosophy. This is what is crucial for keeping a program powerful, consistent, and mobilized toward the same goals.

The creation of a common philosophical base provides a yardstick by which a program can be understood, evaluated, and thereby demystified. From the framework should flow a common language understandable to staff, parents, and children. This language explains why things are done in a particular way. Staff can be more easily trained to perform their roles effectively. The success or failure of a program is evaluated in terms of the goals and the strategies outlined by the philosophy. Staff can readily evaluate their effectivness. Parents can begin to understand the program's successes and failures. This makes it easier for parents to accept the successes of the residential program without drawing inferences about their own inadequacies, and it helps them facilitate changes in their relationships with their child.

Finally, a philosophy helps us know what we are and what we are not. A clearly articulated philosophical base can help a program avoid the trap of trying to be all things to all people. It will indicate the treatment approach of the center and the kinds of children likely to benefit from it.

Characteristics of an Effective Philosophical Foundation

There is no one correct way for treating disturbed children. However, to be effective, even diverse philosophical approaches will have certain univeral characteristics:

1. **The most important task of treatment must be clearly and succinctly stated.** Specific problems and dynamics vary from child to child, but a philosophy of treatment must clearly identify the category of problems that is most essential for the program to confront if successful treatment is to occur.

2. **The philosophy should delineate how other problems or factors fit into the fundamental issues of treatment.** It is not a mechanistic equation that is needed, but a general sense of how different concerns fit together and how focus on one area is likely to lead to gains in other areas as well.

3. **All approaches to treatment contain an implicit set of values.** It is better if these values are explicit and open to scrutiny and

debate. It is fundamentally the program's values about children and treatment that guide its most difficult decisions and prevent it from succumbing to financial or other external pressures at the expense of the rights of children and families or the quality of treatment.

4. **A philosophy must identify the general strategies which will address the primary therapuetic issues.** How will the power of the milieu and all of its components be brought to bear? How will the separate efforts of these components be coordinated into a single overall effort?

5. **A clearly articulated philosophy demystifies treatment.** A useful philosophy is easily understood by staff, board, parents and community agencies. If a concept cannot be explained in simple, everyday language, it will be difficult to implement in a milieu treatment program.

6. **The statement of treatment principles provides a yardstick for measuring the program's performance.** Concepts that sound sophisticated and professional may be difficult to convert to practice. Statements such as, "We provide a nurturing, yet structured environment in which each child receives individualized attention designed to meet his unique needs" is appropriate for a publicity brochure, but it does not identify the treatment principles.

7. **The philosophy needs to be flexible enough to allow for continued growth and change, while it is firmly enough rooted to provide a sense of direction for this growth.** As successes and failures are constantly re-examined and as the knowledge base increases, theory and practice will be modified within the parameters outlined by the philosophical base.

8. **The philosophy of a residential center for children and adolescents should be child-centered.** Despite the importance of family, community, and staff, it is the child or adolescent who is the primary recipient of our efforts. It is on the child's needs and difficulties that the overall residential treatment approach should focus. This does not mean that the role of working with families is diminished, but that it centers on allowing the child to be part of the family without having to play a pathological role.

9. **With the emphasis on deinstitutionalization and permanency planning[N] a philosophy must indicate a clear and consistent approach to the family.** It should guide staff through the dilemma posed by advocating the importance of making the family a partner in treatment, while protecting the child from

abusive, neglectful, or rejecting families.

10. **Most residential centers, as opposed to crisis centers or hospital settings, focus on the effectiveness and power of the milieu.** An approach that downgrades or neglects the importance of the treatment milieu or that places it in a position secondary to an individual program component such as formal therapy sessions or specific academic programs may be appropriate for various out-patient or day treatment programs, but not for a comprehenseive residential treatment center.

The process of developing an effective philosophical basis for residential treatment can be both challenging and rewarding. The process itself facilitates self-discovery and growth. We would not expect any program to totally adopt our philosophy. Rather, it is our hope that a discussion of our philosophy and its implementation by various program components can help others find ways to successfully implement their own philosophy throughout their entire program.

The Treatment Philosophy of Forest Heights Lodge

The founders of the Lodge adhered to the basic philosophy that true changes occur based on intense interpersonal relationships, as opposed to focusing on behaviors per se. Throughout the years that Forest Heights has been in existence, we have adhered to this basic premise. Gradually, however, the philosophy has been refined and articulated in more precise terms that focus on attachment theory and a developmental approach to understanding psychological maturation[N]. Self discovery, ongoing education, and frequent discussions and debates among staff members continue, as we see not only the boys we treat, but also ourselves, as capable of continued growth and change.

At Forest Heights our primary focus is on providing an environment that enhances the development of close interpersonal relationships that are nurturing and honest, in an atmosphere of simplicity, positive warmth, and joy in living. We regard the child's recovery as a re-education process in which we strive to overcome the barriers to attachment while substituting more appropriate and authentic responses within the context of the total life situation. In such an environment the child re-experiences conflict with positive, rather than negative, resolution.

Reducing resistances to change and the re-education process are two basic components of our program. Our residents have come from environments in which they were locked into pathological cycles of interactions. Our goal is to create an environment in which the child's needs will be met and the re-education process will occur. This relearning focuses on several areas:

1. **Re-education about different modes of adult-child relationships.** In general our residents have perceived, for whatever reasons, the adult-child relationship as an adversarial one in which there are "winners" and "losers." From the child's viewpoint such elationships have seemed fraught with danger. A major goal of our treatment is to change this perception and help the young person see the adult-child relationship as an alliance that is beneficial to both.

2. **Re-education about the acceptability of feelings but the unaccept ability of certain behaviors.** Many of the boys' unnacceptable behaviors reflect inappropriate expressions of underlying emotional states. Our goal is to validate feelings, while at the same time we actively teach more acceptable behavioral expressions of the emotions.

3. **Re-education about the worth of the child as an individual.** Most children and youth in residential care have poor self esteem. They do not perceive themselves as capable or worthy of success. Our goal is to treat them with respect and help them increase, and then internalize, their own feelings of self-worth. To do this we must provide numerous opportunities for success and change.

4. **Re-education about reciprocity in groups and power in families.** Again, these children tend to view interpersonal interactions in terms of control. Many believe that if they follow through on a routine request, such as cleaning their rooms, they have in some way "lost." To meet expectations may feel to them like they have in some way diminished their own being. Staff members at Forest Heights work hard to correct this misperception and to teach the importance of reciprocity in relationships.

5. **Re-education about ways to care for and about oneself.** Both in terms of physical and psychological self-care our boys need a lot of help. Frequently they seem to be working against themselves, rather than for themselves.

6. **Re-education about ways to care for and about others.** It is virtually impossible to accomplish this psychological task until the individual's current needs have been met and he has learned to value himself.

7. **Re-education about ways to have fun.** Emotionally and behaviorally disturbed individuals have not learned appropriate ways to have fun and to experience positive

feelings about themselves and others in this context. We
believe that this area of treatment is as important as the
other aspects.

The first step in our treatment process involves sorting out the child's
psychological and developmental needs by identifying how the
individual is "stuck" or fixated in terms of emotional development and
by identifying misperceptions and maladaptive[N] patterns. Then we
must focus on how, in terms of our day-to-day interactions with the
young person, we can meet these needs and provide relearning
experiences. We firmly believe that real change is based on
relationships of trust and caring. All aspects of our program are
designed to support the development of such relationships. This is the
essence of the attachment model of treatment.

We examine the in-coming resident's history with this
framework in mind. How, why, when, in what way, and with whom
were the child's relationships distorted or interrupted?. What factors
within the child, the adult caretaker, and the environment led to the
child's difficulties in getting his basic psychological needs met, thereby
impeding his progress up the developmental ladder of maturation in a
healthy way? It is within these contexts that we formulate our
treatment plans.

This basic philosophy about the importance of relationships
built on trust influences not only the treatment modalities used at the
Lodge, but it also influences the administrative style, the school
program, medical interventions, staff relationships, and work with the
families. We intend it to pervade all aspects of the program. It does,
however, make its strongest statement in the focus on the milieu with all
other aspects of the program being secondary to, and supportive of, the
relationships developed within the living situation.

Within this framework, we work toward the accomplishment
of four interrelated tasks:

1. The child must develop the ability to form a trusting
   relationship with an adult, thereby overcoming the barriers to
   attachment that he has erected in the past.

2. The youth's behaviors must be brought under enough control
   so that he is no longer a danger to himself or to others. This
   control must eventually be internalized.

3. The child needs to learn the academic, social, vocational and
   recreation skills he will need for functioning in a community
   setting after leaving residential treatment.

4. The family must be involved in treatment both to obtain their
   alliance and to facilitate the changes that will allow the child to

play a different and healthier role in the family. The attachments and behavioral gains that the child experiences within our residential treatment center must be transferred to the family, or other caretakers, when the child is discharged.

The Crucial Role of Attachment

The crux of our treatment philosophy is the development of close trusting interpersonal relationships which provide a child with a sense of internal security. Although not all disturbed children have serious attachment problems, it is our belief that those who are referred to a comprehensive residential treatment program, having generally failed in less intensive and more community-based programs, usually do. Their problems with attachment have both contributed to and been exacerbated by previous problems in placements and schools. Therefore we believe that unless we overcome the obstacles to forming primary relationships, behavior controls may be developed but they will not be adequately internalized or generalized.

Attachment is the primary emotional connection that exists between human beings. It provides a socializing influence on individuals. It has been defined by Klaus and Kennell as, "An affectionate bond between two individuals that endures through space and time and serves to join them emotionally."[N] There are several important defining characteristics to attachment. One is transferability. A child who has developed an attachment to a primary caregiver can transfer that attachment to other important people in his life. This becomes the foundation for all significant relationships. Conversely, a child who has never developed the ability to form primary attachments will have great difficulty with anything other than superficial relationships as he grows into adulthood.

Secondly, attachment is the result of a bond that "endures through space and time" (Klaus and Kennell). A child who by loss of parents, institutionalization, multiple fosterhomes etc. experiences many discontinuities in primary caregivers will be likely to have difficulty forming attachments. On the other hand, a child who has successful experiences with attachment learns that emotional bonds can continue to exist even when someone is absent. This, in turn, helps the child to feel secure in the parents' absence and to accept delays in gratification.

Thirdly, a person with a healthy ability to attach has formed the balance that allows him to be autonomous and self-reliant on the one hand, and dependent and trustful on the other. Although the nature of this balance changes as an individual progresses through various developmental stages, the struggle between autonomy and dependency needs is lifelong.

Early parenting is a critical variable in the formation of healthy attachments. However, it is not the only source of attachment disturbances. Biological factors, environmental influences, medical problems, traumatic separations, and perceptual disorders are also important determinants. Any of these factors can disrupt the interactional cycles that lead to healthy attachments. For example, the child who has pain that no one can alleviate will have difficulty trusting that adults can meet his needs. Or, the child who is hypersensitive to touch may experience increased displeasure when a parent cuddles or caresses him. Rather than relaxing with parental contact, this child may experience heightened physical discomfort.[N]

Since the ability to attach is critical to a child's ability to attain his full intellectual potential, to develop a conscience, to learn to delay gratification and cope with frustration, it has a critical influence on the development of the common behavioral problems that we observe in children in residential care.

To facilitate the development of healthy attachments, we believe that our center must help the child feel safe, provide for a continuity of relationships, minimize the number of separations, and provide constant nurturing care for the child in a manner that imparts the message that he deserves to have his needs met on an unconditional basis. Once a child has developed an attachment to one adult, this ability can be generalized and the attachments can be transferred back to the family.

Nurture, both physical and emotional, is a child's right. It is inappropriate for nurture to be provided only when it is earned by desirable behavior. Under the pressure of major behavior problems, it is often tempting to use nurture as a reward in an attempt to gain a more powerful lever over behaviors. However, that undermines the re-education process about the worth of the child as an individual and the nature of a healthy adult-child relationship, both major components of successful treatment. A child who has had a miserable day may be especially in need of individual attention. This is even more important for the child who has learned to use negative behaviors to keep adults emotionally distant, because of their own fears of closeness and attachment.

At Forest Heights we are going to see Kenny's primary problems in terms of a failure to trust that adults will be available consistently for safety and emotional nurturance. Although we may do some speculation as to how the problem started in his early life, we will be more interested in interrupting the negative cycles of behavior that currently reinforce his perceptions of adult-child relationships. Our primary goal will be to increase his trust level for adult availability.

When we look at the functioning of children and families, we utilize a developmental framework. Children's dependency needs must be met before they can utilize their independence in a healthy way. If the child first learns to trust others, his subsequent trust for himself is on a firm foundation. The balance between dependency and autonomy although changing from one developmental stage to another is critical. Assurance that others can and will provide behavioral controls, in the context of nurturing, precedes the development of healthy self-control. Behavioral controls at Forest Heights include not hurting self, others, or destroying property. Through time the youngster needs to be able to follow routine requests without their escalating to a "make me" situation. Thus, both the second (behavioral control) and the third (skill acquisition) tasks identified earlier will be addressed within a developmental framework at Forest Heights.

We emphasize understanding children in terms of their developmental levels, strengths, and needs, as opposed to centering on pathology, problems, and deficiencies. Rather than focusing on "curing an illness", we prefer to focus on teaching children the skills they need as they grow to adulthood. Skill development is an essential part of treatment. We work on identifying the skills to be developed from the beginning of treatment. However, we know that skill acquisition becomes much easier once the attachment process is well underway. For this reason, our initial focus in treatment is on the attachment process, and the focus on skill development is usually postponed until the middle period of treatment.

Seven areas of skill acquisition will then be focused on:

1. **Academic/Vocational:** Children need to learn the basic academic/vocational skills to function in community schools or jobs. This is essential to a successful adjustment in our society. Without these school/work skills, the odds for successful emancipation are greatly reduced.

2. **Self-care:** Many children in residential treatment centers do not know how to take care of themselves or their possessions. Physical self-care skills include personal hygiene, grooming, care and selection of personal property including clothing, shopping for food, cooking, managing a personal budget, etc. Psychological self-care skills include learning ways to take care of one's self emotionally and developing the ability to ask for help. An inability to ask for help can become a major inhibiting factor in the development of autonomy and a sense of self-worth.

3. **Recreation/entertainment:** The need to enjoy life and have fun is universal, basic, and especially difficult for emotionally

disturbed children. Recreational skills are important by themselves, but they also provide the context for the learning of
social skills and relationship development.

4. **Social:** The person who does not have the social skills to
   interact with others in an acceptable way is immediately
   marked as a "loser" even if he is highly successful in other
   ways. Such skills range from small interactions, such as
   answering the telephone, asking directions and purchasing
   groceries, to much more complex interactions such as asking
   someone for a date, interacting with a potential employer or
   being a good sport in a competitive situation.

5. **Emotional management:** Everyone has to contend with
   emotions such as anger, sadness, joy, excitement, fear, etc.
   Having the skills to express these emotions appropriately and
   to manage them in a constructive way is essential. We are
   talking about skills that have to be taught and learned. How,
   for example, can a child learn to handle anger? What
   behavioral expressions of this emotion will lead to adequate
   relief without getting the child into trouble with adults, which
   may lead in turn to an escalation of the underlying emotions?
   This is a different question from one that asks how one can
   work through basic anger about abandonment, a task that
   would more appropriately be addressed in the formal
   therapy setting.

6. **Relationship skills:** All of these skills bear on relationships, but
   there are, in addition, a whole separate set of skills that are
   particularly important to the development of meaningful
   interpersonal relationships. These include communication
   skills, sensitivity to others' needs and feelings, recognition of
   realistic expectations of others, etc. These skills may be the
   hardest to develop, but they are perhaps the most essential.

7. **Conflict resolution:** Interpersonal conflict is an inevitable and
   potentially growth-producing part of our lives. One of the most
   needed and underemphasized skills is how to approach
   conflict in a healthy way. This is where the importance of
   reciprocal, rather than power based, relationships becomes
   most evident.

Emotional management, relationship skills and conflict resolution are
all related to the basic task of behavioral control. Only when the child
feels safe and secure in his environment will he be ready to focus on
learning these skills.

  With the possible exception of academic and vocational skills,
child care staff are the major instructors children will have in learning

life skills at a residential treatment center. These skills can be taught by modeling, by coaching children through situations in which particular skills are needed, by utilizing groups, activities, and daily routines to help children discuss and practice the skills and by approaching the many little interactions with children in the milieu as potential teaching opportunities. In all of the problem solving interactions that occur between staff and children, the primary goal is not to solve the problem or accomplish the task for the child, but to help the child become successful in accomplishing it himself.

> *Using a developmental framework—we are going to approach many of Kenny's problems in terms of skill acquisition. At Forest Heights we will see him as having never learned 1) that others can provide adequate external controls in a non-punitive manner; 2) to adequately control his own behaviors. After developing beginning relationships and alliances with child care staff, the focus will switch to skill acquisition in the seven areas listed above, with special emphasis on several areas. Kenny has not yet learned to behaviorally express his strong underlying emotions in ways that will work out well for him. He has very poor relationship skills. He does not know how to resolve conflicts with either peers or adults. Because of his underlying problems, he seems to have had few opportunities to experience true fun and joy.*

The Role of the Family

When an attachment model is used, the role of the family in residential treatment is critical. The goal of treatment in this context is the development of close interpersonal relationships, which become the foundation for behavioral gains. Both attachments and behavioral gains are transferrable. When they are transferred to the family at the end of the residential work they become the foundation for further positive growth and change.

However, even prior to admission, we find that the family is a very powerful influence in determining the course of treatment. We believe that successful treatment can only occur in the context of an alliance with the family. Even with very disturbed parents or disrupted family systems, treatment is seldom successful if the parents are in opposition. For all of the potential power of the treatment milieu, it cannot begin to counteract the power that the family has over the child

if there is head-on confrontation between the two. It is not enough to
neutralize the family. Its power must be used to enhance that of the
milieu and become part of it. This is the underlying goal of all of our
work with families.

How we make families our ally is a question that is asked
repeatedly during all stages of treatment. With some families it is a
simple task, but with others, particularly when the placement is
involuntary, it is a greater challenge.

We have made some basic assumptions about families.

1. We assume that all families are experts about their own
   children, even if they cannot handle them. We treat them as
   experts, asking their advice and respecting their knowledge.

2. We are convinced that no family wants to reject, mistreat, or
   neglect a child. However, parents may feel they have no acceptable alternative due to their own needs, the stress of the child,
   or their lack of parenting skills or other necessary resources.

3. By the time residential treatment is sought, most families have
   organized themselves around the child's disturbances to the
   point where the child's behaviors may help preserve the family
   system in some way. This does not necessarily mean that the
   child's problems arose because of family dysfunction but
   rather that the problems themselves may have impacted on the
   family system. This means that part of the treatment has to be
   aimed at helping families reorganize in such a way as to
   encourage the child to play a healthier, more appropriate role
   in the family system. If the child's misbehaviors, for example,
   provide parents with their only avenue for communication, it
   may be very costly to the entire family, child included, to cease
   the misbehavior. If, however, the parents can learn to refocus
   on their own communications then the child's misbehaviors
   will no longer be necessary to maintain the family intact.

---

*Developing a firm alliance with Kenny's parents will
be a top priority at Forest Heights. Their knowledge of
him and their past experiences with him will form the
foundation of our initial assessment of his needs,
strengths, and weaknesses. We will depend upon them
to empower us in Kenny's eyes.*

*During the course of the residential work, we will
help the family recognize the role Kenny currently
plays in the family system. We will help them determine which aspects of this role are helpful and which
are unhelpful both in terms of Kenny's striving for*

continued growth and development and in terms of the family's overall functioning.

Finally, at the end of the in-patient treatment process we will utilize our relationships with both Kenny and his family to transfer the trust he has developed in both staff members and himself back to the family setting.

Guide for Parents

When parents, or others, are looking for a treatment center to meet a young person's needs, they should understand, and feel comfortable with, the facility's philosophy. Questions to ask yourselves include:

1. Do I understand the philosophical basis of treatment?

2. Does it make sense given what I know about this child?

3. Do I understand how the philosophy is to be implemented on a day-to-day basis and do I feel comfortable with that?

4. Are the values inherent in the philosophy congruent with family values?

5. Does this program have experience working with children like this child? How does the philosophy address the type of problems this child has?

Conclusion

A treatment philosophy should be a living, changing, dynamic part of the program, reflected in all aspects of the treatment. The end result of a successful philosophy may best be measured by the attitude that the staff demonstrate toward the program, the children, the families, each other, and perhaps most importantly, themselves. If that attitude is one of optimism, self-confidence, pride, respect, and enthusiasm and if staff genuinely like their work and the other members of the treatment community, then the philosophy is working and a therapeutic milieu exists. Without that attitude, the most elegantly stated philosophy or finely articulated program will not work.

pg 48 The Wide Range Achievement Test (W.R.A.T.) is a standardized test which indicates educational functioning by providing grade level scores. For example, a score of 2.3 indicates that the student is functioning at second grade third month level in that subject.

The Bender-Gestalt test is used by psychologists primarily to test eye-hand coordination. A series of 9 cards, each with one design, is presented and the person being tested is asked to copy the designs. In addition to visual-motor functioning, it also yeilds other information, such as organization skills, inhibition or expansiveness (represented by size of figures), anxieties, problems of impulsivity, etc.

Projective testing is a form of psychological testing used to determine an individual's underlying personality structure as reflected in how a person organizes and describes vague visual stimuli. It will also elicit material about unconscious motivation that is not openly recognized or acknowledged by the person taking the test. There are a variety of projective tests including the Rorschach Inkblot Test and various story-telling tests which involve pictures of animals or humans interacting. The person taking the test is asked to tell what they see or to make up a story about the picture.

pg. 50 The reader will note that although these represent three different treatment approaches all focus on the way that adults react to the child's behaviors. They all represent examples of external   internal change process.

pg. 52 In recent years there has been a strong emphasis on decreasing the number of people living for long periods of times in institutions. In general now institutional living is geared toward helping individuals gain the skills necessary to live in a more open setting.

The combination of deinstitutionalization and permanency planning has meant that nowadays growing up in an institutional setting is rarely seen as a viable alternative. Twenty or more years ago it was viewed as acceptable for children and youth to be raised in institutions with minimal or no contact with their families.

pg. 53 Attachment theory looks at the ways that close interpersonal relationships come about and how attachment relates to normal child development. For complete discussions about attachment theory the reader is referred to John Bowlby's books on *Attachment, Separation, and Loss* (3 volumes). from

Basic Books, New York. A much shorter reference that looks at the importance of attachment and how it usually develops is *Putting the Pieces Together: Attachment and Separation* by Vera Fahlberg, M.D. published by the National Resource Center for Special Needs Adoption, A Division of Spaulding for Children of Michigan, Chelsea, MI.

pg. 56   This definition of attachment is a quote from the book *Maternal-Infant Bonding* by Klaus and Kennell published by Mosby Co. of St. Louis.

pg. 57   The arousal-relaxation cycle and its relationship to the development of attachment is discussed in Chapter 5, The Milieu. This cycle can break down when the child does not signal discomfort or feels none; when adults are not responsive to the child's needs; or when no matter what the adult caregivers do they are unsuccessful in helping the child achieve the relaxed state. These concepts are more fully discussed in the Fahlberg reference listed above.

C O N T E N T S

Organizational and Staffing Structure

Kenny's Case	67
Congruency with Philosophical Base	73
The Role of the Executive Director	74
The Central Role of Child Care Workers	75
Hiring and Training of Child Care Staff	76
Continuity and Staff Turnover	80
Staffing Patterns	81
Staff Interrelationships	82
The Role of the Board of Directors	84
The Role of the Professional Staff	85
Relationships with Outside Agencies	86
Guide for Parents	87
Conclusion	88
Notes and Elaborations	88

C H A P T E R 3

Primary Contributor Russell Colburn

Organizational and Staffing Structure

It seemed warm as Martha and John left the airport to catch the shuttle bus to the car rental lot. It had been a hectic three day trip. They had already visited two different residential programs in different areas of the country. The first they viewed as totally unacceptable. It was very large. Even though there were cottages, it definitely had the feel of an institution. They had not been reassured at all by their contacts with the administrative staff there. The tour through the facility was rapid, and they had no opportunity to visit with any of the residents. The second facility had been smaller, with a warmer more intimate atmosphere, but it had been 1500 miles from home. It seemed so far.

Hopefully, Forest Heights would be more like the second place, and in contrast 500 miles did not seem so far. As they got into the rental car and headed for the freeway, Martha took out the written directions as to how to get to Forest Heights. It was about 40 miles from the airport, mostly by freeway. Soon they were climbing Mount Vernon canyon. They passed the exit going to Buffalo Bill's grave and climbed to the top of the first major rise of the Rockies. The view ahead looking out over the higher peaks was beautiful and peaceful. There were even buffalo near the roadside. At least it was a pleasant ride away from the hustle and bustle of a major city. They followed the road signs to Evergreen, passing a small mountain lake before entering the obvious Main Street. A short distance further they turned onto a dirt road which was winding steeply up a mountainside. Surely, no treatment center could be at the top of this hill. Then Martha remembered being told that she would probably think that she was on the wrong road.

Apprehensions returned. They must have a lot of snow in the winter. Could a car possibly get up this hill then? She wasn't certain that she would feel safe with her child living on such a mountain in the winter. Yet, the trees and the blue sky looked inviting. A mile up the winding road they saw the Forest Heights Lodge sign in front of what looked like any other house. The brightly painted front door stood open. It was certainly cooler at this altitude than it had been in Denver. Entering the house, Martha and John went up half a flight of stairs and were greeted by an older woman who was busy typing at the reception desk. Martha recognized her voice from the initial phone contact. She was just as friendly in person as she had been over the phone. The woman introduced herself as Melody and asked how the weather was these days in their hometown. They had arrived a few minutes early for their appointment. Melody offered them coffee as they waited to meet with Mr. Colburn, the Executive Director.

While waiting, the Summers went out onto the deck which provided a panoramic view of the lake below and of nearby Mount Evans. The waiting room looked like a living room. They later learned that the director and his wife had originally lived in this house. It had subsequently been converted into an Administration Building. No wonder the people who worked here seemed so "at home."

Shortly, Mr. Colburn, dressed informally and accompanied by a large German Shepherd dog, came out to greet them. He was a large man with a short greying beard. It all seemed quite different from the other places they had visited. As they entered his office, Martha noted that the dog accompanied them. She wondered how Kenny would do if he saw the dog. He alternated between cruelty to small animals and fear of large dogs. Mr. Colburn leaned back in the chair at his desk and reassured the Summers that after reviewing the case materials he thought Kenny might be an appropriate candidate for placement at the Lodge. Although there were no openings at the moment, he anticipated that there would be several toward the end of the summer. All but one of these was already committed. However, he seemed confident that if John and Martha wanted to pursue placement here, and if after meeting Kenny he continued to think that the Lodge could help him, the opening would be available for him.

Mr. Colburn then asked further questions about Kenny's behaviors since he had returned from University Hospital. He also posed a few additional queries about Kenny's history. The thing that Martha noted most was his empathic attitude toward her and his recognition of how frustrating living with such a child could be. It was as though he really understood what she was saying. She did not feel that it was she rather than her child who was being assessed. The thing that struck John most was that Russ, as he insisted on being called, was straight forward and down-to-earth. He was the type John described as a "man's man."

Russ wanted to know what questions John and Martha had after reading the materials that had been forwarded to them prior to this visit. What questions? How ridiculous. Each of them had so many that they hardly knew where to start. Martha certainly wanted to know if the road was really passable in the winter. She also had concerns about what kind of boys were at the Lodge. Both parents had questions about the school program. They were worried when they learned that it was rare for the boys to immediately be placed in the on grounds school program and that they had to ask to go to school before they were enrolled. That might be all right for some boys, but they weren't certain that that tactic would work with their son. They also wondered how Russ could ever get a commitment from a child to want to be at the Lodge. This seemed to be a prerequisite to admission. However, Russ seemed certain that it could easily be done. Although he seemed to think that he had met many such children, maybe he really had never met a boy like Kenny.

John had further questions about the financial aspects of the placement. Materials had been sent to his insurance company and even though the Lodge did not meet some of the criteria for hospitals, they had accepted the explanations given. They had indicated that because of the acceditation by the Joint Commission for Accreditation of Hospitals as a Psychiatric Facility for Children and Adolescents, they would pay a major part of the monthly fee.

While waiting for one of the residents to come and give them a tour of the facility, Russ explained the staffing patterns of having child care staff on duty for three and a half day shifts. What he had to say made sense to them. It seemed like the family aspects of the living situation were being maximized. Curt, a 13 year old boy, was introduced to them and Russ asked him to take the Summers on a tour of the Lodge. Curt wanted to know if he could take them through the school as well. Martha noted that Curt also referred to Mr. Colburn by his first name. The Summers toured the schoolhouse on their way to the main residence. This building looked newer than the others. There was a small lighted sculpture of "Rocky" in a niche in the entry way. When John asked about it, Curt explained that it had been donated by the sculptor of the original "Rocky" statue used in the film. To Martha it seemed to represent a sense of victory. She wondered if Kenny would ever be able to feel like a "victor." The stairs opened into a large classroom with a deck facing Mount Evans. Curt explained that this was Steve's classroom, where older boys like himself had most of their classes.

Curt then took them into Fred's classroom. Curt had already asked them how old their son was. He wasn't certain as to whether Kenny would be in Fred's class or in Carol's class. Fred was in his classroom sitting at a round table talking with a student. Curt explained that the regular school term had been completed last week. Summer school hadn't yet started so most of the boys were either over at the main residence or were home on visits.

The final classroom belonged to Carol who, as Curt described it, "runs the school" and teaches "the little kids." Carol's room was large. There were many toys as well as a large round table with chairs around it. Martha noted that there was a rocking chair as well. That was reassuring to her. She took it as an indication that this teacher felt comfortable mothering as well as teaching. All of the classrooms were light and airy. None had the atmosphere that either parent associated with the classrooms of their childhood. All seemed somewhat informal. John was wondering how much actual learning took place in this school.

Curt then took the Summers downstairs to the shop and the arts and crafts area. He talked of the woodworking projects that the boys had recently completed under Steve's direction. He also indicated that most of the boys were involved in Arts and Crafts at least once a week with Linda. He showed them a project that he was working on and indicated that it was a gift for his dad for Father's Day. Curt further volunteered the information that prior to coming to the Lodge a year earlier, he and his parents had never seemed close, particularly he and his dad. This was the first present he had ever made for his father. He was really happy that his visit home was going to coincide with Father's Day so that he could see the look on his dad's face when he opened the present. He offered the information that since his family lived in Denver he was able to spend one week-end home per month. Things were going much better between his parents and him. In fact, Curt was hoping that he would be able to go home at least by next summer, and maybe even in January.

Curt said that the remainder of the downstairs of the school-house was an office. It was located in an apartment where parents, visitors, students, and occasionally staff might stay.

As they walked up the sidewalk between the school and the playground, Martha commented on the pretty miniature pansies that were growing next to the walk. John made a comment to an older adolescent who was up on a ladder painting the trim on the building. Curt said that Ed hoped to get all of the trim painted prior to his going home "for good" in a week. At the head of the sidewalk two boys were chopping wood and cleaning up around a woodpile. Curt told them that he would be back to help as soon as he finished showing the Summers around.

On the playground, which Curt referred to as "the flat area" several boys were riding bicycles. A few were over by some rocks. They seemed to be playing cops and robbers. One boy who looked older but quite withdrawn was swinging on a swing. A boy whom Curt referred to as Billy approached the Summers as soon as they entered the playground area. Billy started touching Martha on the arm, with a big smile, and asking her lots of questions. A tall young man called to Billy from the doorway of the building, "Billy, that's not appropriate." Martha herself had thought there was nothing wrong with it. It seemed like he was just being friendly. She certainly couldn't understand why the young man thought it was inappropriate.

John immediately noted the tree house over in the corner of the yard. Several boys were playing in it. For a long time he had planned to build just such a tree house for Kenny, but it seemed that he never had enough time.

When they arrived at the side door of the building, Curt introduced them to Mark, the young man who had called to Billy. Curt commented to John and Martha that Mark was "staff." John saw another young man shooting baskets with two boys who seemed to be having trouble getting the ball as far as the basket. Curt told them that this was Steve, one of the teachers.

They entered a large living area which was two stories tall. It was darker in here than it had been in the schoolhouse and seemed nice and cool. A couple of boys were sitting at a coffee table playing a board game. An older man with a graying beard and thinning hair was sitting on a couch with his arm around a boy who was sobbing. Two other boys were just sitting in chairs. As they toured the rooms opening off the balcony which circled the living area, Curt commented that the two boys were "sitting." He noted further that the boy who was crying had received word that morning that his grandfather had died. Curt identified the older man sitting with the boy as Glen. It was apparent from the way Curt spoke that Glen was different from "staff" or teachers but John and Martha weren't certain what the difference was.

In addition to the bedrooms opening off the balcony there were two bathrooms and several other smaller rooms opening off a back hallway. Although most of the bedrooms were quite small each had a personality of its own. There were many posters on the walls and in most rooms it was easy to ascertain the interests of the occupants. One of the larger rooms was striking in that half of it was quite messy with one dresser cluttered with possessions. The walls on this side of the room had many posters and pictures. The other half of the room was in stark contrast. It was quite plain. There was only one picture on the wall and the dresser was clear of possessions. It was obvious that the two occupants had very different personalities. Martha wondered how they got along and who settled the hassles that probably occurred between them.

As John and Martha followed Curt back down the stairs, they noted that the porch area ahead of them had many large windows framing the Mount Evans view. To the right at the bottom of the stairs was another bedroom. It was a large room with several windows. To the left, beyond the living area, was a foyer. Off this was a small office, which Curt identified as Glen's office, and another large bedroom. Halfway down the stairs was what appeared to be a front door. At the bottom of the stairs there were several doors, one of which led to another bedroom. Curt mentioned that this was Ed's room and that everyone was wondering who would get to move downstairs when Ed left. It was apparent that occupying this room was a status symbol.

When they went back upstairs they turned right at the top of the stairs and entered a dining room with three large tables. At one of them two boys were building models. At another two young women were putting out a snack. One wore an apron and was bringing cookies from the kitchen. The other Curt introduced as Sally, who was also identified as "staff." Sally was pouring juice and supervising the distribution of the cookies. She suggested that Curt offer some to the Summers.

After taking a quick look into the adjoining kitchen, they left the dining area and re-entered the living room. They continued across this room and down a hall straight ahead. To the left was the staff office. To the right was a small bedroom. Two bathrooms opened to the right further on. At the end of the hall was a large room with four beds. Curt identified this room as "the little kid's" room.

After the tour, Curt returned with the Summers to the Administration Building. While Curt went back to the woodpile, Russ introduced the Summers to Ray Curtis, who was going to talk further with them about the philosophy of the Lodge as well as policy and procedural matters. After their tour they found that they had some additional questions. John noted that Ray, as he asked them to call him, answered their questions by relating them to the philosophy of the Lodge.

Although the materials sent to them in the mail prior to their visit had contained information about the philosophy of the Lodge, they found that they understood much more after talking with Ray. He stressed that everyone at Forest Heights believed that children change only in the context of close interpersonal relationships. For this reason the staffing patterns of three and a half days on and three and a half days off had been selected to promote continuity of relationships between child care staff and boys. They further learned that administrative staff, most of whom themselves had at one time or another worked as child care staff, firmly believed that it was the child care staff in the course of day to day interactions with the residents who really made the difference. They were considered the primary therapists. When the Summers asked about psychotherapy, per se, they were told that the decision about starting a boy in individual psychotherapy was made on a case by case basis. At the time of admission few boys were immediately placed in individual therapy as the emphasis was on helping them form primary relationships with the child care staff. Every possible attempt was made not to dilute these connections with too many other relationships early in the course of treatment.

Further discussion around the philosophy with regards to
school was held. Martha and John understood that most of the boys
referred to Forest Heights had already had many battles around school
performance and that school had rarely been a rewarding experience
for them. However, they continued to have concerns about Kenny
falling further behind before he was ready to make a commitment to go
to school. Although the way that Ray explained it made sense, they
wondered if the approach would work with their son.

Following their discussion with Ray, the Summers were
introduced to Ruth, the bookkeeper, as they had some further
questions about the billing procedures when more than one funding
source was involved. Even though a final decision about admission
had not been made, John wanted to make certain that he clearly
understood all of the financial arrangements. Ruth was an older
woman, who offered them a refill on their coffee. Then in a quiet
softspoken manner she answered John's questions. She gave examples
of what had occurred in the past when dealing with insurance
companies, but stressed that each insurance company was unique in its
way of handling such matters.

While John and Ruth were talking, Martha stepped out the
screen door. From here the view was mostly of nearby homes and trees.
The reflection of the lake could barely be made out through the trees.
She had noted that two other women were working at desks in this
room. Although people here seemed busy, they also seemed relaxed
and comfortable. Everyone seemed to have time to make visitors feel
welcome. The entire facility had more the atmosphere of visiting at
someone's home than at an institution. She liked that.

John and Martha had a chance to again spend a few minutes
with Russ. They agreed that John would call within two days to let him
know what their decision was. If they decided on Forest Heights Lodge,
then the next step would be to bring Kenny, and possibly J.J. and Sarah,
for a visit. At that time they would plan for an in-home visit by one of the
staff. ∎

Congruency with Philosophical Base

The treatment philosophy provides the foundation for residential
work. Individual staff members, however, are responsible for
implementing the philosophical approach. The quality of personnel is
crucial to the success of a treatment program. Administrative style
influences how various staff perceive their roles and carry them out.
Smooth functioning between the component parts of the program is
most likely to occur when the administrative structure and style reflect
the philosophical base. If there is a lack of agreement between the
stated philosophy and administrative style, staff members will be

confused as to whether to respond to the words or to the actions of the administrators. Disharmony between various components of the overall program is then likely.

The relationship between board and administration sets the tone for the management style which, in turn, has a profound effect on the treatment program. If there is congruency between the basic philosophy of the facility and the types of relationships maintained within the agency, it is easier for everyone to be clear about his responsibilities. The interrelations of all the components of the organization, board, administrative staff, therapists, child care personnel, teachers and support staff, affect the implementation of the treatment philosophy.

Administrative staff members at Forest Heights see their primary function as creating an environment which facilitates cooperation and reciprocity. Attention is paid to establishing a healthy balance between an individual staff member's autonomy and a strong interdependence among those who work together. There is encouragement for continued growth and change both in individual staff members and in the program as a whole. This reflects the basic philosophy of attachment theory and the importance of the balance between independence and dependence.

A treatment center, by the very nature of its work, is faced with needing to be flexible, creative, and constantly willing to re-examine all of its practices, including administrative policies, with a critical eye. At Forest Heights there has been a foundation of a small, cohesive administrative staff and a low staff turnover rate which has facilitated the development of a particular organizational style.

The Role of the Executive Director

As "keeper of the philosophy" the Executive Director establishes a harmonious, effective treatment climate in which all the components of the organization work together. He is charged with creating an environment in which staff members on all levels feel valued. As chief administrator he works with the Board of Directors to insure sufficient funding for a quality organization in which program dictates budget rather than vice versa. He advocates for adequate pay and incentives for his staff.

In charge of the organizational structure, the director oversees the entire program and insures that there are adequate numbers of competent staff to meet the needs of the residents. He holds final responsibility for staff hiring and firing as well as for resident admissions and discharges.

Open discussion about a variety of decisions, small and large, usually leads to a consensus. When agreement is not possible the

director assumes responsibility for decision making. On rare occasions
the Executive Director may make a unilateral decision even though the
majority of staff have a differing opinion. His unique perspective of the
overall organization and responsibility for the total program may lead
to this. At such times it is particularly important that he model
openness and honesty. Staff need to be aware of his struggles, concerns
and plans without feeling the burden of decision making in the broader
sense. With mutual trust and respect between staff and chief administrator, the former will not only accept the unilateral decision but will be
able to support it although it was not their first choice. Essentially the
director models the role of a good parent, being receptive of others'
feelings and input, but assuming final responsiblity for decision
making. This is what he, in turn, asks individual staff members to do in
their interactions with the residents and their families.

In addition the director is accountable for overseeing
community relations. He sets the tone for how the community
perceives the institution. In turn this influences how the residents are
accepted in the schools, neighborhood and community at large. Part of
this administrator's job is political, as an advocate for children's
services as a whole. The entire staff has a right to understand the
political forces that are in practice governing their lives. Yet it is the
administrative staff that must take the responsibility and lead in
confronting and trying to solve such problems. When residential treatment facilities band together to support their interests in this respect,
they are better able to promote the fiscal and therapeutic efficacy of
high quality care. At Forest Heights it is the director who takes on the
role of political advocacy.

The Central Role of Child Care Workers

Because our philosophy emphasizes the development of close
interpersonal relationships, at Forest Heights the most important staff
are the child care workers. They are seen as the primary therapeutic
agents. They are with the boys twenty four hours a day. They share the
child's joys and his pain. They provide the basic parenting and
caretaking. They are the ones who are primarily responsible for
creating an environment which will help each resident feel secure,
learn to trust, form basic attachments, and discover that he can love
and be loved. They open up another world to the child, hopefully a
world that encourages the child to give up his rigid, nonproductive
defenses and find himself free to experiment with life and with
living.

The security a child needs to experience to enable him to give
up his pathology must be provided by the adults with whom he has the
most contact. Those who tuck him in at bedtime, are available at night

when he is ill or lonely, get him up in the morning with the hope that this day can be brighter, happier, and more successful than yesterday are the true change agents. They protect the child from the impulses and fears that may terrify and overwhelm him. They teach him new skills and consistently convey the message that he is an adequate, worthwhile human being, capable of change. The administrator and the therapist, in their respective roles, either facilitate or undermine these primary relationships. However, because of their limited contact with the child, they themselves cannot be the primary change agents.

The manner in which the child care worker carries out the day to day activities and the quality of his interactions with the child will influence how the child views the world, the institution, and the people who staff it. If the administration is not trusted by the child care workers, this will be transmitted, either consciously or unconsciously, to the residents. If the psychotherapist is seen as the one who makes the treatment decisions based on limited office contacts without knowing what it is like to live with the child, then the child care worker's anger, or feelings of lack of worth, will be conveyed to the child. When child care workers feel that they have no input into treatment planning, or that their input is discounted or minimized, when they have little authority to make decisions about the every day life of the child, they will feel powerless and ineffectual. Again, these feelings will be transmitted to the child and will set the tone for the nature of their relationship.

Hiring and Training of Child Care Staff

Throughout the years our child care staff have come from a variety of educational backgrounds, ranging from a high school education to post-graduate degrees. Many have had prior experience as child care staff in other facilties. However, we have found that the following qualities and attributes, which are essential in implementing our basic treatment philosophy, are much more important in child care staff selection than educational or experiential background per se. They reflect the values inherent in our approach to treatment.

1. Staff members need to feel comfortable with the basic philosophical approach of the program. An effective program cannot tolerate people going off in fundamentally different directions. It can, however, thrive with staff giving highly individualized responses that reflect the same basic underlying philosophical approach.

2. Child care staff must be able to function as a members of a team. It is important that administrative staff engender an atmosphere in which there can be free and open discussion. At the same time it is unlikely that total concensus will be reached on all decisions. Therefore, once a decision is made, all staff members need to work to implement that decision even if, as individuals, they don't totally agree with it.

3. All staff members need to be able to communicate effectively with both adults and with children. Communication is a two way process. Not only should staff be able to talk to a child, they must be able to listen as well.

4. Staff members need to be able to respect the authority of the organization. Children are very sensitized to organizational divisiveness and react to it with manipulation and insecurity. While staff need to be assertive and administration needs to allow this, the basic authority of the organization and its leaders needs to be respected. Some things are non-negotiable. Examples include the right of children in residential treatment to be in an environment that provides both physical and emotional safety, the fundamental respect which both children and their families must be accorded, the basic treatment philosophy and the belief in children's ability to change.

5. Staff members must be able to accept constructive criticism and to be self evaluative. This ability to look at one's self, both in terms of strengths and weaknesses, is essential. The children we work with have an awesome ability to find vulnerability in the adult's defenses and to zero in with unerring accuracy. They resurface conflicts that have often been long buried within the adult. How well the worker copes with these inner conflicts will determine his effectiveness. Some will develop new awareness and strength from this experience while others may find it debilitating and intolerable. The support that the staff member receives from other staff and from administration will often determine the extent of the pain and how it is resolved.

6. Child care staff should have good basic intelligence, with particular emphasis on the area of common sense. Children who come into residential treatment are going to need all the skills and brain power that staff can muster to help alter their stereotyped, self-destructive behaviors. Along with intelligence, flexibility and creativity are also needed. Rote responses from staff to children are not helpful. Dependent on the child's underlying needs, two almost identical situations with two

different children may require entirely different responses from the adult. For example, the destructive child who breaks a window may warrant one response, while the child who in the past has kept everything inside and for the first time now breaks a window needs a different response. To react therapeutically to these situations the caregiver in our facility must be quick witted, flexible, and creative.

7. The adult needs to be a loving and emotionally nurturing individual, who at the same time recognizes that setting appropriate limits is part of responsible care taking. Our philosophical approach depends on adults being able to form close interpersonal relationships. We see our residents as frequently needing unearned gratification. At the same time caregivers in our program must feel comfortable saying "no." They must have learned to manage their own anger and frustration in non-destructive ways.

8. They need to be good crisis managers. The adult's ability to keep "cool" in a crisis gives the children a sense of security. They can depend on the staff for protection from themselves and from others.

9. New staff members need to be secure in their insecurity. The children will respect the new staff member who is comfortable saying to a child, "I don't know about that; let's check with Glen." This type of staff member is less open to manipulation by the children than one who pretends to know everything.

10. Child care staff need to be comfortable displaying a broad range of affect. They need to have a joy in living so that the message communicated to the child is, "life is fun and worthwhile." They need to be able to express their own emotions in straightforward ways so that the children need never guess how the adult is really feeling. A person who never changes expression or who never genuinely shows emotion is an enigma to the child and causes him to be confused and uncertain about where he stands with the adult. Whether the adult is happy, angry, or sad with a child or with a situation, it should be on his face and in his voice.

11. The skills and interests staff members share with children help the identification process with positive role models. Caregivers need to share a wide range of normal life skills, as well as a variety of special interests, with the residents. They open new areas of learning for children who, because of their pathology, have had few constructive avenues open to them. A simple skill to many of us, such as throwing or catching a ball, may never have been learned by a child in residential treatment.

12. Adults need to have a life outside the agency. Dedication is admirable, and if we did not have some need to be needed we wouldn't be in this business. However, staff members need to have other gratifications and interests or they are prime candidates for "burnout." In general, those with outside interests and gratifications will stay longer, be more creative, and will have more ability to give to others. The adult's feelings of self-worth cannot be primarily dependent on our residents liking them.

Kenny will be cared for by child care staff who will be able to provide both the emotional nurturance and the limit setting that he needs for learning to first trust adult caregivers and subsequently learning to trust himself. Our goal will be to provide him with staff who are united in terms of philosophy, but who are unique in terms of implementation. Hopefully, they will teach him how to have fun with both adults and with peers. Since they will be communicating well with each other, there will be fewer opportunities for Kenny to set up "let's you and him fight" situations. This, in and of itself, will increase Kenny's trust for others ability to be in charge.

He will have opportunities to observe adults who view their work relationships as reciprocal in nature, rather than primarily power based. He will see that adults can follow rules, take direction and criticism, and resolve conflicts within a "win-win" context.

Once hired, on the job training proceeds utilizing a variety of techniques. New child care staff are provided with a variety of written materials and in-service training videotapes. However, the primary training occurs by having them be involved with current child care and supervisory staff as they work with the residents.

At Forest Heights new child care staff are introduced into the program slowly and carefully, thus providing some measure of protection both for new staff members and for the children. They are not put in charge of the boys. In fact, they are not immediately allowed to give the children permission to go off grounds or out of a supervised area. Instead, they are told to place their emphasis on getting to know the children as individuals and on letting the children get to know them in return. At the same time they are expected to be watchful of how experienced staff members interact with the various children and to ask frequent questions.

It is only after a new staff member has become well oriented to our program and when experienced staff feel comfortable with the new person that it is announced at morning meeting, "Tom is now able to give permission." This indicates to the boys, who have had an opportunity to develop some measure of trust for the new staff member, that Tom is through the initial transition onto the treatment team. This introductory process does not just encompass a shift or two but may involve a considerable period of time, up to several months.

Continuity and Staff Turnover

In a program with a philosophy based on attachment theory, staff continuity is extremely important. At FHL the average length of employment for child care workers is seven to eight years. The result is that even when a staff member does leave, a solid core of staff who have been with the child throughout his stay remains.

Child care workers have identified several important factors contributing to their longevity in this setting. At Forest Heights child care staff feel not only a tremendous sense of responsibility for the care of the children, but also feel that they have a position of power. They are an active part of the treatment planning and play a vital role in all staff conferences. Their input is given equal, or more, consideration than that of other staff members. For example, if child care staff indicate that it is not realistic to follow through on a recommendation of a therapist or consultant, the house staff recommendation will usually take precedence. Also, unless there are unusual circumstances involved, the child care worker, in consultation with the Residence Director or Assistant Director, will generally make decisions regarding specific disciplinary procedures.

Caregivers feel respected by administrative and professional staff, most of whom have at one time or another been child care workers themselves. The professional staff acknowledge, with their support, the demands put on the child care workers. There is open recognition that the real power with the child is in the hands of the child care staff.

Other factors include staff's feelings of success in the job, the availability of immediate supervision and support from other staff, the warm and personal tone of the program, and the beauty of the environment. Staff have indicated that they feel important and respected yet never completely alone. If help is needed, it is immediately available.

Child care staff, many of whom have worked in other institutions, also list continuity of administrative staff as a major factor in decreasing burnout. When there are infrequent changes in administrative staff, consultants and therapists, less energy is spent on acommodating to new personnel and worrying about changes. Therefore child care staff have more energy to devote to their primary job, reparenting the children in care.

While factors of respect, empowerment, security, and fulfill-
ment are important, so are salary and other tangible benefits. As
elsewhere, child care workers at Forest Heights Lodge do not become
rich. However, paying decent wages to child care staff is our highest
budget priority, and the result is a salary scale which is at the top of the
range available for such work in our state. Our goal is to allow child care
workers to maintain a lifestyle that will support a family so that they do
not have to leave the Lodge as their personal lives progress.

At the same time for many of our line staff we do not believe
that being a child care worker will be their life work. Both financially
and through special work arrangements, support is provided if they
decide to pursue their education so that this can be done while they are
still employed by the Lodge. Many child care staff have left the Lodge
only to later return either to the same position or to an administrative
post. This is encouraged as the experiences such staff bring back to this
setting facilitate growth and change in the Forest Heights milieu.

Staffing Patterns

At Forest Heights our staffing patterns reflect our commitment to
providing our residents with primary attachment objects.[N] Child care
worker shifts consist of three and a half days on and three and a half
days off. One shift starts on Sunday morning after being briefed by the
out-going shift about what has been happening with each individual
child. The dialogue may be about problems the boy is having, or it may
be about successes and good times. This communication is extremely
important as it helps insure continuity of the treatment program. A
similar process is undertaken when this shift passes over the care as
they go off duty.

Each shift has a shift leader who is responsible for its day to day
functioning. The shift leader is responsible to the Residence Director
who overlaps both shifts to insure continuity between them. Of course,
there are some differences between the two shifts because each is
comprised of different people with differing styles, priorities, and
values. It is, however, important to avoid competitiveness between the
shifts. For example, one shift may feel the other is too lax about
structure and does not have a high enough level of expectations. At
such times open communication and trust between the two teams is
crucial, and a unifying philosophy is indispensable.

Some facilities organize their shifts with staff rotating so that
everyone works together at some point. This allows staff to share ideas
and learn from each other. However, for us, the advantages of having
constant shifts seem to outweigh the advantages of the alternative
concept. With the two stable shifts, staff members learn to know the

people they are on duty with to such an extent that they can know instinctively when another staff member may need support. They become aware of each other's strengths and weaknesses and learn to complement each other. A sense of mutuality and togetherness is fostered, much as it is in a family, so that staff members feel free to confront and criticize in a manner which is constructive and direct. We have seen this lead to the development of a mutual sense of caring and dedication between staff who work together. Each shift becomes a strong team, in which the communication is often at a non verbal level. Sometimes all it takes is a look and another staff member is able to respond appropriately and therapeutically to a situation.

Staff Interrelationships

Ideally, the entire organization should view itself as a team working towards common objectives and goals. Within the overall organizational team we have many smaller teams, i.e. milieu teams, educational team, therapy team, administrative team, and ancillary personnel such as cooks, office and maintainance staff. Our goal is that each team be characterized by mutual respect, good internal communication, and a clear understanding of its part in achieving the overall goals of the organization and putting the philosophy into practice. Such teams have to function with a mutual sense of purpose in order to view themselves as an integral part of the overall organization. At the same time, they need to recognize how the effective functioning of the other teams enables their own to function well.

The therapist must learn to appreciate child care workers. The milieu staff need to see themselves an an integral part of the treatment process and to view administration and the therapists as their allies. Teachers need to use not only the expertise of the therapists, but to look at child care workers as an invaluable resource in providing a healthy educational climate, one in which the children come to school eager to learn.

At the same time, the teachers supply child care workers with information regarding the child's progress in school so that milieu staff can support the effort and growth the child has made that day. Educational staff should also share with the child care and clinical staff their knowledge about how the child learns best. This can have profound implications as to what management techniques or therapy modalities might be best suited for a particular child.

The Director must see that there are adequate pay and incentives for staff. There needs to be a pleasant and functional living environment for both children and staff. If equipment and grounds are well maintained then staff and children will work harder to see that a pleasant environment is kept up, and destructiveness in the facility will be minimized.

A common observation by visitors at our staff conferences is that it is difficult to discern the hierarchy as the various thoughts and observations regarding a child are discussed. Just as we expect our boys to learn to be open and honest with staff, we encourage the same among line staff and the organizational leadership.

There are several critical factors which enhance openness and decrease divisiveness between various staff members and their component teams.

1. An agreement as to the basic treatment philosophy of the facility is needed by all the staff. While it is important to be willing to hear and consider challenges from staff about philosophy, it is ultimately hard to maintain a cohesive and open relationship where every disagreement or question becomes global because of basic philosophical differences.

2. There must be modeling of openness and honesty by administration. Line staff need to be aware of administration's struggles, concerns and plans, but, at the same time, it is important that these be presented in such a way that the child care staff not feel burdened with additional responsibilities.

3. Administration and therapists have to be able to disagree, criticize and accept criticism from each other. This modeling again reinforces that differences of opinion are acceptable during discussion and ultimate decision making.

4. The opinions of child care staff need to be sought out and afforded respect. They have the most contact with, and therefore the most intimate knowledge of, the residents.

5. There must be development of a sense of trust, respect, and togetherness among all disciplines so that "turf battles" do not get in the way of effective treatment. This trust is particularly important in terms of decision making. Although individual staff members may disagree about a final treatment decision, it is important that they have enough trust in those who make the final decision that they can accept, and do their best to implement, the plan.

6. An atmosphere of receptivity to creativity and new ideas encourages an excitement about learning. An institution should be seen as a living dynamic organism that needs challenges to keep its zest for life.

There will always be some tensions and disagreements when people live and work together, but our goal is to minimize the negative effects of these and to resolve problems. If board, administration and staff see themselves each as crucial parts of the total team, if there is mutual respect, open communication and genuine caring, then effective treatment will be more likely to take place.

The Role of the Board of Directors

The Executive and Assistant Directors work with the board of directors to insure: 1) that adequate funding is available for a quality program; 2) that the goals of the organization are being met; and 3) that the policies determined by the board are being implemented.

The board needs to be adequately informed about the program. It is their enthusiasm and belief in the effectiveness of the program which will determine the amount of energy they put into all of their duties as board members. This is particularly true as it affects fund raising and public relations. If board members believe in the program, they will be less likely to look upon fund raising as an onerous duty. If they are sold on the program they will be better salesmen when it comes to approaching foundations, individual donors and other funding sources. If the facility has an image problem or if a crisis develops within the community, well informed and committed board members are crucial to solving the problem.

At Forest Heights board members are invited to observe staff meetings. Not only does this allow them to know staff on a different level, but they are able to feel the energy and caring that goes into planning for each child and to appreciate the struggles staff go through in attempting to meet the various boys' needs. They appreciate the dedication, the complexities and the attention to detail needed for a successful treatment program to function.

In addition to the primarily lay member board at Forest Heights we have a Professional Practices Committee comprised of well qualified volunteer professionals from the disciplines of child psychiatry, psychology. social work and education. Administrative and professional staff of the Lodge meet with this committee on a periodic basis keeping them abreast of current developments. They are used as a sounding board if changes in the program are contemplated. If the board has questions about the program or the professional staff, this committee is available to it for consultation.

It is crucial that a harmonious working relationship be developed not only between board and administration but also between board members themselves. Here, too, an openness for exploring new ideas and challenging suggestions in a supportive manner is critical to the overall functioning of the facility.

The Role of the Professional Staff

At Forest Heights we depend upon both our full time and part-time mental health professionals to help integrate various aspects of the program into a unified whole. These staff members must be able to translate underlying psychodynamic issues into everyday words. They help line staff devise strategies for meeting the child's underlying needs, thus changing his perceptions of the world through his everyday interactions. For example, their knowledge of developmental theory may help child care staff view a child as a needy two year old instead of an obnoxious, mouthy 13 year old. Their consultation to line staff is a source of support for those who are struggling with everyday treatment issues regarding the child.

Clinical staff members bring in their outside experiences, both past and present, so that the organization's thinking does not become stagnant or rigid. Their various expertises, such as testing by the psychologist, the medical background of the psychiatrist and the systems theory perspective of the family therapist, contribute to providing a treatment plan that reflects the total child. Finally, the quality of the professional staff affects the program's credibility to the outside professional community.

For the professional staff member to provide these meaningful contributions to the effectiveness of a program, he needs to view himself as a team member. In our setting an appreciation of the central importance of the milieu is essential. Confidence in his own abilities combined with humility, genuineness and openess are helpful qualities. Being both down to earth and having a sense of humor help our professional staff work with line staff. The professional should have a zest for life because the message needs to come from all our staff to the children that life is exciting and full of promise. He needs to be open to learning from others, including those who have fewer educational credentials.

As we have emphasized, at Forest Heights we expect total respect for the role of the child care worker from the professional staff. Often child care workers will be brought into individual therapy or family therapy sessions to share their opinions as to what is happening with the child or to share their child care experiences with the parents. This process can be used as an alliance building process with the child as well as with the parents.

At Forest Heights there is a marked degree of informality among staff and children. This fits both with our philosophy and with our physical setting. We have tried to create a sense of family and, as in most families, formal titles are not used in our conversations with one another. Everyone is called by his first name. It is our bias that titles are often used as a means of emotionally distancing people from one another.

The boundaries of confidentiality extend around the Lodge family as a whole.[N] We do not promise confidentiality between therapist and child. The child knows that what is discussed in the treatment hour will be shared with other staff, just as what is told to child care staff at bedtime will be shared with the therapist.

Our experience has been that, rather than interfering with communication, this may even contribute to our boys being willing to take risks in sharing. The child may share some negative, or very personal, thoughts and perceptions regarding a staff member and then wait to see what the individual's reaction is going to be. When the child discovers that there is no punishment, rejection, or adverse reaction, this helps create an even greater trust level in the total therapeutic environment. In fact, it is quite common that if a resident repeatedly complains about interactions with a particular staff member, the therapist will invite that staff member to participate in the child's therapy session, so that both child and adult have an opportunity to air their perceptions and feelings, thus facilitating joint problem solving and increasing the feelings of trust and attachment between the two.

The widened confidentiality boundaries with inclusion of all staff members emphasizes to both children and adults that we can only help if we all work as a team. Information or concerns not shared with the milieu staff ultimately will not help the child's treatment. This practice has helped prevent factionalism among program components and discourages the unspoken alliance that sometimes develops between therapist and child against the remainder of the program. It also serves to integrate the therapist with the milieu staff. This, in turn, enhances his ability to work with the child. This policy has really put to test the stated belief in the primacy of the milieu as the change agent for children in residential care.

Relationships with Outside Agencies

Relationships with outside agencies form an important element in the treatment of the child. Open, sharing relationships with other agencies are also important in building a broad referral base. Considerable time and effort is spent in helping representatives of other agencies develop an understanding of our philosophy and program. Tours of the physical plant are conducted by one of the children in residence. Educators are welcome to observe in our school. Even if the child is not an appropriate referral for us, we receive many phone calls from agencies, both local and distant, asking for recommendations and assistance in finding a proper placement for a child. We try to supply this help.

Professionals who have worked with a child or agencies that are actively involved with the family are frequently invited to staff

meetings. In the interest of continuity of care before and after placement, such individuals have a vital role to play. Rather than being
viewed as a passive observer of the residential treatment center's team
process, we try to make these individuals part of the process. Our
concerns, failures, excitement and successes are all shared. When a
major decision has to be made, such as cancelling a home visit or
discharging a child, this individual's participation in the discussion is
vital. Direct contact between the referring person and the child in
placement is encouraged and made part of the therapy process in a
planful way.

This does not mean that our residential center gives up its
ultimate autonomy or that the agency representative ceases to play the
role of reviewer and community representative. It merely
acknowledges that if we work together we can better meet the child's
needs, both within the center now and in the community in the future.
After the child is discharged, Lodge staff will make themselves
available for any assistance needed to promote the child's adjustment
to his home community. The positive relationships engendered
promote cooperative treatment planning and encourage a continued
flow of appropriate referrals.

Our involvement with outside agencies is expensive both in
terms of staff time and money. However, we believe that the cost is well
justified. Agencies are much more willing to cooperate in achieving
recommended goals and objectives if they feel they are a part of the
process.

---

*At some point we will want to include Dr. Jorgenson in
the treatment planning for Kenny. Although, at one
level this will begin prior to placment, it will also
include sharing staffing summaries with him and
inviting him to staffings. If he is unable to attend
any of the staffings, then other means will be used to
re-empower him at the time of discharge if he is to
provide the post-placement follow-up.*

Guide for Parents

As you visit treatment centers observe the staff interactions,
particularly those between administrative staff and line staff. Ask
yourselves the following questions.

1. Do staff members look relaxed and secure in fullfilling their
   job responsibilities?

2. Do staffing patterns and interrelationships reflect the philosophical approach to treatment?

3. How is communication between staff members/shifts facilitated to insure consistent treatment of the child?

4. What are the qualifications for staff? Are they given extra training by this facility?

5. What is the child care staff turnover pattern? How frequent are there changes in administrative and professional staff?

6. Are there adequate professional and administrative staff to support the philosophical approach to treatment?

7. How will referring agencies, and/or others that you perceive as important in terms of your child's treatment be involved in pre- and post-placement planning?

Conclusion

A strong philosophical base will make itself evident in the nature of the relationships between board, administration and line staff. It will be further evidenced in all staff interrelationships and the associations with outside agencies. When the administrative structure is working smoothly all employees will have more time and energy to devote to their primary task of helping the child in residence change and grow.

Notes and Elaborations

pg. 71   Although the term "staff" can relate to all employees of an organization, the boys who are residents of Forest Heights identify child care workers as "staff" and talk of other personnel by first name and function, i.e. teacher, therapist, nurse, etc.

pg. 81   We realize that few treatment centers have staffing patterns like the one at Forest Heights. We would, however, encourage consumers to explore how staffing patterns and stated philosophy correlate with one another.

pg. 86   Likewise, confidentiality boundaries may vary from one center to another. The consumer should be primarily interested in two things—how and what information is transmitted within the facility (and what is not)? and how and what information will be transmitted to parents and/or referral or post-placement service providers?

C O N T E N T S

Before Admission

Kenny's Case   91
Congruency with Philosophical Base   93
The Crucial First Steps   93
Admission Selection   95
Admission Criteria for the Attachment Model   96
Family Involvement in Decision Making   98
The Child's Involvement in Decision Making   100
The Involvement of Other Family Members in the
       Pre-admission Process   100
The Extended Home Visit
       Kenny's Case   100
       Text   106
Admission Day
       Kenny's Case   110
       The Separation Interview   116
       Entering the Milieu   120
       Staff and Resident Preparation for a
       New Admission   121
Guide for Parents   122
Conclusion   122
Notes and Elaborations   122

Before Admission

The Summers decided to combine their next visit to Forest Heights with a few days in Vail. Sarah was able to get several days off work. J.J. accompanied them only for the weekend and would be flying home Sunday evening. Even though he would not have a chance to meet the staff at the Lodge and tour the facility as they had, Martha and John felt that it was important that he at least see it on the way to the airport. This also gave them an opportunity to have Kenny see the Lodge before he was to go for his pre-placement evaluation.

J.J. had been very opposed to Kenny's going to some "lock up place for spoiled brats." They shared with him much of the information they had received about the various therapeutic programs at Forest Heights, but they knew that his image of it was probably quite different from reality. It had been a worthwhile detour from the freeway. J.J. was envious of Kenny's having an opportunity to live "up on top of the mountains in the woods." They hoped that this would help Kenny see the entire situation in a different light. Maybe he wouldn't feel that he was being sent away because he was bad, but rather that he was lucky to have this opportunity.

The following day the Summers, with Sarah and Kenny, made their third trip up Forest Hill. Martha found she wasn't quite as apprehensive about the drive this time. However, she doubted that she would ever truly get used to it. Again, they were greeted by Melody as they entered the Administration Building. She remembered their first names immediately and followed this up with a, "You must be Kenny."

They all entered Russ' office. Initially Kenny had said he didn't want to go in there with "that dog." Russ had given him a quick reassurance that Clipper wouldn't hurt him. He then just seemed to expect no further fuss. Surprisingly, there was not. Russ incorporated both Kenny and Sarah into the conversation. He expressed disappointment that J.J. was not able to be with them as he commented that what siblings thought about their brother's coming to FHL was important. Russ encouraged both Sarah and Kenny to ask questions. Kenny wanted to know if he could bring his bike and if he could have his own TV in his room. The answer to the former question was yes. To the latter he received a firm no. Kenny started in with, "It's not fair. I'm not going to come then." He had been told ahead that he, too, had to make a commitment to coming to the Lodge.

Russ did not respond directly to Kenny's challenge, but rather started talking about the kinds of problems Kenny had been having at school, home, and with friends. To Kenny, it didn't sound like the lectures he was used to getting and it didn't sound like a scolding. He found that the more that Russ asked him about the problems and talked about them, the sadder he started feeling. In fact he was afraid that he might even cry. Russ seemed to understand that sadness. He asked Kenny if he wanted it to be different. Kenny agreed that he didn't like the way that things had been going and that he did indeed want them to be different.

At that point, rather than asking Kenny if he wanted to come to the Lodge, Russ switched gears and called on the intercom to have one of the boys come over and take Kenny and Sarah on a tour of the Lodge. Kenny was surprised that his parents didn't go with them. Russ suggested that they stay behind. While Kenny and Sarah were gone, Russ commented that he was certain he could get a commitment from Kenny and they started discussing plans for an in-home pre-placement visit. Russ suggested that Linda fly in one morning and leave the evening of the following day.

Kenny, to his own surprise, found himself already starting to size up the boys he saw on the tour, as though they were to be new classmates and he was selecting those he wanted for friends. Each year he had done that, but it had never worked out the way he had planned. The boys seemed to be having fun. A couple were sitting in chairs, and Jacob, who was showing them around, said that that's what happened if you got in trouble here. You had to sit in a chair in the living room. Well, at least that didn't sound too bad to Kenny.

He asked what bedroom he would have if he came, but Jacob didn't know for certain. He said that most, but not all, kids Kenny's age slept in the "back bedroom" when they first came. Jacob commented that he remembered how scared he was the first time he came to visit the Lodge, but he really liked it now and was glad that he had come. Kenny wondered if someone had told Jacob to say that or if it was true.

After the tour, Sarah and Kenny returned to Russ' office and Russ asked if Kenny had any further questions. Kenny asked if he had to go to school and what happened if a kid didn't mind here. He also asked how frequently his parents could call and visit. Russ answered all of his questions and didn't ignore him at all. This sure was different than school conferences, when parents and teachers got together but kids were left out. Kenny liked it. It made him feel important instead of "bad." Russ then said, "Well, Kenny, you said that you wanted things to be different between you and your folks and that you would like to be able to make and keep friends. I'm sure that's true. I think we could really help you with these problems here at the Lodge if you want help. Is that something you would like?" Kenny was surprised to hear the words "Yes, I do" pop out of his mouth. Oh, boy, what had he gotten himself into? All of a sudden he wasn't certain that he liked people asking his opinion. ∎

Congruency with Philosophical Base

Prior to admission, there will be many, and varied, contacts with the child and his family. At some time during these communications, the basic philosophical approach of the treatment facility usually will be explained. More importantly however, during these pre-admission contacts the philosophical framework will undoubtedly be demonstrated in the interactions between the facility staff and family members. In centers in which the philosophical basis of treatment is strong and pervasive throughout all components of the program, it will be evident in the nature of the pre-admission contacts. In programs in which the basic philosophical approach is fragmented, or poorly articulated, again it will probably be evident during this period.

It is our intention at Forest Heights to transmit to the child and family during the pre-placement period our emphasis on interpersonal relationships, on enhancing feelings of self-worth and self determination, the importance of the family, and the creation of reciprocal rather than power based relationships. We do this by both our words and our actions. Our pre-admission policies and procedures are designed to reflect this basic philosophical approach to treatment.

The Crucial First Steps

In the initial contacts with family members, the stage is set for the type of relationship that will be established between them and the treatment center. Since these intial contacts are usually made by telephone, it is important that the person who answers the phone conveys the type of message the facility wants to impart. An individual who sounds warm and caring, and who in the future will indicate that she remembers having previous contact with the family, helps set the stage for the treatment process. That first call can provide reassurance and strengthen the family's resolve to obtain appropriate care for their child, or it may leave the family with an increased sense of frustration and futility.

The first contact may not be from a family member, but rather from a referring clinician who comments that the family "has not accepted the need for residential treatment, but that they are willing to explore the possibility further." For others, that first call is a desperate plea for help NOW. Whatever the specifics of their story, most families seeking residential treatment for a child have some things in common. By the time they contact a treatment center, they have usually experienced a series of failures. Their trust level for professionals may not be high. Whether inpatient or outpatient services were provided in the past, the family can describe feelings of failed hopes and unfilled promises. In addition, they may have felt blamed for the child's problems or for his lack of progress.

Residential staff must be sensitive to the feelings of pain, fear, sadness, anger, and distrust that families may bring with them when they are asking for help. Most families have experienced a struggle to get appropriate services for their children. There is no greater testimony to the courage, strength, and tenacity of families than the fact that they persist in their search for appropriate care for their child. Usually they must do this at a time when the entire family is under tremendous stress and pressure.

Even when it is apparent early in the course of a telephone contact that the services provided by a facility are not appropriate in this case, it is important to be sensitive to the parents' pain and to try to help them locate more appropriate resources.

When families make their first trip to a treatment center, they are particularly sensitive to the attitudes of those with whom they come in contact. It is helpful when they are greeted by someone who is expecting their arrival and who can help them connect with whichever staff member is to meet with them. The physical setting, as well as the attitudes of the staff, helps set the stage for the subsequent relationship between facility and family.

During this trip, we give the family considerable information about the facility, our philosophy, the types of children that we have successfully treated in the past, and the modes of treatment utilized. They are afforded an opportunity to tour the facility, to observe residents and staff interacting, to see the living accommodations, and to ask a variety of questions, both large and small. They are not rushed. This is their opportunity to assess our program in terms of our abilities to meet their family's needs.

Basic entrance criteria should be clear, not only to those who make the admission decisions, but also to referral sources. Placement in a residential treatment center, in and of itself, provides a major disruption in the child's life by separating the child from family members. Schooling and peer relationships are both interrupted. Such massive changes should never be undertaken lightly. Residential care is usually reserved for the child who is having problems in all three major areas of his life—family, school and peers—and even then only when the problems have not been amenable to out-patient treatment.

At the same time, it is important to be sensitive to the need for insuring a treatment environment that truly meets the child's needs in as timely a manner as possible. If a child moves from institution to institution, always a step behind the level of intervention that he needs, he eventually becomes unresponsive to virtually all treatment approaches.

For this reason, we believe that it is imperative that any residential center have clear guidelines in place for selecting children for admission—children who are truly in need of out-of-home care and who, at the same time, are amenable to the treatment approaches and philosophy utilized. The needs of each individual child must be met.

For example, children who are chronic runners may not be appropriate for an open facility. Those who are a danger to themselves or others need to be in a facility with adequate adult supervision. Children whose medical or physical handicaps require special equipment or staff training deserve placement in facilities which can provide these services. The child's educational needs must be met. At times, admission decisions may be made on the basis of the overall composition of the group, rather than focusing on a particular child's needs. Two examples come to mind: 1) in a facility that tries to keep a balance between children of various ages or between those who are more aggressive versus those who are more withdrawn, admission decisions will be made which support these balances; 2) although a facility may usually be able to provide adequate staff supervision for the child who is prone to hurting himself or others, it may not be able to adequately, at this moment in time, provide for the needs of a particular child seeking admission because there are already several children needing one-on-one attention in residence.

Admission Criteria when the Treatment Philosophy is Based on an Attachment Model

At Forest Heights we have identified some specific criteria for those whom we think are appropriate to consider for admission to our program. With attachment as an assumed goal of treatment, it is crucial that we determine that the child has the potential for developing attachments, even though he may be highly resistant to doing so. Furthermore, with this particular treatment philosophy, where transferring the attachments gained during the treatment process is a necessary part of helping the child move on, we must always ask, "Where does the child go from here?"

Those who do best in our treatment setting are:

1. Those who have attachment problems.[N]

2. Those who have experienced parental loss/separation.

3. Those who are fixated at earlier developmental stages and who need an environment that is conducive to meeting earlier needs to help them continue along the course of psychological maturation.

4. Those whose perceptual problems, whether they be visual, auditory, or tactile in nature, have interfered with their forming normal relationships with others.

5. Irrespective of the nature of the particular problems it is important for residents in our treatment program to exhibit some discomfort in their present condition, or at minimum that there be a potential for getting that discomfort.[N]

Children who meet these criteria may be referred to us with a variety of diagnostic labels, including conduct disorders, attention deficit disorder, the various anxiety disorders of childhood or adolescence, oppositional disorders, pervasive developmental disorders, schizoid disorder of childhood, and childhood schizophrenia. These labels are dependent upon current behavioral manifestations of problems. In general we are more interested in the pathogenesis of the disorder in a particular child and how it has affected his relationships with himself and with others than the diagnostic label per se.

Again, with the attachment model, our goal is to help the child experience adult-child relationships which, by meeting his underlying needs, will be conducive to the change process. At the termination of treatment, we must transfer the attachments that have grown, as well as the behavioral gains made, to the permanent primary caretakers. That means that the child must have a family that is able to make some form of long term commitment to him. By the time of discharge a family

must be willing to be involved, at some level, in the child's
treatment.

At the same time, we must recognize that the family may need to see some evidence of change on the part of their child before their commitment and involvement can be extensive. Previous treatment failures may have undercut the family's belief that change is possible. That lack of hope in turn may result in an appearance of limited investment or in resistance to therapeutic intervention. Sometimes changes in the child are needed before the parents regain their ability to invest in the therapy process. Therefore, in some cases family therapy will be postponed for a period of time. During this period the focus of the family contacts will be on interpretation of the child's treatment program, his progress, visit management, and alliance building.

Likewise, we have identified some children who we do not think are appropriate for admission to our facility. Because we are a long term residential facility we do not see ourselves as providers of short term or crisis intervention on an in-patient basis. In general, short term care requires a different treatment approach than longer term care.

Children with physical handicaps that preclude their participation in most of the usual activities and routines will not be available for our true avenue for change, the milieu. Those with severe or profound mental retardation may not be able to benefit from the subtleties of the milieu. They may respond best to the consistency of a behavior modification approach to treatment. On the other hand, we have taken a variety of children with emotional problems co-existing with varying degrees of developmental disabilities. We have found that we may be able to help such youngsters change their relationship skills sufficiently that they can then fit into a program that is designed primarily for developmentally delayed individuals. In general, these children have had severe enough behavioral problems that they had previously been precluded from such programs.

Adolescents with character disorders are not very amenable to our treatment model. In general, they have little or no discomfort related to their pathology and are extremely resistant to nurture and re-parenting. However, we recognize that many of the signs and symptoms of unresolved separation problems and severe attachment problems closely resemble the symptoms of character disorder. Discomfort is a key factor in determining which of these youth may experience positive changes via our treatment approach. If such internal pain or anxiety is not present, the youth is more likely to need a program where the focus is on creating discomfort than unconditionally meeting needs.

Although many of our residents have a history of running, because of the basically open nature of our facility we do not see ourselves as an appropriate placement for the chronic runaway.

Likewise, because of the construction of our buildings, we do not view ourselves as a viable treatment alternative for a chronic firesetter. On the other hand some of our residents have a history of firesetting as a behavioral response to underlying feelings, such as loneliness. We think we can successfully treat these children without endangering anyone.

Although we accept a broad age range, there will still be some children who fall outside this range. A child has to be old enough, usually early school age, to be able to participate in at least some of our activities and yet young enough to have completed treatment by the common age of emancipation. Therefore, our usual age range at the time of admission is 5-15 years. As described in the introduction we accept only boys into our inpatient program.

Family Involvement in Decision Making

The admission process, per se, has an infinite number of variations. This relates to the fact that this procedure is the initial step in the treat- ment process. Right from the beginning, in our setting, we want to personalize relationships and start building alliances.

The first contacts with the family are usually by telephone. Although he may use input of other staff members in the decision making process, the Executive Director is in charge of all admission decisions. The primary reason for this is that we usually have a very limited number of openings which will be available in the foreseeable future. It would undermine the credibility of the program if we had several different people making, but being unable to keep, plans for these limited openings. Calls about admission are preferably referred directly to the Director. When he is not available the Social Services Director will take the call. If neither is available, one of the other administrative staff may talk with whomever is calling and relay the message to the Executive Director, who will return the call.

Usually sufficient information can be gleaned during the initial telephone contact to give some sense of the appropriateness of considering a particular child for placement in our facility. Unless it is decided that the child is totally inappropriate for consideration, the family is asked to have copies of past assessments—psychological, medical and educational—sent prior to their first visit to the center.

The first face-to-face visit usually occurs at Forest Heights. During this contact a careful interpretation of our program is undertaken. This begins with a statement about the philosophy of our treatment approach. We then usually move on to a description of the characteristics of children with attachment disorders. The most prominent characteristic is the physical or emotional distancing of adults. Frequently the child gets little satisfaction from tasks well done

or may see himself as undeserving. There is nearly always an inappropriate-for-age balance between dependency and independency. This may manifest itself either with premature or excessive autonomy or over reliance on adult interactions or supervision. Delays in
conscience development are frequent. Impulsive behavior is common. Relationships may be shallow. Peer problems are usual. This child may try to gain control of all situations or he may avoid taking any responsibility for his own actions. Problems expressing feelings appropriately are universal. Learning problems with a poorly developed sense of cause and effect and subsequent problems with abstract thinking are frequent.

Rather than never having developed a primary attachment, the etiology of the child's problems may be interrupted attachments or unresolved separation issues. In these circumstances the child's energies may be so tied up in past relationships that he is not able to make use of current relationships. He does not develop new attachments and progress up the developmental ladder of psychological maturation is arrested.

Parents frequently express amazement at how the description of attachment problems fits their child. By this point most parents have gained a clearer understanding of why their child is disturbed. The question that usually follows is, "But what can we do?" The discussion then centers on how our residential treatment process addresses the issues presented by the disturbed child.

This is a crucial point, for, while the family may not be able to meet the child's needs, they usually do have some sense of what he needs. Further is it important that they be given adequate information for judging whether they think that Forest Heights can meet these needs. We believe that the family should take a major role in the decision making about admission. Success in the treatment process is based, to some degree, on developing and enhancing the trust of the parents for the facility and its staff. Secondly, we never intend to disenfranchise the family as primary caregivers or decision makers in the child's life overall. During these initial contacts the stage is set for the open communication which must exist between our center and the child's family throughout the treatment process. Encouragement to question reinforces the importance of the family in the decision making process while it enhances the building of trust.

Many times at the conclusion of this visit, it is possible to offer the family an opportunity to place their child. Other times, it is necessary that further assessment of the child be undertaken by our treatment center staff prior to a decision about the appropriateness of placement being made.

In spite of the omnipotent and controlling stance presented by many, emotionally disturbed children often feel little control over their lives. For this reason, at Forest Heights an important aspect of our pre-admission procedures focuses on getting a verbal commitment from the boy. This commitment does not have to be given with great enthusiasm, but the fact that the child is involved at some level in the decision making sets the stage for building an alliance with him for the treatment process as a whole.

Therefore, the most common sequence when parents want to pursue admission after the initial visit is for a second visit including the child to be set up. At the time of this contact, the boy has an opportunity to tour the facility, meet staff and other residents, spend some time with at least one staff member, and ask questions both of adults and of peers before being asked to make a commitment. If all three parties—the child, family and facility—agree that admission is appropriate, arrangements are made to complete assessments and facilitate placement.

The Involvement of Other Family Members in the Pre-Admission Process

We have found that it is important to involve siblings and sometimes extended family members in the pre-admission process. When possible, brothers and sisters of the child to be placed visit. Frequently, siblings have fears that need to be allayed. Often they perceive their brother as being sent to a "lock up" with windows with bars, high fences, and guards. At the same time they may need help with their feelings of anger about the difficulties they have had with him and the stress he has placed on the family as a whole. Their feelings of guilt, and occasionally their feelings of jealousy, may have to be addressed.

Parents may be facing negative or resistant attitudes on the part of extended family with regards to the placement. Including such relatives in a pre-placement visit can sometimes assist the parents in interpreting the need for treatment and garner support for placement. In addition, observations made during this visit enhance the clinical staff's understanding of the overall family dynamics.

The Extended Home Visit[N]

It was 10 a.m. Kenny and his mom were on their way to the airport to meet Linda, who was coming for the two day pre-placement visit. Martha was rather anxious. She felt that it was she and John who were going to be observed just as much as Kenny. She had been told that they were to do nothing out of the ordinary. The goal was to observe how it usually was in their home. Well, "usually" they were not anticipating having their child enter residential treatment. "Usually" they did not have a stranger staying with them for two days.

At least she had briefly met Linda at the Lodge, so she would recognize her. Here she came now, an attractive young woman with a ready smile. En route to the Summers home, Linda asked Kenny a variety of questions about what he had been doing since his visit to the Lodge, about landmarks that they passed. She seemed very comfortable in this situation. It was apparent that visiting homes of people whom she had barely met was a common occurrence for her. Martha wished that she could feel as assured in new situations.

En route home, Linda reviewed with Martha and Kenny the schedule for today and tomorrow. She wanted to make certain that Kenny knew about her various meetings. Even though school was not in session Martha had been able to set up an appointment with Kenny's teacher from last year and with the principal, Mr. Torres. During the telephone call confirming her travel arrangements, Linda had indicated that during the school year she liked to spend time in the school observing the child in the classroom, on the playground, and in the lunch room, as well as time talking with teachers. Since it was summertime and direct observations were not possible, she would like to talk with the teacher. Martha had thought that she should also talk with the principal since he had known Kenny since kindergarten and had had many contacts with him.

The remainder of the day would be spent at the Summers home. The following day there was a 1:00 p.m. appointment with Dr. Jorgenson. Linda had decided that appointments with the pediatrician and developmental specialist were not necessary. The Medical Director at the Lodge had gone through their reports and had not found anything that indicated any major health concerns.

Except when asked questions, Kenny was very quiet in the backseat as they were driving home from the airport. Martha knew that she could never count on his behavior. When she wanted him to be quiet he rarely was. Now, for once, she didn't care how much he acted up. In fact, she rather hoped that he would act up so Linda could see him at his worst—and here he was, quiet.

On arrival at the Summers home, Martha had Kenny show Linda where she would be staying. He took her overnight case upstairs. Linda was to sleep in what had been J.J.'s room prior to his moving out. There were still a few old high school pennants on the walls and some models on the bookcase.

Linda asked Kenny to give her a tour of the house. She had learned that a lot of information could be obtained in this manner. It provided a feel for the layout of the house. In addition, it was frequently possible to get a clear picture of how the child viewed the home in terms of the boundaries indicative of each individual's privacy. She noted that Kenny viewed no rooms as "off limits." He entered his sister's room, showing off her possessions in the same manner as he had done in his own room. When they entered the master bedroom, Kenny plopped on the bed, commenting, "Someday this will be my room and my bed."

It was apparent that the family spent most of their time in the family room that adjoined the kitchen. At one end there was an area for family meals, although there was also a more formal dining room as well as a formal living room. In the basement there was a large recreation area with space for Kenny's toys to be spread out and ample room for the ping pong table.

At lunch Kenny immediately took six half sandwiches from the plate on the table. Martha tried diversionary tactics and pleading to no avail. Kenny was up and down from the table four or five times during the meal. At one point Kenny wrapped himself up in the drapes at the window of the room. Mom's remonstrations met with no response.

In the early afternoon, while Kenny was taking swimming lessons from a neighbor, Martha and Linda talked further about birth and developmental information. At Linda's suggestion, Martha had gotten out Kenny's baby book and the family albums. She was right. They did help Martha remember the particulars of Kenny's development as an infant. He had had some sleep disturbances even then, being fussy much of the night. At age two to three this pattern had switched and Kenny had started rocking his bed "for hours on end" before he went to sleep. His speech had been somewhat delayed. In retrospect, Martha remembered how she had worried that maybe he would never speak. Nowadays there were times when she would give almost anything if he would only be quiet.

Following the review of developmental material, Linda completed a genogram[N] of Martha's side of the family and got further information about Martha's past history.

Then it was time to go to the school for the meeting with Mrs. Street and Mr. Torres. Mr. Torres reviewed the types of behavioral problems they had observed throughout the years. Of most concern to him were the explosive outbursts when Kenny would suddenly physically threaten other children. The infrequency of such eruptions made such incidents particularly unpredictable. Adults would be lulled into thinking that previous disciplinary measures had indeed been successful and then another outburst would occur. Mrs. Street said that because of Kenny's behavioral problems it was very difficult to assess what underlying learning problems, if any, he might have. She had the impression that he was brighter than he usually let on, but it was impossible to get any kind of consistent performance from him.

While Martha completed dinner preparations with Sarah's help, Linda completed the genogram for John's side of the family and obtained further social history from him. Dinner went somewhat more smoothly than had lunch. John's presence at the table seemed to make a difference. Kenny did much less testing. Linda had learned from previous home visits that boys coming to the Lodge wanted lots of additional information about daily routines, mealtimes, activities, allowances and recreational activities. Dinner time provided an opportunity for this discussion. She told Kenny that she had brought some pictures of the Lodge for him to have to share with friends, neighbors, teachers or others if he chose. She had already shared them with Mrs. Street and Mr. Torres.

After dinner, John asked Kenny to come sit by him on the couch. Kenny made a running jump, landing on Dad. Dad's comment was "See, now that didn't hurt." Kenny sat quietly for about three minutes watching T.V. He then reached up and slapped his dad twice. Dad playfully slapped him back and they continued this type of interaction until Martha was able to distract Kenny.

During the evening, Linda noted a recurrent pattern. Confrontations between Kenny and any of the three adults in the family were never resolved directly. The words "no" and/or "stop" were not used. A third member of the family always intervened to settle the confrontation or else the adult backed down and rescinded the demand.

After Kenny had gone to bed, Linda asked if Kenny had been behaving in his usual manner. She wondered if they thought their reactions to Kenny during the evening were the same as usual. Both parents and Sarah noted that just in the past two weeks Kenny's behaviors had become progressively worse. He had crawled out his window one night and it took them an hour to find him. Actually he was hiding in the back yard. The next night he again crawled out the window and threw a rock, breaking his parents' bedroom window. He had also put water in the lawnmower gas tank and had turned the thermostat in the house up to 100 degrees even though it was 80 degrees outside. He had purposefully cut up two pairs of his pants and a new shirt.

When Linda pointed out some of her observations as to how the family seemed to handle Kenny's behaviors, both parents and Sarah related that the usual pattern in the family was for John to intervene in Martha's conflicts with all three children, and for him to ask Martha to stop the children from behaving in ways that displeased him. Linda asked what they thought would happen if adults kept confronting Kenny about stopping the inappropriate behaviors. Everyone agreed that the more they confronted him, the worse Kenny's behaviors got.

Kenny called his mother to his room at least five times in the hour after he went to bed. She always went. She related that he was constantly saying, "I'm afraid to go to Forest Heights" or was verbally expressing other fears.

During the evening, Linda completed an Eco-Map^N with the parents. The resulting picture helped the family see how they related with their social and work environment. It identified areas of support and strength as well as areas of stress and emotional drain on the family.

There was also an opportunity to answer many of the very practical questions that John and Martha had. Questions about appropriate clothing for the Lodge, laundry, and marking the clothes were raised by Martha. Both parents had questions about visits, telephone calls and letter writing. They wondered when Linda thought that Kenny would be able to come home for his first visit. They had further questions about which of his possessions he should bring to the Lodge and which he should leave at home.

The following morning everyone was up by 6:30 a.m. Linda and Kenny did some building with Legos while Martha was fixing breakfast. Linda again reviewed her schedule for the day with Kenny. As they were building she noted that Kenny followed the diagram given on the box very well and that during this task his concentration span seemed quite normal. While they were playing, Martha commented that she was fixing pancakes for breakfast. Kenny expressed great dislike for pancakes, yet before anyone else was seated he had placed four of them on his plate.

After breakfast Kenny wanted to go outside. It was raining, and Martha felt it was too early for him to be out in the neighborhood, as he tended to go and ring doorbells, seeking other children to come out and play with him. Kenny tried unsuccessfully to sneak out. He then said he was going to his room to play. There he proceeded to turn over all the chairs and to throw everything from his drawers and closet onto the floor. He then climbed out the window and came around to the back, making certain that Martha and Linda saw him through the sliding glass doors. Martha went out, retrieved him and spanked him. Kenny ran into the bathroom and started breaking things. After 15 minutes, he came out more calmly. When Martha told him that as discipline for these behaviors he would be grounded to the yard for the day, Kenny's comment was, "Good, I don't want to go anywhere today."

Later, Linda involved Kenny in some drawing activities and then they played a game together. When Kenny saw that he might lose, he started blatantly cheating and disrupted the game. His parting comment as the game was put away was, "I've never lost a game yet." This was undoubtedly true, as whenever he saw that he might lose he found a way to disrupt the game.

Sarah was off work that day so she took care of Kenny while

Linda and Martha went for the appointment with Dr. Jorgenson. Dr. Jorgenson confirmed that he had noted that both parents had difficulty following through with requests of Kenny. In general, Kenny did better during highly structured sessions when he knew just what to expect than he did during less structured sessions. Dr. J. had noted, however, that when he had gotten into more direct confrontations with Kenny his behavior had indeed escalated, and unless he was physically controlled at those times he would start to destroy the playroom toys.

When Martha and Linda returned home, Kenny had two neighborhood friends over playing in the yard. There were continuous conflicts among the three and Kenny frequently entered the house screaming, "They aren't playing fair. I hate them." Martha would intervene with suggestions as to how to work things out, but nothing seemed to work for Kenny. Finally, Martha sent the neighbor children home. At that point Kenny switched all of his anger from his friends to his mother, blaming her for his having no friends.

After Kenny's anger subsided some, Linda asked if he was interested in knowing what Dr. J. had said about him and his family. She asked Kenny what his hopes had been when he had started therapy with Dr. J. What had changed and what hadn't changed? She shared with him Dr. Jorgenson's observations and comments.[N].

Although Kenny had been on tranquilizers following his evaluation at the medical center, Russ had explained the Lodge's philosophy of not using medication to control behaviors and had requested that Kenny be tapered off medication prior to the pre-placement assessment. As Linda was packing to leave, Martha asked if she couldn't again place him on medication until his admission as it seemed as though his behavior was further deteriorating. Linda reassured her that if Dr. J. approved it would be acceptable, but that Kenny would be taken off the medication following admission to Forest Heights.[N]

As they were driving to the airport Martha commented that the home visit hadn't been "as bad" as she had anticipated. Kenny just looked relieved that it was nearly over. Martha asked if it would be okay if they called Linda if either she or John thought of additional questions before they brought Kenny to the Lodge. She expressed the thought that if the rest of the staff were like Linda then it wouldn't be so bad having Kenny at Forest Heights.

The in-home observations had confirmed both the necessity for in-patient treatment and also the appropriateness of this particular child for the Lodge treatment program. Linda's notes written en route to Denver included the following: "I do not feel that Kenny can be managed on an out-patient basis. Some of his behaviors will have to change before his parents, particularly Mom, can invest in trying to change their behaviors. Kenny is very adept at setting Martha up to feel guilty. This results in her giving in to his demands. John is progressively leaving earlier in the mornings and coming home later in the evenings. He is not providing much support for Martha in her management of Kenny. Everyone in the family seems to be feeling overwhelmed and exhausted." ∎

The Extended Home Visit

Over a period of years, Forest Heights has made extended home visits an integral part of its intake process. The homes our in-patient residents come from vary from one extreme to the other in terms of socio-economic background. It is important that we understand the child's living situation so that we can help him with transition both into the treatment residence and, at the end of treatment, back into his home environment.

When we started doing extended home visits, a variety of clinical staff were involved, dependent both on their particular areas of expertise and on their schedules. However, we gradually came to recognize that for maximum gains from this assessment tool, the person doing the visits needed to have an opportunity to develop extensive expertise in the process itself. For several years now there has been one clinical staff member assigned to this task.

The extended home visit is useful in a variety of ways:

1. **It is a major tool in building trust between facility and family.** The trust initiated between home visitor and family during this visit usually generalizes fairly quickly to other staff. The clinician who lives in the home for several days becomes keenly aware of the family's pain and of their difficulites in living with the child. This provides a balance of treatment planning meetings when other staff members are only aware of the child's pain with regards to the family relationships.

2. **Information about both child and family that is not readily available in any other setting comes to light.** It becomes much easier, in this setting, to get a complete picture of the child's range of behaviors and of the parental attempts to cope with the child. Sibling relationships are easily assessed.

3. **Information about what specific changes will be necessary before the child can successfully return to his family and community is identified.**

4. **Separation trauma is decreased and the transition from home to treatment center is facilitated.** The home visitor is able to help prepare child, parents, and other family members for the

feelings and the procedures connected with the separation 107
experience at the time of admission. During the early hours
and days of placement, the home visitor is a reassuring figure
to the child in placement. She provides a known source of
information for the family. Affording a supportive link
between home and milieu she diminishes both the child's
tendency to compartmentalize home and treatment center and
also the likelihood of the child being successful in setting up
"let's you and him fight" situations between staff and
family.

5. **Direct contact between a representative of the facility and people
who have intimate knowledge of the child's functioning in a variety
of situations—school, peer group activities, therapy, the
neighborhood, etc.—is possible.** Communication lines are
established which allow support services to be current with the
child's progress while in placement. Face-to-face communication with referral sources or others who have had contact with
the family frequently accesses information and observations
that were not included in written reports.

6. **Post-placement planning, taking into consideration the services
available within the home community, begins during this pre-
placement phase.** The personal relationships established with
community support services go a long way in facilitating a
rapid and effective transition back into the home community
at the time of discharge.

7. **It is during this home visit that extensive social history, medical
history, immunization records, etc. are gathered.** Time is
devoted to reviewing patient rights, discipline policies, treatment agreements, and releases. This means that on the day of
admission the focus can be on the separation process rather
than administrative tasks.

The parents are usually asked to set up appointments for the home
visitor with the school therapist, etc. Upon arrival in the family's home
community, the clinician assumes a somewhat dependent role, relying
on the family for food, shelter, and transportation. This not only
enhances the family's sense of competence at a time when they may feel
particularly vulnerable, but it also models that it is acceptable to have
shifting roles of dependency/independency that vary with the
situation.

In order to get the most out of the observation period, the home
visitor joins in the family routine, whatever it may be. Conversation
during family activities such as meal preparation, outings, shopping or
exercising tends to be less defended due to the primary focus being
directed toward the task at hand. Daily routines reveal information

about family roles, problem solving behaviors, interpersonal communications and even family priorities. With active participation in family tasks, the visitor's role becomes less that of a guest and family members behave less like hosts.

Observation potential within the home and community is endless. Decor, room placement of the children, variations in children's rooms and toys, destruction or the absence of it, interactions with neighbors and friends, hobbies, bedtime and mealtime routines are all revealing details of the family dynamics. A tour of the neighborhood on foot or bicycle with the child reveals the extent of the child's awareness of the community. It can yield information in terms of the youngster's perceptions of peers as well as the neighbor childrens' perceptions of him. The task of touring directs the child's defenses away from the discussion, often resulting in revealing insights that would not be readily shared in an office setting.

Another major advantage of the home visit is the potential for a wide variety of interviews. Family members can be interviewed individually or in any combination desired. There is ready access to family picture albums and baby books. These often provide a stimulus for further memories and information. They usually provide an added dimension to understanding the family. Without the time pressure of the usual structured intake history interview, more emphatic responses are likely to occur and the parents are more apt to share their greatest concerns. Frequently one finds family members bringing unfinished business to the interviews: unfinished grief over a death, educational or career disappointments, a risk-taking admission of drug or alcohol abuse or an affair.

By having access to both family members and community resources there is an opportunity to facilitate communication between the two, to clarify misperceptions and sometimes to decrease tensions that may be present in these relationships.

We learn more about siblings' perceptions of the family problems. The clinician can address their fears and worries about their brother's future and their own and can gain further understanding as to how they have coped with the family tensions. Again, the concept that we care about each individual in the family is reinforced. At the same time, the observations of brothers and sisters may give the home visitor an opportunity to help rebuild the parents' self-esteem. Feeling guilt and a sense of failure can be decreased through identifying the strengths observed in the siblings.

By the time that residential treatment is necessary, parents are frequently distanced from and angry with the child. Sides have been taken and the treatment center can quickly become seen as "taking sides" with the child. Empathic caring extended to each family member during this visit enhances the awareness that treatment will be a family process.

During the home visit, whenever possible, the child is observed in the classroom. Teachers, and possibly principals, are interviewed regarding their observations and work with the child. Contacts with previous teachers as well may help in clarifying the overall picture of the child's educational history.

Appointments are made with clinicians who have worked with the child or family. This may include visits with pediatricians or other physicians as well as with psychotherapists. On occasion the clinician from the Lodge has the opportunity to participate in a family or individual therapy session during the visit.

Many times it is possible to have contact with extended family members who live in the area. Such individuals have a great effect on the family and their decision making process. They provide a unique source of knowledge about the child and nuclear family. They have known the child and parents over time in an intimate manner without necessarily being a direct part of the day-to-day family functioning. An opportunity to gain what knowledge they have about the child and family and to assess their support, or lack of it, for placement is afforded.

Throughout the visit family members' concerns about residential treatment in general, and the Lodge in particular, can be addressed. Questions frequently relate to techniques used at the Lodge for controlling behaviors that have been difficult or impossible for family and school to manage. Comfortable and sure responses provide reassurance. At the same time, the parents' guilt about their lack of success in handling these behaviors may be lessened by identifying the numerous resources and skills available within the residential facility. Placement is seen as finding resources adequate to meet the child's needs which are beyond the scope of the family. Admission to the Lodge can then be viewed not as a parenting failure, or abandonment of the child, but rather as a caring and appropriate act of parenting. Children are reassured and less anxious when they have their questions about daily routine and care answered prior to placement. Our home visitor has intimate knowledge of our residential program. She must be able to answer any question about the program clearly and accurately. An inability to answer basic questions about the daily routine and management within the milieu would quickly undercut the family's trust.

The individual doing our home visits must be able to fit comfortably into many different family situations. Economic, cultural and ethnic differences must be readily accepted and enjoyed. Sleeping on a couch, sharing a room with a child, limited bathing facilities must be as easily accepted as being picked up at the airport by limousine and staying in a home with servants.

Our home visitor must always keep paramount the primary objective of observing and gathering information. The temptation to confront behavior or to attempt to get changes in the family during these early contacts is resisted. If the family asks for suggestions about behavior management, the most appropriate response at this point in time is, "If I could give you a quick remedy that would work at home then we would be considering out-patient treatment. We have already determined that your son needs residential care precisely because he hasn't been able to make use of the usual out-patient suggestions." If there is disagreement between the parents about approaches to intervention with their child, both must be given emotional support for caring enough to consider a variety of approaches, while, at the same time, the home visitor must be careful to not side with either parent against the other.

At Forest Heights we are convinced that the extended home visit is an exceptionally cost effective tool. Successful treatment planning is dependent on the depth and accuracy of assessment. The more rapidly complete data is gathered, the more quickly efficient planning and intervention can take place. Successful treatment is, to a large degree, dependent on a strong alliance with the family. Both are greatly facilitated in the course of the usual home visit.

The Extended Home Visit Facilitates

1. Alliance Building

2. Assessment of Family Dynamics

3. Identification of Specific Behavioral Goals

4. The Child's Transition from Home to Treatment Center

5. Gathering Information from a Variety of Sources

6. Post-placement Planning

7. Accomplishing Administrative Tasks Related to Admission Procedures

Admission Day

It was a day of mixed feelings for all. Yesterday the Summers had left home with ambivalence. Both parents were hopeful that they were making the right decision. Simultaneously they were sad that the situation had come to this. At the same time they were looking forward to having some relief from the constant hassles. The anticipation of relief led to feelings of guilt. "What kind of parents would be relieved to have their child in residential treatment?" they asked themselves.

Martha especially felt the guilt. It had been so difficult to tell friends, neighbors and family of their decision. At first she had hoped to use, "He's going to a boarding school in Colorado," as an explanation for his leaving. She had nearly convinced herself that it was a lot like a boarding school. However, she had noted that when she had used the term with Mr. Colburn on their last contact, and on Linda during the pre-placement visit, each had stressed that the Lodge was a residential treatment center, not a boarding school. With casual acquaintances and neighbors to whom she was not close she continued to use the term boarding school, but she had decided that with the others she should be honest.

Although Martha's mother had not directly disagreed with the decision, Martha was certain that she did not really approve of it. Her mother had a way of rarely approving of what Martha did. Yet, she never said anything directly. If Martha tried to explain her decisions she ended up sounding defensive. Why did she have so much trouble with her mother in this way? Her brothers certainly didn't have the same problems.

One of the neighbors had come right out and said, "I could never send my child to a place like that!" Others were not so blunt but she felt that few really understood. Her best friend was an exception. She knew what Martha had been living through with Kenny and how miserable they all were. Sarah as well was understanding and supportive of the decision. J.J. was less supportive. He had commented, "It's a big waste of money for basically a spoiled brat," but at least he didn't go on and on about it. He was so busy with his own life that he had barely made it over to the house for Kenny's good-bye dinner.

John wasn't one to talk about family problems when he was at work. He was able to avoid the situation with most of his business acquaintances. However, he had talked some about the problems with Kenny and the decision at his Christian Men's Breakfast Club. His friends there seemed supportive and offered their prayers.

In spite of not liking the necessity for residential treatment, John was certain that they were making the correct decision. Today he was mostly hoping that neither Martha nor Kenny would cry or "raise a big fuss" when it was time to say good-bye. If there was one thing he disliked, it was people being emotional. By this, he usually meant crying.

He knew it was unfair of him, but part of him still held Martha responsible for the problems with Kenny. After all, his role was to be the breadwinner, and certainly no one could say that he had been remiss in his duties there. Martha's role was to keep the house running smoothly and that included raising the children. Well, that certainly had not gone as planned when it came to Kenny. With the other two she had done a pretty good job.

He thought back to how he had eagerly anticipated Kenny's birth. When J.J. was born, John was just getting his feet on the ground in the business world. It seemed as though he had neither the time nor money to spend with J.J. When his first son became a teenager, John had all of a sudden realized that he had missed out on J.J.'s childhood. He had hoped that the latecomer to the family would be a boy so that he could enjoy doing things with him. By then, they were becoming financially secure. He should be able to free up more time from work to spend with a son.

However, those plans had again gone awry. From early on, Kenny had been difficult to have fun with. Then the more major problems had started. Taking time off from work to be at home certainly wasn't pleasant. There were always hassles of one sort or another going on there. Martha was frequently in tears. If she wasn't in tears, she was yelling and Kenny was in tears. No man needed that after a hard day at work. Then Martha had started to intimate that maybe if he would spend more time with Kenny things would improve. Dr. Jorgenson had even seemed to support her in this. Well, his taking off work to go to therapy hadn't done the trick either.

They had decided to drive to Colorado so that they could take Kenny's bike and all of his belongings. It had been a long drive, but it hadn't gone too badly. With permission from the doctor, they had given Kenny a double dose of his tranquilizer prior to leaving. Martha felt guilty about this also, but she didn't think that she could put up with Kenny's usual car antics for a whole day at this point in time. Luckily he had slept much of the time in the car. Of course, they had paid for it last evening when he wasn't sleepy. The hotel had a pool and a lot of activities and eventually he had been tired enough to fall asleep watching T.V.

On the drive up to Forest Heights, Kenny was mostly scared. However, this was something he was not about to admit even to himself, much less to anyone else. Instead he was very hyperactive in the car even though he had had his usual dose of medication that morning. He had tried to get his parents to stop at a store to buy a new tape recorder on the way. He had broken his the week before. The delaying tactic had not worked. His dad had stood firm saying they were already running late for their appointment. Too bad. Kenny was certain that if he had had only Mom to deal with, he would be successful. He usually could get his way with her. With Dad, he could never tell. One time his bullying would work. Another time it would not.

He started wondering about the adults at the Lodge. Would they be easy to bully or not? Probably the women would be. It was always easy for him to manipulate females. If pleading didn't work, tantrums or threats did. Sometimes he was scared of how easily he had been able to get his way with adults. On the other hand, it was fun, too. It made him feel powerful.

The times he was most frightened were when he started to get out of control and couldn't stop himself. That was when adults

appeared to be the most scared also. Nothing seemed to work then. At
school they had used the time-out room, but he didn't think that helped
him. He knew that he just got more and more scared when he was out of
control and was then left by himself. Really, really scary thoughts
would pop into his head then. They were so scary that he never wanted
to think about them again after such incidents.

On arrival at the Lodge, it was suggested that the Summers
drive over to the flat area to unload the car. When they entered the living
area of the Lodge, Glen, whom by now they knew was the Assistant
Director, introduced them to Rob and Alice, two of the child care staff
on shift. Glen explained that Rob, Alice, and Jack, who was downtown
right then, would be on shift until Wednesday noon. Alice would help
Kenny unpack his clothes and get his things put away while his parents
were over at the Administration Building. Then they would have a
chance to say good-bye to each other. As they started to unload the car
many boys crowded around. Kenny recognized a couple of them from
his first visit to the Lodge. It looked like it would be real easy to make
friends here. He had always wished that he had more friends.

Alice went with Kenny to the back bedroom where he would be
sleeping. As they unpacked his clothes, she marked his initials on those
that didn't already have name tags. She told him some about the other
boys with whom he would share the room.

While she was putting his initials on his toys and helping him
put them away, she explained the two basic rules of the Lodge. "The
reason you are here is to get help with your problems. Staff can't help
you if they don't know where you are, so you are to stay in the yard
unless you have permission to go beyond the fence. You must ask to go
to your room and to the bathroom. Most of the boys here are really
afraid of being hurt or of hurting others. So we have a rule about no
hands on others without permission." Linda had told him about the
rules when she was at his house. They sure seemed like dumb rules to
Kenny—imagine having to ask to go to the bathroom. He bet that no
one followed that rule or the one about not leaving the yard without
permission. He sort of liked the "hands off" rule. He had been told that
you got "sat" if you broke a rule. Well, that wouldn't work with him.
He'd either refuse to sit or else would sit and yell at the adults. He hadn't
yet decided which.

As they were putting away his things, he repeatedly asked if he
could go over and be with his parents. Alice told him that someone
would buzz on the intercom when they were ready for him. As they were
working, Mike came into the room to get his model. He told Kenny that
he had been at the Lodge for six months and, "Really it's not so bad." He
talked about still sometimes getting homesick and wishing he could see
his parents more often. They lived in Illinois and that was a long way
away. Kenny wished that Mike wouldn't talk about missing parents. He
knew that if he started thinking about that he might cry. He didn't want

to cry in front of the other kids. They might think he was a baby.

Just then the intercom in the dining room buzzed and Alice said that she would walk with him to the Administration Building. He didn't know why she had to walk with him. He remembered the way. As they started to leave the flat area, Alice pointed out the boundary beyond which the boys weren't allowed to go without permission. When he commented that he could walk over by himself, Alice didn't say anything but just continued to walk along with him. On the way, he saw a lot of grasshoppers and decided to stop and try to catch one. He wondered what Alice would do if he tried that. He stopped and she stopped and waited, commenting that catching grasshoppers was fun and that she knew it was hard to say goodbye to parents. Is that what she thought? Ha, he'd show her, and he ran on ahead.

It had been decided that since Linda had made the home visit, she would conduct the separation interview with Kenny and his parents. They went into a large playroom that had a camera mounted on the ceiling. Kenny wondered if someone was spying on them. Linda noted his glance and told him that the equipment was hooked to a remote control video set in the next office. She assured him that it was not turned on now and that children and parents were always asked to give their prmission when it was to be used.

Kenny sat between his mom and dad on a long green couch while Linda sat on a chair facing them. Alice was also present. Linda started talking about the problems that he had had at home. He didn't want to hear all that again. Linda then asked John and Martha what kinds of changes they expected to see in Kenny while he was at the Lodge. What needed to be different so that he could live at home? John quickly responded that Kenny needed to be able to mind without always arguing and that he needed to stop fighting with other kids every time he didn't get his own way. Martha added that he needed to be able to mind the teachers so that he could learn at school and that she hoped that he could learn to make friends—and to keep them. Linda asked some other questions about whether or not they had been feeling really close to Kenny lately (the answer, after considerable hedging, was no) and whether or not it was important to them that that change.

She then asked Kenny if there was anything else that he could think of that he wanted to work on while he was at the Lodge. He couldn't think of anything. Linda commented that she hoped that maybe he could get over some of his fears and scary thoughts while he was here. Kenny wondered how she knew about his scary thoughts. He had never told anyone about them. Could she read his mind? Now that was a *really* scary thought.

Linda then asked Kenny how he felt about saying good-bye to his parents. He quickly said, "It's okay," and tried to hold back the tears. Linda responded with an, "I don't believe that. Your face is telling me that you feel something else. You know it's okay to have lots of feelings about coming here. I bet that your parents have a lot of feelings too." John felt very uncomfortable with the turn of conversation. He was hoping that they could just say good-bye and leave without being emotional. Martha didn't know what to think. En route to the Lodge she had thought ahead to when she must say good-bye to Kenny and to leaving him there. Part of her hoped that Kenny wouldn't cry and protest. She knew that she would feel guilty if he started that. On the other hand, how terrible it would be if he didn't cry at all. What if he really didn't even care about being away from them. Sometimes, she wondered if that was how he really felt. Sometimes he looked at her with so much anger and hate that it frightened her.

Linda asked him again how he felt about saying good-bye. He didn't respond. She then asked how he thought his parents felt about saying good-bye to him. His quick reply was, "Well, they're the ones who decided to send me here, so probably they are happy." Linda asked Martha, "Are you happy right now?" Martha couldn't, no matter how hard she tried, keep the tears from coming. As she started to cry she reached out and hugged Kenny and told him, "I'm going to miss you a lot." Linda asked, "Even though you are going to miss him, do you still feel that he should be here?" Martha gave a rather vehement "Yes" in reply. At that point, Kenny too started crying. John noticed thought that it wasn't his usual whiney cry. This time there were real tears. He seemed genuinely sad, not angry or manipulative.[N]

Linda asked John, "With Kenny away from home what are you going to miss most?" His response was that he would miss their fishing times together. He had hoped that they could do more and more of that as Kenny got older. Linda commented that maybe sometime on a visit dad and son could go fishing at Evergreen Lake. Kenny could try it out ahead with the other boys and staff and find the best place for his dad and him to fish. Kenny reached over to hug his dad, and John to his surprise found that he too had a few tears springing to his eyes. It had been years since he had known that feeling. They clung to each other for a few minutes. Linda commented, "I'm glad to see that, in spite of all the problems you have had together, you also still have some good close feelings."

Then she asked both parents if it was okay with them if Kenny learned to get close to Alice and the other staff at the Lodge. Martha commented that one of her biggest fears about having Kenny come to the Lodge was that he might not have anyone to feel close to. In fact on their first tour of the Lodge it was seeing Glen sitting with his arm around one of the boys that had made her feel that this was the right place for Kenny. She hoped that he would learn to trust staff and to feel close to them. John, too, agreed that this was important. Kenny, himself, however, doubted that he really would ever learn to feel close to the staff here. Why should he?

Linda switched the subject to letter writing and telephone calls.

It was agreed that Martha and John would call Kenny on Sunday evening to see how he was doing. They planned to call every other week and to write on the alternate weeks. They were advised that they could call Linda or Glen anytime they wanted. It had already been agreed upon that their first visit with Kenny wouldn't occur for about six weeks, both because of the distance involved and because Kenny needed some time to get to know the staff and learn the routine here before visits. John would have a long weekend coming up in six weeks and that seemed like the most reasonable time to schedule the visit. It seemed like a long time away to John, Martha, and Kenny at the moment.

Linda and Alice accompanied the Summers family to their car. Kenny tried to prolong the final good-bye by asking numerous questions of his parents and trying to manipulate the conversation. Finally, Linda said that it was time for his parents to leave. Alice said it was time for Kenny to come into the Lodge and get ready for lunch. She assured him that she knew it was a difficult time for him and that he needed to be close to an adult. "Boy, is she dumb," Kenny thought. He just wanted to be left alone. He wished he could go to his bed and cry. However, he certainly didn't want to ask permission to do that, so he guessed that he was stuck hanging around with Alice.

Martha and John were silent, each lost in thought as they went down Forest Hill. Six weeks seemed like such a long time. Martha was afraid that if she started to speak, she would cry again, and then John might become upset with her. John was thinking how surprised he had been at the tears that had come to his eyes when Kenny had spontaneously hugged him. ∎

The Separation Interview

Obviously, the child's placement in a residential treatment center necessitates the trauma of separation from the family. At the same time, we see the separation process as providing a therapeutic opportunity. The underlying principle is one of fully allowing, and indeed sometimes stimulating, the total intensity of the separation experience. Psychological defenses seem to be particularly weak at the time of separation and loss. Previous feelings of anger or sadness are more easily resurfaced. The emphasis is on intensifying, rather than minimizing, emotions. That intensity, when shared with supportive others, can facilitate new beginning attachments.[N]

By taking care of most administrative procedures prior to this day, the focus can now be on the separation. At Forest Heights our primary procedure on this day is the separation interview. During the interview three issues are explored:

the feelings about the separation process

loyalty issues centering around loving and being loved

Parents and child meet together with a clinician who has previously met with both. In general, both child and parents are asked a series of questions.

The Facts: The interview begins with the facts about placement and includes questions such as:

> **"Who decided you would come here?"** The response needs to reflect the child's awareness that the parents, the facility, and the child himself all played a part in the decision making.

> **"What are you here for?"** will generate some general discussion about what the child and family would both like to be different (i.e. being closer to people, having more friends, doing better at school, having better control over his temper.) The issue is identifying those things in the child's life which he wants to be different and around which he can develop an alliance with the adults toward making change.

> **"How long will you be here?"** It is important that this question be asked even though it is virtually impossible to give a specific answer. This validates for the child that it is acceptable to ask questions even when no one knows the answers. In addition, it allows the clinician to clarify the child's part in determining the length of treatment. A sample response might be, "Of course you are concerned about how long you will be here. I can tell you how long most kids stay, but I can't promise how long it will be for you. Different kids are different. In part, it depends on how well we are all able to work together to change those things we discussed earlier."

> **"Where will you go when you are ready to leave here?"** This question is designed to address the abondonment fears that children have at the time of separation from their parents. For some children, the answer cannot be specifically answered. For example, there may be unresolved issues between divorced parents about custody, or a child may be in the custody of a social service agency. However, this question is a primary concern of the child. It is important that he be aware that we are sensitive to his concern, and it presents an opportunity to identify our willingness to care about his future as well as to care for him now. At minimum, he needs information about how the decision will be made and how and when he will be told about the results of the decision making process.

Many times, family problems are a factor in the child's placement. It is important in such cases that the child's past and future roles in the problem be clarified. Parents may be asked, "Did Paul have anything to do with your getting divorced (your alcohol problem, etc.)? Parents will need preparation and support for answering such questions. They will have received this during the extended home visit. These questions help clarify for the child which are adult issues and which are primarily child issues.

In addition to assuming responsibility for the origin of family problems, the child may assume responsibility for solving these problems. Again, the parent can be asked questions which help clarify these issues such as "Is there anything Paul can do to make you and his mother (dad) get married again?"

During the separation interview the child is helped not only to frame questions, but also to decide whom to ask the questions. Thus the child is given permission to want to know and to ask questions in a straight forward manner of the person most likely to be able to give him an answer.

The Feelings: The feelings of both child and parents are addressed during the separation interview. Initially, we approach the feelings issues from a permission giving and validation point of view. It is okay to feel, to verbalize the feelings, and to have them accepted as normal. A variety of feelings are addressed and explored. These encompass the feelings that are recognized to be part of the grieving process: sadness, fear, anger, confusion, abandonment, powerlessness, etc.

Again, interpretation to the parents may be necessary around a particular feeling such as, "While we adults view this as helping, many children feel like they are being sent away and feel abandoned (angry, etc.). Can you understand how Paul might feel like that?"

The failure of the child to respond verbally to a question about feelings is usually interpreted. "Sometimes kids think that if they avoid thinking about and talking about feelings they will just go away." "Sometimes kids are very angry and they express it by refusing to let us know anything about what they think or feel." At other times the expression of feeling may be inappropriate. Again, an interpretation can be given. "While he is here, we can help Kenny learn more about his own feelings and learn how to express them more appropriately. This will help others understand him better."

During this part of the interview the total focus is not on the feelings of the child. Parents, too, are asked about their feelings and are encouraged to accept that such separations are usually accompanied by a variety of conflicting emotions on the part of adults. Family members may be directed to not only pay close attention to what others are saying, but to also pay attention to facial expressions and body language, thereby facilitating the overall communication process.

Empathic understanding is offered to each family member for his individuality in coping with the separation process.

Loyalty Issues: At the time of admission, most children and adolescents are confused about loyalty issues. The child may fear that if he learns to love staff members, he will either disappoint parental figures and their love for him may lessen or that his own love for his parents will in some way be diminished.

The initial questions about this area are addressed to the parents. "If Kenny lives here for a while he is likely to start caring about, learning to love, some of the staff members. Is this okay with you?" This gives the parents an opportunity to give the child permission to get close to staff. "If he learns to love staff here, do you think that he will stop loving you so much?" This addresses some children's fear that love comes in a fixed quantity and that if you give some away to one person, you have less to share with others. "If Kenny learns to love staff here, will you love him less?" addresses the child's fear that if he loves others his parents will retaliate by loving him less.

Sometimes a child will not invest himself in the separation interview. It appears that he is not processing all, or part, of what is occuring. In spite of these conditions, it is worthwhile to continue to move through all of the usual steps. Children should not be denied the opportunity to deal with these important issues. We know that these concerns are in the minds of most children in similar circumstances. The child deserves validation that they are normal thoughts and questions.

The separation interview can be helpful for other family members as well. Parents can be helped to express their anger, sadness, fear, and guilt. Often they need as much permission and modeling as the child. At times parents have difficulty expressing themselves appropriately. This will be identified as a therapeutic issue for the parent to work on while the child is working on his identified problems.

We sometimes include siblings in the separation interview. They often have a mixture of anger and guilt. Furious at their brothers for "causing trouble at home," they may have wished that the brother were gone and now their wish is coming true. The appropriateness of those feelings needs to be identified, while it is simultaneously clarified that they are not responsible for the placement decision. The possibility of siblings fearing that they, too, might be placed in the future may need to be addressed. Brothers and sisters gain permission to ask about their brother who is in the treatment center and to talk openly about their concerns.

Normally, the focus at the end of the interview will be on sadness. The intensity of the feelings related to the separation, followed by support and closeness of staff, tends to promote the initial stages of trust, security, and attachment. A child care worker, who will be available to the child over at least the next few hours and hopefully days, is present for most of the interview. It is especially important that someone from the milieu staff be present at the closing of the interview to reinforce the commitment to be available to the child. Indeed, the child is encouraged to seek out this staff member when he is feeling sad or lonely. Reassurance that it is okay to not immediately know all the rules and exceptions is given, and the child care staff member can assure the child of his availablity to help him in this area as well.

Entering the Milieu

The child care worker who has participated in the separation interview will be the primary person for providing much of the initial care of the child. That person is selected based on factors such as the age of the child, the kind of care he needs, and his potential behaviors.

This child care worker focuses on many basic care tasks, such as helping the child unpack, marking and putting away clothes, explaining where things are, and teaching the rules and expectations. The child care worker will also monitor and help the child with initial peer interactions. Other residents come and go as the child is settling in. They want to know what toys and possessions the new child has brought with him. The worker is supportive of the new resident's autonomy in these interactions, while at the same time he helps him initiate appropriate peer interactions. The worker is a buffer in the testing that always occurs between peers and the new resident. The new child may need to be afforded some protection from the invasive personal questions of peers.

> **Example:** As Kenny is unpacking his toys, Sam comes in and starts exploring them. He says, "Hey, Kenny, you and I can be best friends and we'll share all of your stuff, okay?"
>
> Alice intervenes. "Sam, I feel like you are trying to take advantage of Kenny. He is just getting settled in. He will need time to get to know all of you guys. Maybe the two of you will become good friends, maybe not. But at any rate, Kenny deserves to have time to get to know you better before he decides who he wants to share with."

All child care staff need to be prepared for the new child. This begins with a staffing prior to admission and continues in the milieu. Proper preparation is crucial. It includes some basic issues that need careful consideration. We must separate the issues of taking care of and liking. Although it is not expected that all child care staff like all children, it is expected that they will provide good caretaking. For this reason, during the pre-placement staffing, special emphasis is placed on the child's behaviors as they relate to basic caretaking issues—i.e. eating behaviors, bedtime and sleeping patterns, usual responses to adult requests, peer problems, and overt fears.

Prior to admission house staff will decide on room placement, types of activities the child will be initially included in and the level of supervision that will be necessary. These decisions will be based on the information given by the home visitor at the pre-placement staffing. Particular emphasis will be placed on safety issues—factors that pose a risk either for the new resident or for other children.

The other residents are also prepared for the new child. They are given his name, age, where he is from and some general information. At the same time respect for confidentiality must be obvious. Personal questions may be responded to with "He will decide what he wants to share with you." The residents need to be prepared for behaviors the child presents that may pose a problem for them and given encouragement to seek adult help and support. Either because of age or behaviors, a current resident may feel displaced in his position by the new child. He may need help in terms of identifying appropriate ways to handle these feelings.

We find that discussion of a new boy's arrival provides an opportunity for effective therapeutic work with the group as a whole. Children are encouraged to remember their first day and all of their feelings. They are encouraged to talk about what was helpful to them at that time and whether this help came from adults or peers. Reminiscing about their own behaviors when they first came and the changes they have made is reinforcing of the change process. These discussions may stimulate truly helpful responses for use with the new child. They also provide an opportunity for reminders that the initial lesser requirements of the new resident does not mean that expectations of current residents will be lowered. Discussion of any changes in room assignments or table assignments needs to take place with concomitant validation of the feelings that these changes may stimulate. Choices about how to cope with these feelings can then be explored. Every new child's arrival provides a therapeutic opportunity for all of the children already in care.

Questions relating to the period prior to admission include:

1. Do the procedures encourage the likelihood of the facility having full information about your child and family? This includes past history as well as information about current problems. Past history includes birth and developmental history, medical, educational, and family social history. It also includes information about past assessments and therapy. Current information includes how your child is adjusting to home, school and peers. It may include recent psychological or psychiatric testing and information about current therapeutic interventions.

2. The interaction between facility staff and your child and other family members prior to the admission is indicative of the type of relationship you will have with them post-admission. Do you feel that this type of relationship will be helpful?

3. What does the facility do to minimize the separation trauma both for the child and for the family?

Conclusion

What is done between the time of initial contact with the family and the child's actual admission sets the stage for subsequent treatment. Having adequate information about the child and family for accurate formulation of the problem solving procedures to be undertaken during the in-patient treatment time is crucial. Interactions with both child and family are particularly critical in terms of alliance building and setting the stage for subsequent therapeutic maneuvers. Admission time is fairly routine for treatment center staff but it is a time of crisis for parents, child, and other family members. They deserve emotional support in dealing with the separation trauma.

Notes and Elaborations

pg. 96 In general children with attachment problems do not perceive the adult-child relationship as being to their benefit; they may perceive these relationships as being either physically or psychologically hurtful. Attachment problems are not synonymous with the terms "lack of attachment" or "unattached children." These terms relate to children who seem to be incapable of emotionally connecting with others.

Those with attachment problems can and do emotionally connect, but not necessarily in the usual ways.

pg. 96   People seem to change and grow only when they feel some discomfort with current conditions. The strength of Forest Heights' program is in identifying and heightening the resident's discomfort so that behavioral changes occur. There are some individuals, especially those who have never developed attachments to others, who seem to experience no internal discomfort. We recognize that we are not successful in treating these individuals in our program.

pg. 100   The extended home visit explained in great detail in this chapter may be unique to Forest Heights Lodge. Parents should not expect that most agencies will provide this service. There are certainly other ways to gather the same information. We have just found this mode to be the most efficient for us.

pg. 102   The Genogram is a pictorial representation of the family history through time, including several generations. Information includes names, birthdates, and birthplaces of family members; dates of marriages and divorces; children born of each marriage; biological parents of children born outside of marriage; education and occupations; medical/health history; dates of death and causes of death; losses, separations, moves. The Genogram helps to correlate various facets of the family history—i.e. the relationship of births to death; or remarriages to moves. During the development of the Genogram it is apparent that the family is the expert in terms of knowledge, while the home visitor is the expert in terms of organizing the knowledge in a manner useful to both treatment staff and family. This process again emphasizes the collaborative nature of the Lodge family relationship. The Summers family genogram is included in Chapter 7 on Working with Families. A complete description of the Genogram can be found in Ann Hartman's book, *Finding Families: An Ecological Approach to Family Assessment in Adoption.* (Sage Publications, Beverly Hills, 1979.)

pg. 104   The Eco-map is a second method used to assess the emotional climate of the family. It assesses the nuclear family's involvement with extended family, as well as its links, both positive and negative, with work, school, church, social services, health, recreation, social network and neighborhood. As the information is pictorially arranged on the paper often family members draw their own conclusions and begin to understand their situation in a new way that enables them to be a little more objective about themselves and their child. The Eco-map for the Summers family is included in Chapter 7. The complete description of the Eco-map is also found in the Ann Hartman reference listed above.

pg. 105   We find that if questions are phrased in ways that are respectful of the child's vocabulary and abilities for logical thinking, the young person is capable of sharing tremendous amounts of information.

pg. 105   Our approach to the use of medication fits with our basic philosophy. If medication will enhance the child's ability to form relationships, it is used. However, it is primarily through the child's behavioral manifestations of his problems that relationships will be built. Medication to control behaviors per se may dampen the intensity we use to build attachment through the arousal-relaxation cycle and we would not want to use it in these cases.

pg. 115   Parents, child and staff are frequently surprised at the emotional reaction during the separation interview. Psychological defenses are particularly low at times of stress; therefore, this provides a nearly ideal time to assess the strength of the young person's resistances to experiencing and sharing feelings. However, without the formalized process which heightens everyone's emotional state it would be quite likely that a child like Kenny would have shown little or no emotion when his parents left.

pg. 116   We are making use of the Arousal-Relaxation Cycle explained more fully in Chapter 5 to enhance the building of trust, security, and attachment.

C O N T E N T S

Milieu

Random Log Notes from Kenny's Case   127
The Milieu   141
Relationship to Philosophy   142
    How Attachments Develop   146
Behavioral Control   149
    Relationship between Behavioral Control and
        Program Philosophy 150
    The Concept of Supportive Control   151
    Techniques of Supportive Control   157
Structure vs Spontaneity   161
The Three Stages of Treatment   163
A Day in the Life of Forest Heights Lodge   170
Guide for Parents   180
Conclusion   181
Notes and Elaborations   181

C H A P T E R 5

Primary Contributors Glen Lein and John McGovern

Milieu

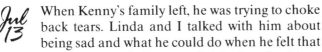 When Kenny's family left, he was trying to choke back tears. Linda and I talked with him about being sad and what he could do when he felt that way. He didn't say much. Later we finished getting his room together and his clothes and toys marked. The rest of the day he alternated between keeping close and playing with other guys or by himself. Played with bike, Legos, and cars. Ate little at meals. Near bedtime he looked scared and homesick. We kept him close and talked to him about those feelings. I checked on him a lot tonight.

Alice Anderson, Child Care Worker

Jul 14 Kenny seemed to enjoy the climbing and water play on outing to O'Fallon. He's strong physically and seems to be well coordinated in gross motor activities. He did show, on a couple of occasions, that he has a hard time stopping himself when adults interrupt his talk or activities. He continues to eat lightly at meals. He has been cooperative in terms of following the basic rules—i.e. asking permission. He had a hard time at bedtime last night when T.G. was loud and whiney, but was able to settle down with support of staff.

Rob McDonald, C.C.W.

Jul 21 Kenny is showing a little more of himself each day. Today he was outside pretending to use a stick as a sword. When I approached, he was unaware of my presence and I had to speak *loudly* to get his attention. Tonight I had to speak firmly 2-3 times to get him to stop bugging others. Kenny said he was "going to vomit" if I kept getting on him so much. I commented, "I know you are sick of people being on your case but I'm going to continue to get on you when you're having a hard time minding."

Jack Ulanski, C.C.W.

Jul 23 Hands on several times. I sat him for this. We're getting repeated complaints from other guys about his hitting them or going by and kicking their ball away or some such thing when adults aren't right there. We pull him in close at those times. Kenny alternates between pouting and denying his behaviors and having a tantrum, yelling and screaming. Overall he does better when he is kept close to an adult.

Mark Jones, C.C.W.

Jul 25 Near bedtime, Kenny is the first one to be ready for a story or close time. This seems to be an easy time for him to take from me. During the daytime, he is always testing limits with me. If I try to keep him close, he sets up one issue after another. I've told him that I cannot take him for outings with me until he learns to trust me enough that he doesn't always need to be testing my reaction. I sure notice a difference when he is close to one of the men during the day. He seems to feel more secure and relaxed than when he's alone with me.

Sally Carlton, C.C.W.

Aug 29 Kenny has a hard time feeling good about himself and showing it. He seems to need permission to be proud of an accomplishment or to be excited about something new. If given permission, then he is able to show it. Kenny finished a model yesterday and when he showed it to Tom, he didn't like the way Tom "looked at it" so Kenny took his newly finished model and smashed it. Kenny gets very angry when he doesn't get approval from others. Had fun on outing this week but wanted his own way most of the time. Occasionally can ask to be close when he's feeling uncomfortable in situations with other guys.

Mark Jones, C.C.W.

Sep 2   Kenny let himself get goofy lots of times on the overnight camping trip this week. He just could not stop himself. He lets lots of different guys and/or situations get to him. He's being naughty more frequently (i.e. ignoring rules) and depends on adults to interrupt his negative behaviors.

Jack Ulanski, C.C.W.

Sep 5   Found Kenny scuffing up kitchen floor with black heel marks from boots while he was supposed to be helping with dishes. He had volunteered for dishes as two of the usual crew were on visits. Needless to say Kenny got his first lessons on mopping the kitchen floor.

Pete Ware, C.C.W.

Sep 8   Kenny came back from first overnight visit with parents. They reported that everything went very well. They were really pleased with the changes. Kenny tried to avoid saying goodbye to them. I wouldn't let him do this and he looked really sad as they drove off. Mom sure tends to baby him while dad gives him the message "be a big boy" which seems to mean "act like a little man."

Glen Lein, Asst. Dir.

Sep 9   Many crying outbursts tonight over small things such as, "He went first" or, "I wanted an orange popsicle, not purple." Kenny looked like a 2 year old who needed a nap.

Fred Washington, Teacher

Sep 15   Parents had hoped that Kenny might possibly be ready for school soon after the onset of the school year. He isn't. He has made no overtures about coming to school, and in general it seems that he needs more time to feel secure in the living situation before he will be ready to put any energy into learning. Sally and I will have him in our Thursday group outings. This will give me more opportunities to assess his strengths and weaknesses and to develop a beginning relationship with him.

Carol Benedict, Educ. Dir.

130

Sep 26 Requiring one-to-one supervision much of the time. Lots of hands on and not minding. Taking others' things, etc. Cries and tries to make adult feel guilty with, "but I didn't know." When confronted, Kenny can drop this and take responsibility for his behaviors. At times he refuses to do things I've asked. I'll keep him next to me until he does what is asked (i.e. put clothes away; take a bath, etc.) After a brief while he'll just do it. He sure enjoys the close time with Sally in the evening—i.e. having stories read, rocking, etc.

Pete Ware, C.C.W.

Sep 30 Kenny has all the other kids turned off now. We used to just hear from others what he was doing. Now he's real open in his verbal and physical baiting. He gave me a pretty hard time on outing yesterday and finally I had to pull over and hold him for five minutes. After a big confrontation he always comes back later to make up. He is setting it up for adults to be in charge of everything (i.e. he stays in bed too long in the morning, runs the bath water but doesn't get in, hands on, lying, profanity, telling dirty stories at bedtime). We need to keep Kenny within eyesight *all* of the time; otherwise he puts himself in dangerous positions. He does respond well to *immediate* support after reprimands.

Rob MacDonald, C.C.W.

Oct 31 Kenny wanted to be Superman on Halloween. I think that he gets too easily caught in believing that he is Superman so I gave him several other choices and finally he decided on being The Jolly Green Giant. He looked really cute and had a lot of fun. He did real well while trick-or-treating with me. It sure is a change for him to be able to go off grounds with me and have it go well without a male around. I like it because he can be so much fun to be with. I told him this and he looked surprised.

Sally Carlton, C.C.W.

Nov 3 Kenny has been asking me about starting school lately. I told him he needed to think about why he wanted to go to school. He came back yesterday and said, "I've always gotten in trouble at school and I want to learn how to not get in trouble there." He asked if we could talk to Carol about starting school. I suggested we get together Thursday—after the staffing.

Glen Lein, Asst. Dir.

Nov 5   Glen and I met with Kenny today. We discussed his goals for coming to school. We talked about his needing to learn to take help from adults without fighting it so much. Told him that when he started school it would be with me one to one for an hour or so. He immediately started to protest, but picked up on Glen's and my interchange of looks and stopped himself. I was impressed.

Carol Benedict, Educ. Dir.

Nov 13   Kenny started school with me this week. On occasion he would start to lose control of himself, but usually he was able to respond to a simple arm around the shoulder. Loss of control would come when he was frustrated about the task at hand. If he approaches a task incorrectly it's hard for him to switch even when I show him how. One day he was so frustrated with his math that I finally just plopped him on my lap in the rocker for a few minutes. At first he was surprised but it didn't take him long to relax. Once he was physcially relaxed we returned to the task and he seemed more open to trying it my way rather than persevering in the unsuccessful approach.

Carol Benedict, Educ. Dir.

Nov 14   Carol, I notice the same thing in the house. When Kenny gets really locked in and needs to be held, I try to switch from the holding to cuddling just as soon as possible. He always seems suprised but sure eats it up. I'm trying to interrupt negative behaviors very early and get to the comforting holding without his needing to escalate to the point of being held for control. It seems to be working.

Mark Jones, C.C.W.

Nov 28   Kenny had a hard time over Thanksgiving. He was homesick and kept saying it wasn't fair that other guys got to go home and he didn't. I kept focusing him back on the sadness. He had talked of a special way that his mom fixed sweet potatoes. I let him call and get the recipe and Margie agreed to fix them this way for Thanksgiving dinner. He felt special although he did find out that several of the other guys had also shared favorite recipes. Kenny was very surprised that the adults did the dishes today for the guys.

Sally Carlton, C.C.W.

132

Dec 15 Kenny's behavior is erratic. At times he strikes out at kids when he's really angry at staff or at another boy. Other times he is being helpful and able to show real caring for others. It's neat seeing that quality coming out more and more. He talked on the phone to his mom and dad Sunday and was straight about being both excited and scared about the upcoming visit.

Alice Anderson, C.C.W.

Dec 16 Kenny finally got to sleep under the Christmas tree tonight. He had been all bent out of shape on Monday when we put the tree up because he didn't get to turn on the lights. It "wasn't fair" that Sam had gotten to do it—he had had a chance last year and Kenny is the youngest of the "new kids" so he felt he should have been able to have the privilege. That's the way he thinks and when he gets locked into it NO ONE can talk him out of it. In fact the more you talk to him the more likely he is to try to talk you into thinking his way. Yesterday he blew it again. Today he tried real hard. He had a very difficult time after supper but was able with a lot of closeness to keep it together and to be chosen to be one of the ones to sleep under the tree. Was very excited about it.

Steve Gills, Teacher

Dec 27 When I picked Kenny up at the airport he seemed rather down. It was difficult to know if it was because he was sad about coming back or if the visit hadn't gone as well as he had hoped it would. He wouldn't talk about it on the way back to the Lodge. However when I was putting him to bed, he asked if I would rock him. Said he was sad about coming back especially because yesterday hadn't been a very good day. He'd gotten into a lot of trouble with both his mom and dad. He had hoped to "make up for it" today and hadn't been able to because of coming back. He was sobbing as he talked—lots of tears. I realized that usually when he cries there aren't any tears; his crying is usually in anger.

Alice Anderson, C.C.W.

Jan 20 Kenny's family left yesterday after their four day visit. Kenny seemed to enjoy them while they were here. He did get anxious when he knew that they were meeting with Russ and Vee without him but seemed very relieved after the sessions that he was included in. Sarah is really good with him. She has a good balance between setting limits and being supportive of him. He was sad when they left but talked about how much he wanted to work on his problems and was wondering if I thought that he might be able to go home by this summer. I kept putting the focus back on what he thought.

Alice Anderson, C.C.W.

Feb 17 I notice that since Kenny's parents were here, he has been asking me a lot about things that I do with my son Bobby, who is four. Whenever my wife, Jennifer, and Bobby come over to the Lodge he watches all of our interactions with great interest.

Rob MacDonald, C.C.W.

Feb 17 Therapy note: Kenny and I have been going through his baby book and the family albums that Martha brought when they came for the family sessions. I've been trying to help him understand further about his early relationships with family members. I've been focusing on the cyclic nature of the family interactions. He has been very interested in this activity. However, he tends to want to focus on who was at fault in various interactions. With some support however he is able to bypass that issue and put himself in other family members' shoes and express how they might have been feeling.

Vera Fahlberg, M. D.

Mar 11 Martha has been spending the day with me today. She went with Carol and me for Thursday group. She was very uncomfortable when David acted up at the park and we confronted him. She sure looks uneasy whenever staff confront any of the boys. She seemed really scared when William had an all out tantrum tonight and Mark and Pete had to hold him. I had more trouble trying to keep her calmed down than I did in being supportive with the other guys, who of course started to act up as they picked up on her anxiety.

Sally Carlton C.C.W.

Mar 12 Martha was very surprised and again seemed anxious when several of the guys started acting up in the back seat en route to the store and I pulled over to the side of the road. She told me later that she didn't know if she could ever do that. She was surprised how quickly they had calmed down when I pulled over. By tonight she was able to really join in on some of the games and fun we were having and she looked more relaxed, like she was having a good time. Kenny has done a lot more testing while she has been here. I have to keep reminding him that that was how he used to act with me all the time, but that I know that he doesn't have to anymore. Usually, he was then able to turn it around without my having to involve one of the male staff members. Martha in a way seemed relieved whenever she saw Kenny giving me a hard time. I think that she was reassured to know that everything does not always go smoothly between Kenny and me and that I get frustrated with him too.

Sally Carlton, C.C.W.

Mar 14 Met with Martha before she left and we went over a variety of areas. She asked lots of questions about the interactions she had observed between child care staff and the boys. The questions reflected her close attention to what was going on. She was surprised at how fast staff switched from confronting to being close and nurturing and was really impressed at how staff members were supportive of and used each other to help the boys express their feelings more openly. She wondered if she and John would ever be able to do that. She is most anxious to have John come and spend a few days with one of the male staff members. She thinks it would be very beneficial to him.

Vera Fahlberg, M.D.

Mar 17 My focus with Kenny today was on his relationships with women. How he had felt when mom and he were alone at home prior to coming to the Lodge. How he had felt with Sally and Alice when he first came. How he had learned to trust Sally and Alice to be able to take care of him when there wasn't a male around. And how all the old feelings resurfaced when his mom and Sally were together. He was able to talk quite openly about his ambivalent feelings when his mom and Sally were together. Part of him was scared about how it might go. Part of him was happy that his mom was learning new ways to help him. At the same time he hated to give up the old ways of interacting with her. He, himself, brought up the fact that he had sometimes disobeyed Sally when his mom was there not to find out what Sally would do ("I already know what she will do then") but more to find out what his mom would do when Sally "took care of me." He seemed to be relieved that staff felt comfortable confronting Martha about how uncomfortable she was when they confronted the boys.

Vera Fahlberg, M.D.

Apr 1 Kenny was so excited about all the silly things we did today— having lunch at breakfast time; dinner at noon and breakfast at supper. He had a ball when we insisted that everyone eat his spaghetti and salad without using any utensils. Al, the new boy, had a difficult time joining in the fun and Kenny kept encouraging him and sharing how he had felt when he first came. He told Al, "Even though staff joke a lot and do silly things like today they can be really strict." It was as though he understood that Al might be more scared by fun times than by adults being strict. I was surprised.

Sally Carlton, C.C.W.

May 4 Kenny's been very excited about the Arts and Crafts project he has been working on for Mother's Day. He has really worked hard on it. I've been surprised how well he has done. He has a creative bent when he decides that something is of real interest to him.

Linda Clefisch, Arts and Craft

May 5 Kenny has been really struggling with "big" vs. "little" conflicts. He is very aware of the fact that many of his behaviors are babyish. He then gets embarrasssed but doesn't handle that feeling well and is likely to do "something stupid". Staff need to help him when there is even a chance that he might be embarassed. It's sort of like when he used to lash out at others because he was afraid others would lash out at him. Once we focused in on his fears the aggressive behavior slowed down. If we can help him deal with his embarrassment around acting "like a baby" it will be helpful. He has decided that one thing that might help will be to be called Ken after his tenth birthday because to him Kenny sounds "babyish". I tried to help him see that there was a certain element of magical thinking in this but agreed that we would go along with it.

Vera Fahlberg, M.D.

May 9 Kenny had a difficult time this morning--so excited about his birthday. For months, he talked of what he was going to order for his birthday dinner, etc. This morning he really blew it. Had to be held for the first time in months. He started out with, "You can't do this. It's my birthday. You can't wreck it." Surprisingly, it was only ten minutes or so before he decided that it was him, not us, who was "wrecking" it. He needed a lot of closeness and support the rest of the day, but was able to keep it together and have a good time. Everyone

136   enjoyed the dinner he picked—steak and baked potatoes. He did a good job in the kitchen with Margie which is a real change from the past. The time that he looked most relaxed and like he was having the most fun was when he was opening his presents. This was a real change from Christmas when he just tore through them. This time he looked excited, but seemed to want to prolong it by opening each present carefully.

Alice Anderson, C.C.W.

Jun 15 Ken's dad was here for two days this week before he and Ken left today for an 8 day visit. John enjoyed the activities with the boys and seemed to feel comfortable with our limit setting. He seemed surprised when I would listen to any of the boys' feelings or encourage them to show their feelings in age-appropriate ways.

Rob MacDonald, C.C.W.

Jun 15 John and I talked for a while before he left with Ken and he brought up that it is difficult for him to talk with family members about feelings. He tends to get into "but there is no reason for you to feel........" rather than just accepting the feelings. I think that he still has difficulty accepting his own feelings.

Glen Lein, Asst. Dir.

Jun 16 Glen, I couldn't agree more. So long as John, Kenny, and I were focusing on areas for each family member to work on during the visit John looked very relaxed. When we started talking about feelings he was visibly more uncomfortable and became more superficial. The only time that I've seen this change for him was during the intensive family work in January when he got a lot of support for expressing his own feelings. I think that we are going to have to come back to that area again and again. Maybe we should have Russ or Glen involved as John seems to be able to make better use of males' giving him permission to express his own feelings than when I try to do the same thing.

Vera Fahlberg, M.D.

Jun 25 Kenny—oops, Ken—was really excited about the fact that in spite of having had problems on the visit he and his family were able to turn it around and have things go well after the telephone contacts with Vee. He wonders if, when he goes home "for

good" they'll be able to call if there are problems. I assured him that we   137
would make certain that there was someone he and his family could
call whenever necessary. By the way, Ken is reminding me with great
tolerance every time I goof and call him "Kenny." He says that he isn't
sure that his mom will ever change. He is adamant that he wants
everyone to remember that he is a "big kid now that I'm ten and Kenny
sounds babyish."

Sally Carlton, C.C.W.

Jul 27 Ken had a lot of fun on the camping trip. he caught several
fish—more than anyone else. He was proud but didn't lord it
over the other guys. In fact he even helped Al and Craig who
hadn't had much experience fishing. I overheard Ken telling them
about his first overnight camping experience here at the Lodge and I
thought back to it myself. Lots of changes in the past year. It's good to
see them. Ken can be a really fun kid.

Rob MacDonald, C.C.W.

Aug 8 Ken was in my group at Elitch's today. He had a good time. Was
a little afraid the first time on Mr. Twister, but then went back
repeatedly. Again, he talked about the difference between last
year and this. "Last year I bragged about how brave I was whenever I
was scared. This year I just say, 'I'm scared' and it doesn't last nearly
as long."

Jack Ulanski, C.C.W.

Aug 25 I took Ken down to Wilmot today to show him where his
classroom will be and to meet briefly with Mrs. Green, his
teacher. He is very excited about going to public school. On the
way home we talked about what frequently happens with him when he
gets really excited—he becomes more active and sometimes makes bad
choices for himself.

Fred Washington, Teacher

Aug 26 Ken looked scared when I took him to school this morning but
he didn't want me to come in with him and assured me that he
knew the way. He looked much more relieved, but also just
plain excited when I picked him up at noon. In addition to Mrs. Green
he will have Mr. Barton for Science and other teachers for specials.

Sally Carlton, C.C.W.

Sep 10 Ken is sure hard to live with after school. He comes home, has a snack and then seems to be on the prowl trying to see how many hassles he can get started between then and supper time. Yesterday he hit a new record I think for starting hassles. It gets tiring especially when the other kids look up to him as a "public school kid." I'm concerned about what kind of message we are giving the rest of the kids.

Pete Ware, C.C.W.

Sep 10 Ken and I met with Mrs. Green today for our regularly scheduled weekly conference. She reports that Ken is doing very well in class. He is following the rules and is completing the work. Seems to be getting along with classmates well. He has two friends that he eats with and plays with during recess.

Fred Washington, Teacher

Sep 13 Remember that Ken is using a tremendous amount of energy just to keep things going at school. This is probably why it all falls apart when he gets home. He needs a lot of support and closeness right after school since this seems to be his most difficult time of day.

Carol Benedict, Educ. Dir.

Sep 17 Mrs. Green reports that things have not gone so well this past week. Ken is pushing, shoving, and being louder than most. The two friends he had last week now seem to be avoiding him. During the most structured classes he is working hard and completing the work. He has asked for help twice in the past week—something that was difficult for him last year.

Fred Washington, Teacher

Sep 21 Got a call from school. Ken had gotten out of control, cussing out a substitute teacher. He was sent to the office. I fully intended to bring him home, but when I got to the school he was talking with the principal about how embarrassed he was about his behavior and how he wanted to apologize to the teacher. No defensiveness. Surprise, surprise. Mr. Flagler and I agreed this was a good plan and Jim accompanied him back to the class. If Ken has *any* further problems today I'll be called immediately.

Glen Lein, Asst. Dir.

Sep 21 Ken looked very sheepish when I picked him up from school today. He was afraid I would be really upset with him. As soon as he realized that I wasn't, he talked openly about how embarrassing it was to go back and apologize but how good he felt about it later, especially when a bunch of the kids came up and talked with him during recess. Apparently, they kept asking him what happened when he went to the office and what would happen when his parents heard about it.

Rob McDonald, C.C.W.

Oct 23 Things seem to be evening out with Ken. There are fewer hassles. When they do occur it is easier to get through them. For the most part he's staying away from the guys he has trouble getting along with. He was invited over to a friend's yesterday for a birthday party. He looked like he had had a good time when we picked him up and the mother said it was nice having him (same as she was saying about everyone). Ken is talking positively about Scouts which meets Wednesdays after school. I think the semi-structured group time is good for him. Brent called this morning to see if Ken could go to a movie with him in Evergreen today. I told Ken he couldn't go as we had an outing with everyone planned, but said that maybe it would work out another time. He took the "no" real well. He no longer acts like "no" means, "I don't like you." He was disappointed and that was obvious but rather than over-reacting his disappointment seemed appropriate for the occasion.

Sally Carlton, C.C.W.

Oct 30 Ken's roomate, William, said that Ken had taken one of his tapes and wrecked it. Ken said that Will had loaned him the tape and that it was fine when he returned it. I sat them both and told them they needed to get it worked out together. After half an hour I thought that this tactic wasn't going to work and I was about ready to intervene when all of a sudden Ken got tears in his eyes and admitted taking the tape without Will's permission. It got caught in his tape recorder and was wrecked. He had tried to pretend that nothing had happened. He looked like he felt guilty which was good to see. I took him down to buy a new tape for William with his allowance.

Pete Ware, C.C.W.

140

Oct 30 Ken again asked to be Superman for Halloween this year. He said that he thought that he could handle it without "fuzzing out" or getting "goofy". I agreed and told him that I thought it was important for both him and me to find out if this was so. So far he has done well thinking ahead about it and planning his costume.

Sally Carlton, C.C.W.

Nov 1 Ken had a good time both at the Lodge party and while trick or treating last night. He got excited and a little silly as the boys were all getting ready to go out but stopped himself with minimal reminders. When I tucked him in last night he said he was proud of the fact that he had handled it well. I told him I was glad that he had had fun.

Alice Anderson, C.C.W.

Nov 5 During the month prior to Mark Jones leaving last week, Ken hadn't shown many feelings about it. Even at the going away party he had had less to say than most of the fellows. However, this week he has given Tom Winter a tough time and has talked constantly about how much he liked Mark and how much he misses him.

Pete Ware, C.C.W.

Nov 10 The focus of my session with Ken today was on his feelings about Mark leaving and Tom coming. I think that Mark's leaving has made Ken start to think about his own and others' feelings when he leaves. I'm certain that right after discharge his parents will get many of the same behaviors that Ken is directing toward Tom now. In talking with Ken, I get the impression that he is checking himself out as much as he is checking Tom out, i.e. "Can I start to hassle an adult and then stop myself?" I think he needs this verbalized for him with a statement such as, "Well, can you stop yourself or do you need my help?" If he needs staff help, provide it.

Vera Fahlberg, M.D.

Nov 13 I think you were right, Vee. With the verbalized choice Ken was able to stop himself most of the time this week. I let him know that I think this is an important skill for him to have before he goes home. He is asking more and more when I think that he will be

ready to go home. I keep re-directing him to either Glen or Vee with
these questions.

Pete Ware, C.C.W.

Nov 19 Vee and I sat down with Ken today. We reviewed with him the new treatment plan and looked back over the early ones. Focused on the changes he had made. He came up with some that Vee and I had forgotten. We then told him that staff had discussed a discharge date, but that we were really interested in what he himself was thinking of in terms of when he would be ready to leave. He said sometimes he thought he should go home for good at Christmas time and that other times he thought in terms of spring vacation. We told him that we were thinking of a date in between. We were thinking that when the semester ended in late January would be a good time. He was very excited.

Glen Lein, Asst. Dir. ∎

The Milieu

The heart of residential treatment is milieu therapy. The child is constantly involved in the environment of structure and interactions. Every interchange has the potential for providing the child with an opportunity to experience growth and change. Within the therapeutic milieu stereotypic conflicts need not be repeated. The kinds of demands the environment will make on a child in relation to his ability to respond adequately can be controlled in this setting. In the therapeutic environment the child re-experiences conflict with positive rather than negative resolution. Therefore residential centers are at a decided advantage in treating the seriously disturbed child or adolescent.

Emotionally disturbed children have not been able to respond in a positive growthful way to the demands of their former environment. While taking into consideration contributing organic or physiological factors, the child's problems of adjustment are seen as arising at least partially from imbalances in his former environment. In the residential treatment facility an attempt is made to establish and maintain a climate which strikes a balance between environmental demands and the child's ability to respond. This does not mean that only easily met demands are placed upon the child, but rather that the demands will be in terms of realities which he can understand. This will lead to consequent re-learning and adaptation. Much of the focus in residential care is on the re-education process as it relates to relationships. To be effective there must be opportunities to form attachments which place demands on both partners. It is in redefining the nature of these interpersonal relationships that true change occurs for the child.

To some measure, the adults are mediators between the environment and the child, providing both the initial impetus and the continuing support toward achieving the ego growth which permits gratificiation and adaptation to occur. A dynamic equilibrium encourages responses that are essentially growth-inducing. In short, the goal of the treatment program is to produce a healthy, adaptable individual who will have the capacity to withstand the inevitable stress and strain as well as experience the thrill and joy associated with living a full and challenging life. For this reason treatment must interject demands in a child's life. These will be demands which he has to struggle to meet, but which must be met to clear the way for attaining comfortable new adequacies.

Within any personality there exists the capacity for producing defenses which are maladaptive.[N] Trauma, lack of affectual flow and gratification or excessive demands may result in any of the symptoms of lack of adjustment. The total personality may then be obscured by fixed patterns of response which are inadequate or bizarre. However, in most cases the potential for more acceptable responses still exists. Moreover, the personalities of children seem capable of adjusting to a variety of life circumstances. It is to this inherent resiliency that most efforts in residential care are directed.

Residential treatment continually utilizes the total living experience. Within such a context apparently static patterns of poor adjustment in the emotionally disturbed child are replaced by new patterns which are demonstrably more gratifying and fulfilling. To effect this, however, first the belief that life is worth living and that the painful changing of the patterns of one's life is worth the struggle must be instilled. This applies whatever the symptoms, whatever the diagnosis, however pervasive the disability.

The child's recovery is seen as a learning experience. Blocks arising out of the past are removed. More appropriate and authentic responses are substituted. It is in the milieu setting that the re-education process takes place as we attempt to create and maintain an environment which embodies and reflects the total life process. From this irreducible core radiate the complex procedures and methods of operation guiding therapeutic concepts, the constellation of professional and non-professional staff, and at the outer edge the awakenings to new possibilities of treatment.

Relationship to Philosophy

Nowhere in the treatment program should the implementation of the philosphical statements be as evident as in the milieu. It is here that the philosophical approach to treatment is either substantiated or denied. The most important tasks of treatment and the general strategies which will be used to address the primary therapeutic issues are defined in the philosophy. Simultaneously it provides child care workers with a framework within which to find the answers to the "what should I do when........?" type of questions.

At Forest Heights Lodge, the relationship of milieu to philosophy is seen in the development of our discipline and control policies as exemplified by our concept of supportive control. It is demonstrated in the three stages of the treatment process that we describe as occurring at the Lodge. Its presence is acknowledged in creating a balance between structure and spontaneity. Most of all, it is apparent in every routine that takes place during each day in the child's life while he resides at the Lodge.

With a treatment philosophy based on attachment theory, the emphasis is on creating relationships of trust and caring. This pervades all aspects of our program. However, it makes its strongest statement in the milieu. Child care workers are the dominant persons in the lives of the boys in our treatment center. They are the primary focus for attachment. Their relationships with the residents is given priority. Other aspects of the program are secondary to, and supportive of, the relationships developed in the daily living situation. Child care staff are perceived as the primary treatment personnel.

Basic to all treatment is the issue of safety. Unless an individual feels safe, it will be difficult to overcome defenses and resistances to change. Unless he feels safe, there will be little energy available for continued growth and change. Therefore, basic to the creation of a therapeutic milieu is the necessity of creating an environment in which children feel both physically and psychologically safe.

It is within the milieu that the children face their greatest frustrations. It is here that they have their needs met. To help our residents progress and move increasingly closer to appropriate levels of self-control and self-care, staff must demonstrate both creativity and flexibility in meeting the boys'varying needs.

The following general principles are seen as necessary to the creation of an environment supportive to the development of healing attachments.

1. Limited number of rules: The absolute rules focus primarily on providing the basic sense of safety and security necessary for any treatment interventions to be successful. Because these rules are so limited in number and scope, we are able to maintain the flexibility necessary to implement the responses which are best for each individual child at a particular point in his treatment. Limited rules permit more effective confronta-

tion of the underlying issues. The focus of interventions can be centered on trust and relationships rather than on rules.

2. Limited number of child care staff: It is difficult for strong attachments to develop if the child is asked to relate to a large number of child care staff. We have three child care staff on shift at a time. For this reason we supply maximum support services for the care givers. Housekeeping, maintenance, and cooking duties, although they may be activities which are done with a child to facilitate skill development or as a means to building relationships, are not allowed to interfere with basic child care and nurture.

3. Staffing patterns and the staff interrelationships supportive of the development of attachments: At Forest Heights, the staffing patterns reflect the emphasis on close interpersonal relationships. Child care staff work three and a half day shifts. This allows for the continuity of relationships that we see as the crucial aspect of our treatment program. The same person who gets the child up in the morning will be involved in the bedtime routines. The staff member who sends a boy off to school in the morning will be there when he returns.

   In addition, we have chosen to have each shift composition be consistent. Strong cohesive patterns of working together are encouraged. Each shift is comprised of two males and one female staff member who together form a treatment unit. Working together continuously, they become increasingly aware of each other's strengths and weaknesses and soon, because of their intimate knowledge of each other, much of their communication is condensed.

   Each shift has its own identity. Basic rules are the same for the two shifts. However, expectations and parenting styles vary from shift to shift. Both staff and children openly acknowledge this. No one asks that each individual staff member respond in an identical manner in his interactions with a particular boy. The development of close interpersonal relationships based on true attachments does not allow for that type of consistency. The strength of true attachments is that they are unique reflections of the personalities of the two individuals involved. However, the measuring stick used by all staff members to guide their responses to a child is consistent. They are expected to respond in whatever manner will facilitate their relationship with the particular child.

4. Child care staff must be powerful and competent: Children will only trust those who have power to effect change in their lives. The amount of power possessed by child care staff determines the degree of trust they can inspire in the residents

of the facility. At Forest Heights it is only the child care staff, and only after their initial training period, who may "give permission." They are the only ones empowered to do so except in an emergency situation. This is primarily because they are responsible for knowing where each resident is. They are the ones primarily responsible for each child's safety and security. A secondary effect of this, however, is further empowering of the child care staff. It is an intrinsic recognition that it is child care staff, not administrative staff or therapists, who have the primary power of the relationship.

5. Child care staff have equal participation in treatment planning: The child's behaviors in the day-to-day living situation describe both his underlying needs and his perceptions of the world around him. It is the child care staff who will have the clearest view of these behaviors. This information is an integral part of the treatment planning process. Staffings of individual children correlate the child's current behavioral functioning with the underlying psychodynamic features of the case. Consultants and therapists use their skills in helping the child care staff understand the reasons, feelings and perceptions behind the child's behaviors. They help child care staff develop strategies supportive of the re-education process. These are implemented in the milieu. Since it is the child care staff who both provide the observations and who implement the treatment plan, they must be actively involved in its development.

6. Staff relationships with administration: Staff, too, need to feel safe and protected in order to have energy for growth and change. This is one of the primary functions of the Assistant Director and the Residence Director. They insure that adequate staff and back up are available. No staff member should have to feel that he/she is in an unsafe position by being asked to be responsible for too many disturbed children. Staff know that additional back up is only a phone call away. Just as we try to set the boys up for success by setting reasonable expectations, we also attempt to set child care staff up for success by providing adequate supervision for them.

7. Confidentiality: Confidentiality boundaries are inclusive of child care staff. To appropriately care for children, child care staff must be knowledgable about the child. If child care staff are excluded from certain information, it implies a lack of trust between the adults responsible for care.

8. Discipline and control policies support closeness: Our basic philosophy dictates that the more trouble a child is having the

closer he needs to be to an adult for help and supervision. When attachment is the goal it does not make sense to use any form of discipline which encourages physical or psychological distancing. Therefore, the use of isolation techniques or medication to control behaviors is avoided.[N] On the other hand, if the child has a condition, such as psychosis, where medication will enhance his availability for relationship building then it will be used. As a child once commented in describing what happens at the Lodge, "No matter what you do, you end up being closer to adults."

9. Gratification must come from the child care workers: Effective treatment occurs when there is a balance between confrontation and gratification, between conflict and resolution. The most hours and the most opportunities for gratification occur within the milieu. Gratification is based on the child's immediate needs. Rapid and consistent responses to the child's needs for gratification build trust.

How Attachments Develop

As mentioned earlier, the focus of the Forest Heights treatment program is on the development of attachments. To understand the adult-child interactions that take place at the Lodge, it is important to first understand attachment theory. In the milieu we attempt to translate this theory into daily practice. Our primary task is to create an environment that facilitates the development of intense interpersonal relationships. Simultaneously we confront those behaviors that keep children emotionally distant from adults. As residents develop more trust for caregivers, they will have more energy available for trying new behaviors. In turn, success with new behaviors leads to increased trust of caregivers.

From theoretical and developmental materials, we recognize that there are three distinct ways in which attachments develop. One is based on the arousal-relaxation cycle. (Fig. 1)

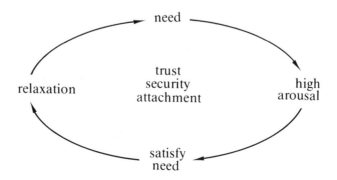

Needs lead to states of high arousal, with concomitant
autonomic nervous system changes. Pupils may become larger or
smaller, mouths drier or wetter, muscle tension increased. When needs
are met relaxation follows and the individual is open to forming interpersonal connections. This is a potent way to develop attachments,
being dependent upon emotional intensity.

With the distubed child, the needs that initiate the cycle are
more likely to be psychological than physical. Intense emotions may be
unpleasurable, such as anxiety, fear, anger, rage, or sadness. On the
other hand the feelings may be positively charged. Examples would
include joy or excitement. Frequently, the need revolves around
acceptance of and support for the strong feelings until the body tension
that accompanies these emotions subsides. It is at this point that the
child is most open to attachment.

For this reason, early in placement there is little attempt to tone
down emotional responses. We do not try to side step states of high
arousal. Instead each of these instances, viewed in a positive light, is
seen as providing an opportunity to facitilate attachment. Once
attachments are formed, we will help the young person develop
alternative, more socially acceptable, means of signalling his
discomfort, asking for help, demonstrating his emotions.

Some children in residential care are constantly under strain.
While feeling this tension, perceptions of what is occurring around
them are seriously limited. As a result, intellectual development
dependent on such perceptions is inhibited or blocked. Usual modes of
decreasing tension seem to be ineffectual with these children. The
tension frequently needs to peak before it can be discharged with the
child becoming relaxed and available for new learning. Therefore, for
two different reasons it is helpful to facilitate the state of high arousal,
thereby helping the child release the tension and attain relaxation.
Simultaneously, we facilitate attachment and help the child become
available for more adequate processing of the world around him.

At the time of admission, the new resident will be dealing with a
wide range of intense feelings. Most will be experiencing considerable
sadness, anger, and fear. Possibly there will be concommitant
excitement and hope over the prospect of a new beginning. Because the
early hours of treatment are crucial in terms of setting the stage for
being able to trust adult availability, we try to admit children early in a
shift. We want the staff person involved in the separation interview to be
available for interactions over the next couple of days.

We use this time of intense feelings to facilitate the attachment
process. No effort is made to diminish the strong feelings or to avoid the
internal struggle that the child is experiencing. Indeed, intense feelings
and internal struggles are seen as the source of energy for change.
However, simultaneously we provide support, closeness, warmth,
caring and empathy for what the child is experiencing during this

difficult time. We decrease external demands of him during this early period. The message we want to convey is that adults here understand the child's feelings and internal conflicts and that they will provide support to the child coping with them. We want to take care of the youth's needs, emotional as well as physical. For most of our residents prior to admission the adult focus was on their behaviors. We help them focus on their feelings. We help them learn more about themselves. The better they understand themselves and their feelings the more likely they will learn new behavioral adaptations.

A second mode of developing attachments relates to positive interactions. These interactions are not so emotionally charged. They are low keyed positives that help increase the individual's self-esteem and feelings of self-worth. This is the focus of many of the interactions between child care staff and residents during the early weeks of treatment. Opportunities for this type of interaction are numerous during the hours when most of the boys are in school. It is one of the reasons that we do not want to hurry the new boy's entry into school.

The third mode of developing attachments relates more to the group process. It is described by the word *claiming*. Claiming behaviors are those that describe the "we's" and the "they's" of the world. Disturbed children, traditionally, have felt isolated. A major goal of treatment is to help them learn to be part of a group—a family group, a school group, a peer group. We start with helping them feel part of the Lodge family. There is a conscious emphasis on, "This is the way we do things here." "Lodge kids do.........Lodge kids don't do.............. in public" etc. These statements are conveyed in an inclusive manner, implying, "Since you are now a member of the Lodge community we will help you meet expectations." We consciously avoid statements that might be internalized as, "If you don't behave in the prescribed manner you will be ostracized from the group."

Unconditional giving is an important aspect of developing attachments. Just as the baby doesn't have to "earn" food or having a wet diaper changed, our residents have their needs met because all children, by virtue of being, are deserving of having needs met. Initially, the child doesn't have to earn anything by his behavior. Someone will go with him to select and buy some new toys because kids need toys. Attractive clothing will be provided when needed because it is important that he look good in order to help him feel good. Food will always be provided because children need phycial as well as psychological nurture. Adults are responsible for initiating positive interactions irrespective of the child's inital response to them. Most disturbed children have perceived their environment as ungiving, rejecting and unrewarding. They have come to the conclusion that they indeed don't deserve anything. Our job is to help them see their environment in a new light. In this way we facilitate the child's

Behavioral Control

No residential treatment program can successfully function unless the basic issue of who is in charge is beyond question. The treatment approach must include a means of addressing negative behaviors. If staff are afraid to confront the action of a child or if a child correctly perceives himself to be endangered or dangerous to others, then a therapeutic environment cannot exist. To be able to confront behaviors without abusing authority, staff members must have confidence in their own power to handle problem behaviors. If staff members do not have adequate measures for coping with problem behaviors they may resort to harsh punitive measures to deal with unacceptable behaviors.[N] Yet the need to maintain a safe, orderly and predictable environment must be viewed in connection with the other needs of children. Acceptance and emotional nurturing are just as important as maintaining a sense of order and discipline.

Disturbed children usually perceive life as a series of ungovernable, irrational, hurtful events. Each child placed carries an accumulation of experiences which have inhibited normal psychological growth. Indeed, the child who is a potential prospect for residential treatment is one who has been unable to achieve age appropriate self control. It is as though the children we accept for treatment are racing down a hill in a vehicle which has an opaque windshield or a broken steering wheel and, in either instance, no brakes. To leave such a child in complete command of his behavior is ridiculous. Some kind of buffer or mediator must be interposed.

Most children in need of residential treatment either fear their own capacity to harm others, or are fearful of others' potential for harming them. Therefore, safety issues are primary. We must let the child know that he will be safe, both from his own destructive urges and from those impulses in others. Staff must be able to provide adequate controls for keeping behaviors within acceptable limits. Residents must know that if the behaviors go beyond acceptable boundaries there will be someone available to take care of the threatening situation. If children do not feel this sense of safety there will not be an atmosphere that allows them to take the risks necessary for growth and change.

A firm, consistently applied set of limits must be established to give staff, families, children and referring agencies a clear sense of the program's boundaries. There are two kinds of limits to establish—behavioral and programmatic. Behavioral limits identify the types of behavioral problems that the program believes it can successfully address. Each program must decide if they are equipped to meet such problem behaviors as running, firesetting, drug usage, assault, or promiscuity. This does not mean that these behaviors are permitted, simply that they are not automatic grounds for dismissal or referral to a more structured or secure facility. If a residential treatment center is willing to accept a fire setter, staff must believe that they can successfully treat the disorder which underlies the behavior and that in the meantime they can contend with the behavior itself.

Programmatic bottom lines are the limits of intervention a facility is willing to provide. Some programs are willing to keep children on one-to-one supervision. Some use time-out rooms. Others use physical restraints. Some use medication to control behaviors. Others are unwilling to go beyond the sanctions implicit in a phase system or sending a child to his room. If a youth's behavior cannot be contained within safe limits by the most potent tools an organization has at its disposal, then the child does not belong in the program.

Both sets of limits are essential for all residential treatment centers. They provide the guidelines which help a program define which children it can help. They prevent staff from feeling overwhelmed by behaviors. They allow the children to feel more secure. For these boundaries to work, a program must occasionally be willing to discharge a resident or refuse admission to an applicant whose behaviors fall outside these limits.

Relationship between Behavioral Control and Program Philosophy

As mentioned earlier, it is important that the mode of controlling behaviors be congruent with the facility's philosophical base. In a program with attachment as the base of its treatment, we believe that limits, geared to the child's developmental level, are ultimately based on adult-child relationships, as opposed to an impersonal system. At Forest Heights Lodge we feel comfortable providing one-to-one supervision. We see it as facilitating attachment. Time out rooms, corporal punishment, physical restraints, or medication for behavioral control are all seen as hindering the development of close interpersonal bonds. Therefore they are not used. These are our programmatic bottom lines.

Complex rule structures lend themselves to manipulations and to varying interpretation by the different staff who must enforce them. They diminish the role of interpersonal relationships and attachments. In contrast, the attachment model emphasizes control based on relationships as opposed to institutionalized rule structures. Disturbed children test boundaries constantly, particularly when they first arrive in a new placement situation. The most important of these boundaries has to do with the limits on behaviors. Maintaining limits must be achieved in a way that facilitates addressing the underlying needs or issues the child is facing at any given moment.

At Forest Heights, there are two basic rules that are always enforced. Transgressions are never ignored.

1. "No hands on. You will not hurt yourself or others." The basic message is that a child will be safe and will neither hurt others nor be hurt himself.

2. "We must always know where you are. If we don't know where you are, we can't take care of you." Therefore, when he is inside the boy cannot leave the living/dining area, even to go to his room or the bathroom, without the knowledge and permission of a child care worker. When he is outside the child may not leave the fenced in area of the yard without this same knowledge and permission for the same reasons.

The underlying message of both of these rules is, "We will take care of you. You will be safe." Obviously, there are certain behaviors that are never condoned. Sexual play, drug usage, stealing and property destruction are examples. But these fall under the auspices of the "you will not hurt yourself or others" and the "permission" rules. Beyond these two rules, there are many expectations which may shift in response to the needs of the child and the judgement of the staff. Although the institution says to the child that here he will be safe and cared for, it is the individual staff member who, based on his daily contacts with the resident, delineates the many other norms to which a child must adhere.

The Concept of Supportive Control

Our interventions to control behaviors are done in a nurturing way that supports a primary focus on attachment, trust, and the development of relationships. Our approach to discipline rests on the concept of supportive control. The purpose of supportive control is to serve as a mediator between the disturbed child and the world which he does not understand and with which he cannot yet cope. It serves to support the child through the period of growth toward adequacy.

Behavior is controlled in a spirit which bolsters the child's ego. The concept of supportive control acknowledges the child's attempts to live a comfortable, rewarding, and productive life. We do not view behaviors as good or bad but as helpful or non-helpful in the child's effort to have things go well for himself. The ultimate goal is to teach the child "self control." Therefore, control procedures support the child's growth and help him internalize self control as opposed to taking control away from him. The underlying message of supportive control interventions is one of caring and concern for the child. They are intimately connected to our efforts to help a child form attachments. Issues of control and order are not separated from concerns about relationship and trust. Interventions are done to protect the child or group and to maintain order, not to take a problem away. Adults own responsibility for protecting the child and maintaining a healthy environment. We do not own responsibility for solving the child's problems. Only the child can accomplish this task.

The following principles are associated with the concept of supportive control:

1. Feelings and actions are constantly differentiated. Children are always permitted, even encouraged, to experience their feelings and to express them in an appropriate manner. There are no "shoulds" about feelings. As one of our boys once said, "Feelings just are. They don't know any better." They can be expressed, discharged, understood, and reflected, but they cannot be dismissed. On the other hand, inappropriate behavioral expressions of emotions are confronted and controlled. When a child is hurting inside, we do not try to take the pain away. Instead we try to help him experience the hurt in as genuine and intense a way as possible. At the same time we help him to learn more appropriate behavioral outlets for his pain. When a child is angry we do not try to convince him that he should not be angry or try to take away the source of the anger. Instead we help him express his anger in an overt but appropriate manner. We try to help him say what he is angry about or at whom he is angry. We do not discount his perceptions.

2. Behavior is not punished, it is controlled. When a child is asked to sit because he has hit another child, it is not in the spirit of preventing future misbehaviors by making the consequence so odious that the child won't repeat the transgression. Instead, we sit a child in order to help him interrupt his current behavior while providing him with an opportunity to think about his actions and consider acceptable alternative responses in future similar situations. The goal is for the child to learn self control.

3. A child must not be allowed to use behavior to maintain distance and avoid relationships. Children with attachment problems frequently use behaviors to keep adults emotionally distanced rather than to encourage continued interactions. For this reason we do not use isolation as a response to inappropriate behavior. A child who must be controlled through sitting or holding remains in the living room or otherwise close to the center of group activity. The behavior thus results in interactions with, but not in the exclusive attention of, an adult.

4. Behavioral outbursts provide opportunities for developing attachment. They are associated with physical and psychological arousal. A child having a temper tantrum puts out a tremendous amount of emotional energy. As the tantrum fades it is usually followed by a period of calm and quiet. At this point, while his barriers to attachment are lessened and he is open to new learning, an adult needs to be available to him.

5. Adults intervene supportively when behaviors are just starting to be problematic. They do not wait for problems to get out of hand. The intervention may be very low key. It may consist only of a comment such as, "Can you stop yourself or do you need my help?" Some children connect best with interventions of low intensity. Others are only reached through high intensity interactions. Adults modify their reactions to mesh with the child's mode.

6. Although we may mitigate the natural consequences for certain behaviors, the child is not protected from reality. If one child steals from another, the latter is allowed, even encouraged, to be angry at the child who has stolen. He is not, however, allowed to express his anger in a hurtful manner. If a child misbehaves on home visits, they may be shortened or temporarily discontinued, but other means of ongoing contact with parents will be encouraged.

7. The child is included rather than excluded from the group. Statements such as, "we do not act like this," or "to live happily together we must do these things" emphasize to the child that certain behaviors are part of being a member of an identified, coherent group. The child who has progressed to some understanding of the results of his own behavior will, when destructive of group activity, be helped to recognize several key concepts. First, he will be helped to realize that his behavior has been destructive for the group and for himself. Second, the behavior could have been controlled. Third, his own control is not only possible but definitely preferable as an indication of growth.

8. Individualization should be connected to the needs of the child rather than to overt behavior. Even in the group setting all children cannot meet the same demands, nor is their behavior remotely identical. Expectations for the new resident will be different than for one approaching discharge. With each individual child, the demands placed on him for self-control are determined by his progress, maturation and personality. Likewise, gratification and positive attention reflect the child's needs rather than his overt behaviors.

Limits are not only necessary, they are usually welcomed by the child. Youngsters need to know what the behavioral boundaries are. When appropriate limits are set, a great worry is removed from the child's shoulders. He knows that he can move about, explore and try out new behaviors, and that if he moves beyond the boundaries of acceptable behaviors adults will let him know. Indeed, boundaries free as well as restrict.

The goal of discipline is always to help the child meet expectations not to provide retribution for unmet expectations. With supportive control measures, adults meet the child's needs for both affection and discipline in a manner that conveys, "I want things to go well for you." When the child is out of control, an adult supplies the external control that is necessary until the child regains control over his own behavior. In this situation the underlying messages are twofold. First, it is too scary for anyone—adult or child—to feel totally out of control of his behavior. Second, the long range goal is for the child to be able to control his own behavior so that external controls will not be necessary.

Discipline provided within the framework of supportive control enhances a child's self-esteem by encouraging him to conform to appropriate expectations. All children need adults to hold such expectations for them and to place controls on their behaviors. At the same time all children need love, acceptance, and emotional nurturing from adult caregivers. In addition they need adult role models who show how to express feelings in acceptable ways. They learn from observing adults who demonstrate self-control. It is important that staff not be drawn into child-like retaliation when faced with provocative behaviors. Adults must display maturity.

For children in residential treatment, the modeling of appropriate behaviors is especially important. As we restrict behavioral manifestations of underlying problems, we must actively teach alternate acceptable behaviors. Adults teach by their own behaviors. The adult who makes a mistake and is able to comfortably say, "I goofed," teaches the child that no one is, or has to be, perfect. Adults who model appropriate ways to deal with frustration teach the child how to cope with similar feelings. Adults who express both positive and negative feelings in direct and appropriate ways teach youth about expressing a wide range of emotions. Adults who physically and verbally demonstrate love for the child teach him what love is and how to show love in return.

Behavior problems in children have a variety of causes. Many behavior problems begin as a way for a child to express feelings or describe needs. Particularly prominent in the population of our treatment center are behaviors which reflect the child's attachment/ trust problems. Some seriously disturbed individuals experience marked distortions of reality and may react to internal stimuli as though they were external attacks. Other behavior problems are a result of children's visual or auditory misperceptions of the world around him.

Some behaviors are indicative of a child's delayed development. For example, a child of ten may be expressing negativism in a way that would have been appropriate at age two but is atypical at age ten. Or a child may be exhibiting a problematic behavior because he is engaged in constant control battles with adults. Sometimes, behavioral patterns that begin for any of the above reasons persist because they have become habits.

Successful management of a particular behavior depends on the underlying cause. For example, if the child's behavior occurs because he is "stuck" at a particular stage of development, then the approach to managing his behavior is to meet those earlier developmental needs. If the behavior exists as an inappropriate expression of feelings, the child is taught new ways to express affective states.

Similar behaviors in two children may have differing underlying causes. On the other hand the child's behavior patterns may have more than one cause. We believe that in a setting that is supportive of the child's continued growth, the initial focus must be on ascertaining the causes of the various negative behaviors. This needs to precede much active discipline. This assessment will help us determine the appropriate expectations for a particular child and will help us devise disciplinary strategies that are aimed at helping the child meet expectations rather than being focused on punishments for past transgressions of the rules.

Most of the widely accepted child management techniques in our culture are based on two premises. 1) The child has a normal attachment to adults and wants to keep them emotionally close. He learns that he can do this by pleasing them. 2) Most children believe, or at least hope, that they are deserving of good things happening to them. These premises have led to the development of a series of disciplinary techniques that 1) create emotional distance between the child and parent when the former misbehaves and 2) provide rewards for "good" behavior. Although these techniques are successful with most "normal" children, they do not work well with children who suffer from attachment disorders or with children who see themselves as undeserving.

Those with attachment disorders have either never learned to desire emotional closeness, or have learned that it is painful to do so. In adapting to earlier life experiences, they have learned to seek relief by creating an emotional distance or barrier between themselves and adult care-takers. Therefore, when adults use techniques based on emotionally distancing children for their misbehaviors (i.e. sending them to their room; expressing disapproval either verbally or non-verbally) they are in reality rewarding the child (giving him what he is seeking or desiring). Clearly, this is not going to encourage the child to change his behaviors.

Many severely disturbed children do not believe that they deserve to have their basic needs met. They see themselves as undeserving of positive experiences and rewards. This reflects a feeling of lack of self-worth that is different than poor self-esteem. Disciplines based on helping children earn rewards (i.e. "You have to do your homework before you can play" or, "You must earn the privilege.") may not work with these children because they don't believe that they deserve to go out or have privileges. Some may start to earn the reward but then undermine it before completion. Others will "give up" before they even start. We believe that using a total behavioral modification approach in working with disturbed children has an inherent danger in that the disturbed child is put in charge of the amount of gratification he receives. Adults respond only to what he initiates. We do not believe that disturbed children should be in charge of their treatment program, but rather that it is the responsibility of adults to determine what the child needs and to insure that his needs are being met, irrespective of his behaviors.

What then are disciplines that do work with such children? Those who have not learned to be emotionally close need to have physical closeness encouraged, possibly even mandated, especially following misbehaviors. In this way, we are not inadvertently providing secondary gains for their misbehaviors. We are also giving the child the message that, "No matter what you do, I want to be close and caring with you." Since most of these children also exhibit poor self-control, we are at the same time putting adults in a position where they can easily provide the necessary external controls until the child can learn more self-control.

In addition to needing limits, all children deserve to feel loved and accepted as unique individuals. It is the everyday happenings in a child's life that give him this feeling. When he is hungry he is fed. When he is tired, he is tucked in bed. When he needs comforting, he receives it. All of these things happen not because the child has been good but because these things are good for children.

Children who see themselves as undeserving usually have never experienced the unconditional meeting of needs that teaches them that they are deserving of gratification. For these children, adults need to clearly identify the young person's legitimate needs for his particular age and provide unconditional giving in these areas. Once a youth has gotten gratification from good things and starts believing that he "deserves" them, adults can move to the more usual expectations and disciplinary techniques which involve some form of "first you do this and then this will happen."

Techniques used within the framework of supportive control are intended to convey the message that the child is being cared for as opposed to being punished. All techniques are founded upon the two fundamental principles that the child will neither hurt nor be hurt and that the child will be cared for.

Our aim is to help both the individual child and the group as a whole attain levels of self-control and social awareness that will allow them to interact with the community in a more satisfying way. We assume that each child has the potential for such self-control.

Supportive control measures used at Forest Heights are varied and numerous. The specific techniques mentioned are designed to promote the child's ability to attach, connect discipline with nurture, maintain behaviors within acceptable limits and further the aim of self control. Which measure is used with a child at a particular time depends upon several factors. The underlying cause of the problem behavior, length of placement, current group dynamics and individual staff member's style of interacting and current emotional state all influence the selection process.

1. Support and modeling for the appropriate expression of feelings. Permission and support for having and expressing feelings is given by staff reflecting the feelings that children have. When a child is struggling to express what he is feeling, caregivers will help the child articulate his emotions. Child care staff may actively encourage the child who has difficulty outwardly demonstrating emotional states. Staff model the appropriate expression of affect by being real, direct and open in the expression of their own feelings in the context of the milieu. In general, prior to admission our residents were repeatedly told to stop their misbehaviors. Here, we will actively teach them more appropriate behavioral expressions for their underlying needs and emotions.

2. Control of rhythms and intensity of interactions. The pace of a child's response to a stressful situation has a characteristic rhythm. A child will often build himself up to an outburst or he may gradually reduce his pattern of participation prior to a period of withdrawal. Staff interfere with this pace by presenting demands or engaging in communications that interrupt the child's resistance to cooperation or participation. The rhythms of interaction between adult and child and the rhythms of self-expression are areas that staff can influence with positive results if they become aware of a non-productive pattern. For some we need to increase the rhythm. For others,

we need to slow it down. The degree of intensity of interactions is likewise used as a mode of supportive control. Some children seem oblivious to low keyed interactions. Others are overwhelmed by loud, fast, or physically confrontive behaviors. To emotionally connect with a child we must respond to his individual needs.

3. Two good choices. A child may be provided with two or more acceptable choices as an alternative to continuing undesireable behavior. For example, if two residents are having a hassle while playing a game, a staff member might suggest, "The two of you need to agree on a solution to the problem or else put the game away and find something else that can be fun for both of you." Such a comment not only suggests acceptable alternatives but stresses that the object in playing a game is to have fun.

4. Reframing. In most situations we confront, there is both a positive and negative aspect to what occurs. As important as it may be to confront the negative behavior, it is equally vital not to ignore the positive. Reframing involves restating a negative, polarizing or challenging statement in terms of a positive striving. It allows for many potential confrontations to be turned into a constructive problem solving process.

Example: Brian and Joel are cleaning the dining room after lunch. Brian quickly completes his task, but Joel, who is very disorganized and has some organic impairment, is still working on his table. Alice, the staff member on duty, asks Brian to help Joel finish his task. Brian gets angry, throws his sponge down and says he is tired of having his jobs take longer because "stupid Joel" is such a lousy worker. Alice pulls Brian aside saying, "Brian, I think you are very good at cleaning tables. You really care about doing a good job. I am always glad when you help me because I know that the job will be well done. It upsets you when you are working with someone who either doesn't care as much or who isn't as good as you are at doing the job. Maybe you and I can find a way of helping Joel do his part of the job better." Alice goes on to suggest other ways for Brian to express his frustration without namecalling.

5. The One Minute Scolding. This technique, described in a book of the same name, was developed by Gerald Nelson, M.D. It seems to be particularly well suited for use with children with attachment disorders. As noted earlier, the attachment process is particularly likely to occur in those moments when a drop of

energy level follows a period of high arousal. The one minute scolding makes use of this theoretical concept. It combines confrontation of behaviors with affirmation of caring for the child. For the first 30 seconds or so the care giver states clearly, firmly, and forcefully that he or she does not approve of a certain behavior. Then the statement is turned into a statement of concern, caring, and optimism indicating that the adult wants to help the child find better ways of meeting his needs.

Our experience with this technique is that it defuses many situations quickly, while creating a closeness that allows us to move on without dwelling on the behavioral incident. We find that it must be used without further disciplinary interventions.

Example: Instead of reframing, Alice may choose to use the one minute scolding. Using a confronting tone of voice and overall demeanor she starts out with, "Brian, I really do not like it when you call other children stupid. It sounds cruel and uncaring to me, as though all you care about is yourself. Lots of us have helped you when you were having trouble with something like homework or chores. It seems we should now be able to ask for your help with others every once in a while without having to put up with namecalling. I get angry when I ask for something that simple and get no cooperation. Switching to a softer voice and a more nurturing attitude Alice goes on to say, "And you know, Brian, I think you can learn how to help others now because I have seen you growing in so many ways already. That makes me feel good because I care about you. You always do a good job on your chores. It's a pleasure for me to work alongside you. I want you to learn how to work even better with others because I think it will help you make friends more easily. I know that is important to you. I want to help you with this, Brian, because I like you."

6. Environmental Manipulation. Many times the environment can be organized to minimize problems, remove unnecessary sources of disorder, and create a calming, optimistic and cohesive atmosphere. For example, extra attention at bedtime is provided for those with sleep problems. A child who usually has difficulty at the table is positioned next to an adult who provides the supervision and support necessary for mealtimes to go well for this child. One-on-one supervision is a frequently used mode of environmental manipulation at the Lodge. We

find that with close adult supervision, many children with problematic behaviors can be successfully included in a variety of enjoyable and productive experiences.

7. Sitting. A child who is out of control, misbehaving, or having difficulty making an activity go well, may be sat in a chair in the living room. Sitting interrupts the behavioral pattern. Simultaneously, the child is provided with an opportunity to think about what he was doing and to consider alternative behaviors for coping with specific situations. The sitting is seen as an opportunity for the child to work on his problems as opposed to being punitive.

8. Holding. Should a child not be able to regain sufficient control to sit in a chair, or if his anxiety, fears or anger are such that he requires assistance in regaining control, he may be held. Holding is presented to the child as, "I will take care of you until you have regained self control." Holding is done without inflicting pain. It helps the child find that he can be cared for and controlled without either being hurt himself or hurting anyone else. It is imperative that the holding be done in a way that is safe for both the child and the adults. Likewise it is done in a manner that minimizes the sexual arousal that sometimes accompanies restraint. The holding is supportive and lends itself to an easy transition from control to nurture.

9. Restriction of Privileges. If a child has had difficulty maintaining self control, he may not be allowed to participate in certain activities. This restriction is seen as supportive.

Example: "Today has gone poorly for you. I don't think you can go to the swimming pool tonight and have it go well. To go wouldn't be a good choice right now. We need to work on having things go well for you here at home first."

When a child is restricted from an activity, he remains behind with a staff member who provides a pleasant alternative activity within the Lodge. Again, the goal is to set the child up for success rather than to punish. An activity restriction is presented with a conviction that at another time the child will be able to handle a similar outing.

10. Logical Consequences. Logical consequences may be used in a variety of situations. For example, when a child has damaged property, he may be asked to help repair the damage. In addition he may be asked to give up a portion, but never all, of his allowance for a period of time to reimburse for property that is destroyed or stolen.

There are many ways of understanding behavior and many systems of behavior control. Regardless of how one looks at specific systems of discipline, the fundamental understanding that control is aimed at meeting the needs of the child, enhancing his feelings of safety, trust, and strengthening adult child relationships seems to us to be the basic element of treatment.

Structure vs Spontaneity

Creating a therapeutic milieu entails shaping a healthy balance between providing adequate structure for insuring feelings of safety and security combined with the flexibility necessary to meet the constantly changing needs of each individual resident. Most children referred to residential treatment centers benefit from a high level of structure. Many residents experience such fragmented thoughts and explosive feelings that such structure becomes their anchor to reality. This provides the basis of trust both for adult caregivers and for the environment. Residents of treatment facilities usually have difficulty with transition times. Times of change from one activity to another seem to trigger feelings of loss of control and the subsequent behavioral manifestations of these underlying feelings.

At the same time, we know that many have not learned how to have fun. Many fun filled experiences seem to be associated with spontaneity rather than rigid planning. Both sets of needs must be met for adequate treatment to take place. To do this we provide for both structured and unstructured periods during the course of the day.

"Islands of structure" provide residents with an opportunity to re-enter a consistent framework. These are periods in the day when children can count on specific things happening at specific times. The routines are just that—routine. These islands of structure are especially important for youth in treatment who have had difficulty trusting adults. They see that on a regular and consistent basis we come back to the same kinds of things. This provides a sense of safety and security. They can count on us.

Our islands of structure tend to be centered around transition times during which the adults consciously change the rhythms of the group. Early morning routines are important in terms of helping the resident transition from sleep to awakening. Particularly for the psychotic child transitions between sleep and awake periods are critical because they are fraught with confusion. Mealtimes and snack times provide obvious choices for routines and islands of structure. Again, these are transition times. Staff set new rhythms for the group as we move to a different activity. Prior to meals all staff and boys come together in the living room and sit down for a few minutes. The primary purpose of the gathering is to help ease the transition by providing an opportunity to settle down and prepare for a pleasant meal. It is a time of quiet interactions. Staff members consciously slow the rhythm of interactions from the more intense one associated with play and unstructured time. The slower pace decreases both internal and external tensions and facilitates co-operation at the table.

Bedtimes again provide an opportunity for structure and routine before sleep. Adult supervision and routine are particularly attentive for both the younger and the more disturbed children, who are especially dependent upon adult interactions to help them keep in touch with reality and to maintain adequate levels of self control.

During structured activities, many adult interactions will be those in response to behaviors of the boys. They will be redirective or limiting of behaviors. In contrast unstructured times provide staff with opportunities to interact from a proactive stance. They provide opportunities for staff to be available for positive interactions with the boys. Such interchanges can be used to teach new skills and competencies, to consolidate previously acquired gains, and most importantly, to share positive experiences.

Even within the islands of routine there are opportunities for spontaneity and fun. For example, occasionally we have a "no utensils" meal, during which the usual manners are put aside by everyone, adult and child alike. It is quite likely that the meal provided will be one not easily eaten without utensils. The fun is joined in by all, but only with difficulty by those who are overly dependent upon routines or who are compulsively neat and clean. On a day such as April Fool's day, breakfast may be served at the usual time but consist of foods normally served at dinner. On another occasion there may be a "backwards" meal during which dessert must be eaten as a prerequisite to getting meat and vegetables.

Spontaneous outings are encouraged. A staff member in the evening realizes that there is a new covering of snow outside. A snow walk is planned even though it might interfere with usual bedtimes. However, spontaneous events need to be infrequent enough to maintain their positive aspects. They must not become routine in and of themselves. They must not interfere with residents building a basic sense of trust about continuity of routine and their expectations for consistency. It is truly a delicate balance which achieves the advantages of both routine and spontaneity while minimizing the disadvantages of each.

Traditions and rituals are another important aspect of the milieu. They help consolidate the sense of unity of the group and provide for more "claiming" to enhance attachment. Although there are the minor rituals, such as those that occur at mealtimes, getting up times and bedtimes, here we are talking about the less frequent rituals.

Traditions which accompany major transitions in our lives are particularly significant. They provide mile markers and enhance feelings of specialness. They mark major events in each individual resident's and staff member's life. Rituals are associated with the child's movement through our treatment program. They occur at the time of a child's admission to and his discharge from the program. For example, on admission a child care worker will help the new resident set up his room. It is important that children see themselves as unique, important, and special. Things of interest to the child—be it cars, space figures, sports figures, or whatever—become part of the room decor. Although adults' judgement of what is good for the child influence decisions, we want the room to reflect its occupant's personality and interests. Prior to discharge, there will be a going away party for each resident. Traditions are an important aspect of this celebration.

There are also ceremonies involving staff members. There is a ritual when a new staff member is accorded the privilege of "giving permission." There are traditions to be observed when a staff member leaves the Lodge. These all provide a sense of unity for members of the Lodge community.

At the Lodge we have, like most families, developed a series of ceremonies that provide continuity from year to year. We observe traditions around holidays. Halloween celebrations, Thanksgiving dinner and other holiday events follow a recurrent pattern. Staff and boys together cut the Christmas tree, which must be tall enough to touch the ceiling of the two story living room. A series of traditions accompany the decorating of the tree.

Traditions and rituals surround birthday celebrations. The child selects the dinner menu for his birthday. He and a staff member together set the table for his special meal. He is the center of the group's attention as he opens his gifts in the living room following dinner.

The Three Stages of Treatment

Our two absolute rules, outlined earlier in this chapter, relate to safety issues and to caring enough about the children to know where they are and what they are doing. Expectations, however, are variable, but specific depending upon the child's particular needs and where he is in the course of treatment. On admission, expectations will be minimal. It is unrealistic to demand the same level of behavioral control of new residents as is expected for those approaching discharge. If our new boys were capable of that there would be no reason for them to be in placement. On the other hand, by the time a youth is ready for discharge we expect his behaviors to be similar to those of individuals his age living in a family setting and attending public school. This is why we make a strong differentiation between rules and expectations.

Expectations are constantly changing throughout the course of treatment. They may change from caregiver to caregiver. They are dependent not only on adult personality variations, but more importantly upon the strength of the relationship a particular adult has with the child. As relationships become stronger, adults place higher expectations on the child. Gradually, these are transferred to other adult-child relationships. "You don't treat me that way. I don't expect you to treat other adults that way." "You've learned to trust me. What can I do to help you learn to trust Alice?" These are common statements as children progress in treatment.

We divide the treatment process into three parts. During the first period of treatment the focus is on building a base of security and trust. In the middle phase of treatment the emphasis switches to skill acquistion while during the final period the focus is on consolidation and transferring the gains made to the post-discharge setting.

The phases of treatment correlate with the three levels of trust that are basic elements of the attachment process. The first stage concentrates on building an increasing trust of care by others and a concommitant trust of control by others. During the second and third periods of treatment the child learns to internalize both the caring and control initially provided by child care staff. In that way the youngster develops the final level of trust, a trust of self.

> **Example:** Charles' father was accused of murdering his wife. The trial date had been set. Charles was certain to have many strong feelings during the court proceedings. Therefore, it was decided that it would be therapeutically advantageous for Charles to be admitted immediately prior to the trial. John, the Residence Director, talked daily with a court observer and then would relay the information to Charles. During the early weeks of his placement, Charles was under continual and considerable tension. Sometimes he would become enraged by the information. At these times his behavior would exceed his abilities for self-control and he would have to be held. Other times he would fall into the depths of despair, sobbing uncontrollably. On rare occasions he would deny having any feelings. No matter what the news or his behavioral responses, Charles was given emotional support in coping with his strong feelings about the testimony and about the subsequent conviction. The emotional support he received from staff members facilitated a rapid attachment process. During the middle period of his treatment, Charles learned how to express his emotions in ways that encouraged inter-personal closeness rather than distancing. He learned

new ways to handle his frustrations. He became less impulsive. In the group setting he learned more about conflict resolution. Throughout his treatment he was exposed to adult male role models who showed caring and concern. At the same time they were able to set limits and deal with frustrations without resorting to physical violence. In individual therapy Charles was aided in resolving the grief issues relating to his mother's death and his father's incarceration.

As we started anticipating Charles' discharge, it became apparent that he needed to see his father face to face. Contact with the prison psychologist was made. Although a prison guard would be present, it would be possible for Charles and a staff member to meet with dad with some modicum of privacy. In therapy sessions and in a staff meeting consideration was given as to who should accompany the youth on the visit. With input from Charles it was finally decided that it should be John. Although Charles had developed a good relationship with his female therapist, he continued to feel emotionally closest to John, who had been the consistent adult in helping him cope with his strong feelings during the trial. During the drive to the prison in a nearby state Charles was very anxious. He verbally reviewed the questions he wanted to ask his dad and the things he wanted to tell him. Although Charles' father seemed happy to see his son, he avoided answering his questions. Dad continued to deny responsibility for his own actions and to cover his underlying feelings with a brusque exterior.

On the drive back to Evergreen, John and Charles talked of how prior to coming to the Lodge, Charles' approach to problem behaviors had been similar to his dad's. Denial and avoidance had been his primary defenses. They talked of all the changes Charles had made. They also talked of how sad it was that Charles' dad had never attained the same skill levels. In the past Charles had worried that he would turn out just like his dad. He no longer had that fear for he now had choices available to him. The overall effect of the trip was one of freeing Charles from the past while strengthening his relationship with John in the present.

Early in the treatment process, adults take responsibility for the child and his behaviors. Our caretaking message is, "We are responsible for you. We will take full responsibility for seeing that you are safe and that your needs are being met." Child care staff are responsible for identifying and meeting needs. The emphasis is on safety, nurture, and unconditional giving. The child is not expected to "earn" rewards. He is given to because it is important that all of his needs be met. We want him to know that at the Lodge kids get things because they need them, because they are special and deserving and because we enjoy giving.

New boys are not expected to conform to the same behavioral expectations as those who have been in residence for some period of time. Indeed, their inability to meet such expectations is openly acknowledged. However, at the same time, we verbalize the anticipation of the child's learning to meet such expectations at some point in the future.

The new child is likely to be fearful. He is uncertain as to whether or not he will be safe in his new environment. Commonly, he is hypervigilant, paying close attention to all interactions between staff and residents as well as to those involving peers. He may keep himself separate from these interactions. He may avoid drawing attention to himself. Instead, he will hover, watching and listening. During this observation period, he will be assessing the safety of the environment.

For some new boys there is a "honeymoon" period. They are busy observing the interactions between other residents and the adults. It is a time when they become familiar with their surroundings. They form initial impressions of what it will be like to live here. During this time there may be a quiet resolve on the part of the new resident to make the best of the situation. He may exhibit this by such good behavior initially that at times we are left to wonder why he was admitted.

The "honeymoon" period can provide us with many openings for getting some "hooks" into the child. There will be many opportunities to show him that he will be taken care of, that he will be nurtured and that his needs will be met. Initially, this is done by making the child responsible for very little. We take a fairly omnipotent stance that we will take care of virtually everything. We may even provide care in areas in which the child himself appears adequate. Some children come to us appearing to be very independent, too adequate in terms of never allowing others to care for them. They do not experience enough trust in caretakers to allow themselves to be put in the position of needing or wanting someone else's care. Because we want them to begin to see us as people who can take care of them, we do many things for them. We may help a boy make his bed, comb his hair, select his clothes for him, or see that he gets some of his favorite foods. We do these things not because he is incapable but because we want him to learn that our staff enjoy caretaking.

For other new residents there is only a very short period of time during which they allow themselves an opportunity to look things over. Instead of observing, this child will jump in immediately with testing. We view this as an effort on his part to find out whether we can, and will, take care of him. Our response is one of heightened caretaking, rather than punitive in nature. We realize that the newly admitted resident may go through an extreme period of exhibiting problem behaviors such as sexual provocation, hands all over everybody, stealing, inability to talk about what really is happening to him, and blaming others. Such behaviors are seen as indicating his need for treatment.

In most residential centers, on occasion there will be residents out of control of their own behaviors. There will be adult-youth interactions of high intensity. We pay special attention to providing adequate emotional support for the new resident observing these interactions. Fearfulness may increase if most intense interpersonal interactions take place behind closed doors, if the new resident is hustled off during these interactions, or if he is told that they do not concern him. Just as all occurrences in a family basically impact on the children within the family, we believe that all occurrences in the residential center impact on the child. The new resident deserves our help and support in understanding these occurrences and their impact on him.

For those children who have developed skill at avoiding adult interactions, the rules relating to asking permission provide for several points of contact with adult caregivers throughout the day. When the youth asks permission to go to the bathroom, a staff member may realize that he has not had many interactions with this particular boy today and will make it a point subsequently to initiate interactions.

Another positive side effect of the rule relating to permission to go to rooms and to the bathroom is that it provides opportunities for adults to say, "yes" to children. Many disturbed youth are adept at making requests to which adults will surely respond "no." Feelings of rejection and lack of worth are thereby furthered. No child is denied the opportunity to go to the bathroom. Although early in the treatment process boys are not allowed to isolate themselves from others by spending excessive time in their rooms, rarely are they denied the opportunity to go to their rooms for an identified purpose. Therefore, many requests for permission lead to "yes."

Even going to school requires permission, as it is outside the fenced in play area. This again iterates the philosophy that school attendance is a privilege. If an administrative staff member, or a therapist, wants to meet with the child outside the living/playing area, that staff member asks permission of the child care staff to have the boy leave with him. Again, the message of, "We can't adequately treat you or protect you if we don't know where you are" is conveyed. These rules say nothing about diminished trust for either children or adults, but rather are phrased in more positive terms which convey being responsible for the caretaking of residents.

When there is evidence that the resident feels physically and psychologically safe and secure in the Lodge environment and that he has developed at least one attachment to an adult caregiver, we can move on to the second part of treatment. The emphasis during this middle period is different than during the initial phase. The child now feels safe and secure. He has developed an important reciprocal relationship. He now has energy available for skill acquisition. The focus of treatment turns in these directions. Most are learned in the context of milieu relationships. The child care staff are the major instructors in the child's acquisition of these life skills.

Seven Areas of Skill Acquisition

Academic/Vocational

Self-care

Recreation-Entertainment

Social

Emotional Management

Relationship Skills

Conflict Resolution

The two basic rules remain constant. However, permission for longer stays in unsupervised areas is likely to be given. A public school student may be given permission to study in his room rather than in study hall. A resident who has demonstrated a healthy level of self-control will be given downtown privileges. This means he may go, with permission, downtown without direct staff supervision. He may go by himself on an errand, such as getting a haircut, or with another child swimming or to a movie. The child enrolled in public school may go on outings with school friends. Such privileges always connote that one has moved beyond the initial stages of therapy.

The final period of treatment focuses on internalization and consolidation of the earlier gains and on transferring these gains to other settings. The child has learned to interact with the Lodge environment in a healthier, more satisfying manner. However, he will not be spending the remainder of his life in this setting. He must be able

to transfer these gains and successes to subsequent environmental
settings. He will be encouraged to take part in more activities away from
the Lodge as we prepare him for living in a less restrictive
environment.

Considerable time will be spent with the child and his family
actively transferring the behavioral gains to the family setting. He will
be provided opportunities for demonstrating his newly acquired skills
within his family setting and with peers in his home neighborhood
during more extended or more frequent home visits. He may attend
public school in Evergreen prior to discharge and thus have an
opportunity to demonstrate newly acquired skills and behavior
controls in a less structured setting without adult staff members being
immediately available.

By now, the youth will have not just one attachment
relationship but will have extended his trust to encompass a series of
attachments. Those staff members close to a particular child will use
the power of their relationships to help internalize the youth's gains.
They help him learn to depend upon himself in his interactions with
others. Just as the pre-schooler carries the parental representation
within himself, using it to aid in maintaining self-control, the adult
caregiver will help the previously disturbed youth internalize the
formerly externally imposed expectations.

The youth is confident of his ability to control his own
behaviors, to ask for help when he needs it, to identify, and
appropriately express his emotions. What were once externally
supplied behavioral controls have now been internalized. He has
learned that he is a worthwhile individual who is deserving of love,
acceptance, and positive relationships with others. Peer relationships
will have improved. He will have learned how to help friendships grow.
He no longer sees conflicts primarily in terms of winning and losing, in
terms of a power base, but rather as a necessary component of life
providing opportunities for further growth and change.

Throughout all three periods of the boy's treatment, the two
basic rules of the Lodge remain constant. The daily routines remain
fairly consistent. Most of the adults he interacts with will be there
throughout his stay. Indeed, these changing growing relationships
involving the same child and the same adult caregivers give a strong
impetus to ego growth and emerging ego strength on the part of the
child. However, increasing demands, expectations and responsibilities
have been placed on the resident throughout his stay. Behaviors that
were tolerated as expressions of pathology on admission are no longer
acceptable. They no longer serve the same purpose. They are no longer
necessary for contending with the environment. The youth has learned
new coping skills and can count on them to aid him in successfully
facing the challenges that lie ahead.

Expectations at the time of admission are minimal.

Expectations at the time of discharge are, in general, those that would, for the youth's age, be considered usual in a normal family and school environment. The milieu has, in some ways, stayed the same throughout his stay. Yet as treatment has progressed, the expectations of the milieu and caregivers have been modified. Change has occurred. Both the responsibility and the credit for the growth lie within the child. However, change has occurred not in isolation, but in the context of adult-child relationships.

A Day in the Life of Forest Heights Lodge

The strains of Beethoven, initially subdued in the background, gradually swell to extend throughout the Lodge. It is 6:30 A.M. on a Friday morning in early October. Stan and Irwin, already dressed, are sitting in the living room talking quietly with Sally, a child care worker. They both like getting up early on occasion to have a few minutes of quiet time with a staff member prior to the hubbub of the day. Today they have been speculating about the weather. It is overcast and the threat of snow is in the air. They have looked at the chart posted on the wall to see who will win the yearly "snow contest" if indeed today holds the first significant snowfall of the year. It will be Kenny, one of the newer residents.

As Sally goes to the back bedroom, Stan heads for the dining room. One of his chores is setting the breakfast table. He has learned that his day goes better if he doesn't feel rushed in the mornings so he sets his alarm to get up twenty minutes ahead of the usual wake-up time. That way he gets into the bathroom ahead of others and has a few minutes to converse in the living room prior to starting his chore.

A second child care staff member, Mark, enters the living room, freshly shaved, dressed neatly but casually. He starts upstairs to awaken the boys. Meanwhile, Pete, the third staff member on shift makes the downstairs rounds. "Good morning, Tom Asher" he says as he turns on a light. "Time to wake up, Ralph." A staff member enters each room, awakening each resident with some personal interaction. One may need a hug to get his day off to a good start. Another does best if there is no immediate physical contact. Some are slow to emerge from sleep. Others literally bound out of bed. Morning has differing meanings for various boys. Some need considerable care and support to get their day going. They will most likely have rooms on the first floor where there are fewer children sleeping and where more individualized attention can be given.

Sally is awakening the younger boys in the back bedroom. It is apparent that David has already been awake. He quickly gets out of bed and into the clothes that he and Sally laid out the night before. Kenny awakens in an argumentative mood. He verbally tries to engage Sally in a battle. "I'm not going to get up today! You'll have to make me!" Sally chooses not to respond to this verbal ploy. She continues to talk soothingly with Todd who has problems differentiating between reality and fantasy, between being awake and dreaming. As she makes her rounds of the room, physically and verbally interacting with each of the four residents, she comes to Kenny. Knowing that underlying his frequent control battles is a feeling of lack of overall control, she starts the day's interactions with Kenny by asking if he still wants to wear what he selected last night or if he chooses to change his selection. In addition, Sally starts tickling Kenny's tummy. Initially he giggles and squirms but rather quickly says, "Stop it." This Sally does promptly. This is an appropriate area for Kenny to exert control. Some days these tactics are enough to counterbalance his desire for total control. However, today Kenny remains lying in bed throwing out the verbal "hooks." "See, I am not getting up. You can't make me."

Sally continues to help the others with their clothes as needed. She quickly straightens up the beds. There is only one that needs changing this morning. For now, she just strips the bed. She and Todd will remake it after breakfast as they complete the housekeeping chores in the back bedroom. Since she bought the comforters with their brightly colored washable covers, bedmaking chores in the back bedroom have been greatly eased. As is common, Todd tends to just stand around waiting for Sally to tell him what to do next as he prepares for the day. Sally and Alice have both tried a variety of tactics aimed at helping him be more responsible for himself in the early mornings. However, they have learned that if they provide Todd with positive interactions and support as he gets up and starts his day, he is able to gradually assume more age appropriate control by the time breakfast is over. If they do not provide this support early on, his day tends to go from one bad scenario to another. The overall goal is to help him have a good day.

Kenny is the only one not dressed and ready to go to the living room. It is 6:50. The music of Beethoven continues to be a backdrop for the various early morning activities. As Sally leaves the back bedroom, she quietly comments, "Breakfast will be ready in ten minutes. I hope that you are ready to join us Kenny. I like sitting next to you at the table." Again, she has learned that Kenny is sometimes able to drop the argumentative stance if adults refuse to be engaged by it.

Meanwhile, Mark and Pete have again made the rounds of the various bedrooms about five minutes after the wake up call to remind the boys that now it is time to get up. For some that is all that is necessary for them to meet the expectation of being to breakfast on time, dressed, combed and ready for a new day. For others, considerable adult support is necessary. Today, Chris is having a difficult time getting started. His parents are coming this afternoon. They will be joining Chris in his therapy session with his psychiatrist, Joyce. He is concerned about how it will go. Because of his preoccupation with this and his anxiety, he is having trouble focusing on the tasks at hand— getting dressed, getting his bed made, his hair combed, etc. Mark knows that Chris tends to be very anxious about parental visits. Although Chris has not verbally mentioned the visit today, Mark comments, "It sure looks like you're having a hard time focusing on early morning tasks. I bet you're wondering how it will go with your folks this afternoon." Initially Chris responds with, "No problem. There won't be any problems. I know." Mark comes back with, "Of course, you hope that there won't be any problems. However, I'm certain that you, your parents, and Joyce can work together to solve any problems that might come up. I've seen you really working with staff to solve problems here at the Lodge. You've made a lot of gains in that area. Now it's time to start using some of those skills with your family. Joyce will help you. She's really good at that." As he is commenting, Mark reaches over and straightens Chris' shirt and helps him make his bed.

Gradually, he can see some of the tension leave Chris' face. "You know, your parents won't be here until about 3:00 p.m. The session this afternoon will probably go better if you have had a good day than if you get sent out of school or have a lot of other problems earlier in the day. When you have trouble, you seem to really get down on yourself. I'd like to help you have the early part of the day go well for you. I think you and I should meet briefly with Fred before school and see if we can work out some ways that he can be helpful if you have trouble paying attention in school. In fact, it probably would be good if you brought up your feelings about the visit at morning meeting. Some of the other guys might have suggestions for you. That way all of the staff will be tuned in to your needs. Kids your age really need to learn how to ask for help. This would be a good opportunity for you to practice this."

As Mark heads downstairs, he comments to Carl, who joins him on the steps, "Gee, you're looking good today. That shirt sure looks sharp on you."

In the living room, Sally and Pete are helping insure that the boys are looking nice in preparation for going in to breakfast. Mark turns off the stereo and announces that it is time for the group to gather in the living room, sit down and get ready to go to breakfast. Kenny comes tearing in from the back bedroom with hair not brushed and shirt tails out. As he takes a seat in the living room Sally moves over next to him, tucks his shirt in, brushes his hair for him, and ties his shoes. She recognizes that he is signalling that he will need considerable adult intervention to get this day off to a good start. She will have to decide which is the best time to treat his behavior as an outright control battle. If she can provide enough external support to get him through breakfast, she will have more time after that to devote to his control issues without it interfering with her caretaking of others. This is her goal.

As everyone, adults and boys alike, takes a seat in the livingroom prior to going in to breakfast, a new calmer rhythm is set. The more hurried pace of early morning activity is replaced by a slower more relaxed tempo. Voice levels are softened, movements are not so hurried. It is the adult responsibility to facilitate this change in the rhythms of the group. During the few minutes that staff and boys share together in the living room prior to entering the dining room the stage is set for the tone at the table. As a group, the members of the Lodge family enter the dining room. Everyone stands behind his chair. Mark asks Sally to take her seat, and then invites Pete and the boys to take theirs. A goal of having tasty, hot, attractively presented meals on time is set for all meals. Mealtimes are times for socialization as well as for nurture of the body. An adult at each of the three tables helps facilitate appropriate behaviors. Those boys who need more individual attention at mealtimes are seated immediately adjacent to an adult. Kenny's place is next to Sally on her right. She visually, and sometimes physically, insures that each child has food on his plate.

As could be expected today, Kenny starts complaining about the food. "I hate pancakes. Why do we always have pancakes? We never have anything I like." Sally places a single pancake on Kenny's plate. She butters it and pours syrup over it. Kenny yelps, "You know I hate syrup. You wrecked it. You wreck everything!" If Kenny were older, or had been at the Lodge longer, he might be excused to take a seat in the living room until he was ready to rejoin the group and have breakfast go well for himself. However, Sally realizes how dependent Kenny is on immediate adult presence when he is having this much difficulty. Rather than excusing him from the table, she chooses to move his chair away from his place, closer to her. While continuing to verbally converse with others whose table behaviors are more appropriate, she puts her arm around Kenny's shoulders providing him with a modicum of external body control. Although his mouth is rejecting of her, the tension in his shoulder muscles decreases. Again, he attempts to engage Sally in a verbal battle. "I'll probably starve. You never let me eat." With the arm around his shoulder, Sally gives him a gentle hug. She asks Todd what he is working on in Math. Unless actively engaged by an adult, Todd rarely initiates conversation at meals, especially at breakfast. Once he starts talking about school, the others join in. As voices start to rise, Sally reminds them that everyone will have his chance to participate and that it is difficult to hear anyone if everyone is shouting. As Sam starts to interrupt Todd, Sally gives him a nonverbal signal reminding him to wait his turn.

Kenny is verbally trying to engage Sally in a control battle centering on food. She long since learned that such battles are impossible to "win" and indeed are futile. Kenny alternates between threatening to eat everything so no one else will have anything and warning to never eat another bite. "I'll just starve to death." Sally reminds him that he will be provided with an adequate serving of food, but that it is his choice as to how much of it he eats. With her arm intermittently about his shoulders, she can feel when he is physically calmer. At that point she asks if he is ready to rejoin the others. He pulls his chair back around to his place and resumes eating the food on his plate.

Meanwhile at Pete's table, Chris is having a difficult time paying attention to others' requests, even when Pete reminds him that he needs to focus on the meal and his tablemates. He is excused from the table. As he passes by Mark en route to the livingroom, the latter pulls him aside commenting, "Things will go better for you all day if you focus on getting things turned around quickly this morning." After several minutes in the living room, Chris re-enters the dining room telling Pete that he is ready to retake his place at the table. He comments that he knows he's been thinking about his upcoming visit rather than paying attention to others at the table. For the remainder of the meal it is obvious that Chris is exerting considerable energy just staying engaged with others.

As the meal approaches its end, Mark leans over to scan the job list posted on the wall close to his place. He identifies those who are on dish crew this morning. He asks for a volunteer to help Jim with the trash today. Last night was a birthday celebration and the cans are more loaded than usual. Individualized comments about morning chores are made to all those who need this type of verbal reminder. Although Chris usually does not need such support, Mark realizes that today he will be dependent upon adults to help him focus on each succeeding task.

Sally and several of the younger boys head to the back bedroom to finish straightening and cleaning it. Sam is responsible for dusting the floor each day. Sally and Todd put fresh linens on his bed. The other boys are asked to straighten their belongings. Once again, Kenny starts arguing. Sally decides this is the best time to push the issue, rather than trying to de-escalate it. Kenny is one of those children who frequently needs to escalate before he can physically relax, be positively engaged with others and have a good day. Intensifying her responses with him now will not deprive the others of the support they need to get their day started. School and supervisory staff are starting to arrive. Sally can easily engage herself in the nose-to-nose confrontation that seems to be inevitable with Kenny at some point this morning. When he refuses to help straighten his things, Sally takes Kenny by the arm and leads him to the living room. She puts him in a chair. Glen, who is walking by, sits down next to Kenny and comments to Sally, "You can go back and help the others with the back bedroom chores. I'll be here with Kenny." At that point, the latter starts kicking and screaming. In the past, he would also attempt to leave the chair. Now, so long as an adult is physically present, this no longer occurs.

Mark has gone upstairs to check on the boys' rooms and to supervise the various upstairs chores. Chris is cleaning the bathrooms. Although he seems preoccupied, he is working consistently on the task at hand. Again, Mark asks what Chris thinks might be helpful in terms of keeping him focused on the tasks at hand. Together they decide that maybe Chris should talk with Glen about some of the issues that are certain to surface during the therapy session today. It will probably be helpful if he does this right after morning meeting, prior to going to school.

Pete is in the dining room and kitchen helping, and supervising, the morning dish crew. In the living room Irwin is moving furniture while vacuuming. His compulsive traits work for him in completing this particular job. He is certain to go off to school each day filled with praise for a chore well done. Sometimes at school his compulsive traits work against him. He is gradually learning to maximize the advantages and minimize the disadvantages of this characteristic of his personality.

The teaching staff, Carol, Steve, and Fred arrive as breakfast comes to an end. Steve is outside on the patio putting bikes in the bike rack and conversing with Carl who is sweeping the patio. They are speculating as to the likelihood of snow today. Carl is sure hoping that he won't have to shovel, instead of sweep, tomorrow. Jim and Stan are arguing as they struggle with the trash cans. Steve asks if they plan to agree on a solution or if they are agreeing to continue arguing. Stan starts laughing. Jim becomes verbally defensive. However, the job gets done.

As the morning chores reach completion, Sally asks Curtis if he has all of his things together for school. Since she helped him insure that both books and assignments were placed in his backpack at the end of study hall the night before, she knows that the answer should be yes. However, Curtis when anxious still has a tendency to automatically answer "no" to everything. Although he has been in public school for about six weeks now, his anxiety level still tends to be fairly high. Staff members are working on setting up situations in which "yes" can be a comfortable response. They want Curt to head off to school with a "yes" rather than "no" headset. As morning meeting is about to begin, Sally and Curtis head off for the drive to Wilmot.

Morning meeting provides another transition time. Again the pace is slowed from that of busy involvement with morning chores to the more thoughtful sedentary rhythm that accompanies attendance at school. Although Kenny's outburst has peaked, and he is now physically relaxed, he needs to be close to an adult in a positive way. Since Sally is taking Curt to school, Carol goes and sits in a chair with Kenny curled up comfortably against her. All of the boys and adults involved in the house and school come together in the living room. The meeting provides a visible connection between two of the major aspects of the therapeutic program at Forest Heights. Glen, as is usual, leads the meeting this morning. He starts out with a comment about the weather. There is considerable discussion about last night's forecast, the appearance of the sky today, the amount of snow that is necessary to identify it as the first snow of the season, who will win the contest if it snows today, tonight, etc. Pete mentions that he is planning to take a group to Denver in the evening to go roller skating. Several boys immediately ask if they can be included. Pete indicates that he will be watching throughout the day to see who is demonstrating the levels of self-control that are necessary to make such an outing an individualized success for each participant, as well as the group as a whole.

As Glen opens the meeting up for comments by anyone, Chris raises his hand. When Glen calls on him, he talks briefly about his concerns and excitement about his upcoming visit. He notes that he has already been experiencing difficulty in keeping things going well this morning and asks if he can talk individually with Glen before going to school. By this time, Sally has rejoined the group. As she sits down, she motions to Kenny to come sit next to her. Carol non-verbally encourages him to join Sally. No words are exchanged until the end of the meeting but Kenny has gone over and snuggled in against Sally.

At the close of the morning meeting, teachers and students walk together from house to school. Meanwhile Sally and Kenny remain sitting together. Sally comments, "I missed having some quiet close time with you earlier today. I really enjoy it when we can be close in a comfortable rather than argumentative way." Kenny's only reply is a kiss on Sally's cheek.

Chris accompanies Glen to his office. There Chris talks about his ambivilance about his upcoming visit. Glen reminds Chris of the various gains he has made since coming to the Lodge and of his previous fears about his own and his parents' abilities to transfer these gains to the family setting. Chris asks if Glen will sit in on part of the session with his parents and Joyce. He wants to confront his parents about some of his feelings about past interactions. He believes that he needs support not only from his therapist, but from someone in the house. Glen indicates that he is really pleased to see that Chris is making so many gains in the area of identifying when he needs others' help and asking for it verbally rather than by negative behavior, as has so often been the case previously. He reassures him that he will be present at this afternoon's session. Glen then switches the focus to the present asking Chris, "What do you need to do this morning, to help yourself feel more confident this afternoon?" Chris heads off to school, with his anxiety at a more manageable level, ready to focus on his academics.

Kenny hasn't started school yet so he will be involved with adults in the house during the school hours. Todd's first school

experience each day consists of an individual half hour with Carol later
in the morning. Sally suggests that the two younger boys each get some toys from their room and play in the living room while she checks to see if anything else is needed when she makes a trip to the local drugstore later in the morning. Kenny asks if he will be able to go with her. Sally's responds, "You were having a difficult time early this morning. It looks like you have gotten things turned around. Let's see how it goes between now and when I go on errands." Kenny starts to whine, but then notices the look that is on Sally's face and quickly stops with the comment, "I think I'll get my Legos out."

Todd is still just standing in the living room. Mark comes over and starts talking with him. He suggests that maybe today they should get their twenty minutes of ball playing in early because of the weather. He knows that any changes in schedule tend to be difficult for Todd, but that if the changes involve one-to-one attention they go better. This is an opportune time to interject one more such experience into Todd's life. Catching and throwing a ball are still difficult skills for Todd. He is unable to participate in group activities which involve these skills. On the other hand, he is very agile and quite sure on his feet. Mark and Todd start out their gross motor time with a few minutes of "follow the leader." Mark takes the lead, hopping off with Todd following. He then switches to skipping, another of Todd's skills. Todd is then able to take the lead. Gradually the activities switch from Todd's strengths to his weaker areas—ball throwing and catching. He is well focused on this activity today and seems more sure of himself.

Meanwhile Sally has completed her list. She tells Kenny that she has some time for them to spend together and asks if he would rather she work with him on the Lego project, play a game or read a book. It still is difficult for Kenny to choose from three activities. He tends to focus on what he is missing out on, rather than what he is doing. He needs lots of opportunities to gain enjoyment from an activity he has chosen. Sally, understanding that this choice is difficult gives him two minutes to make it and goes off to put some clothes away. When she returns she asks for his decision. Kenny has chosen a game this time.

Throughout the course of the school day, boys are coming and going between the house and school. Some will have free periods during which they return to the house. Some who are just starting school may be involved in a one on one situation for only a brief period. Some who are having difficulties having things go well for them at school will be excused to come back to the house to work things out with an adult there prior to returning to school.

Shortly before ten Sally invites Kenny to join her in the kitchen to help Margie put the finishing touches on the morning snack. This morning it consists of apple wedges and celery stuffed with peanut butter. Sally and Kenny take the trays over to the school building. This provides Kenny with an opportunity to observe the school structure and expectations without having to yet be part of it.

Kenny and Sally have just completed their game when Todd returns from the first of his several daily periods in school. He is clutching several papers in his hand. Sally is surprised that he comes over and quickly hands them to her. She has not had to remind him that she wants to see them. She comments positively not only about the work per se but also about his initiating the sharing. He says, "Carol told me to bring them to you." Sally's comment is, "I like you sharing them with me without my having to ask first." Sally suggests that Todd keep his jacket on as she is planning to leave for downtown Evergreen as soon as the game is put away. Kenny has been able to be involved with her in fun activities for over an hour. Sometimes he has difficulty on outings alone with a woman. However, she knows that this will be a good opportunity for him to practice having things go well with her away from the Lodge. "We've had a good time together this morning. I want to be able to enjoy more of it. I think it can go well for you downtown, what do you think?" She gets a verbal commitment from Kenny to 1) keep close and 2) comply with car and store expectations.

Lunch, with the usual mealtime expectations and satisfactions, provides another island of structure. Following this there is about a half hour period before the afternoon group meeting which prepares the boys for the resumption of the school day. During this free time, the residents involve themselves in a variety of activities. Usually an adult or two will have some activities going, both for those who have difficulty keeping themselves busy and for those who enjoy the particular activity.

Afternoon school begins at 1:00 p.m. after a short group meeting to aid in transitioning from house to school again. Those not in school once more become involved in activities in the house. Shortly before three Mark goes to get Curt at school. If at all possible he tries to go by himself. This early in the school year, Curt needs some one-to-one time right after school for sharing both his daily frustrations and successes. Helping Curt transition from the expectations of public school to the Lodge activities and expectations for the week-end seems to be an important factor in determining how things will go for him over the next couple of days. Mark helps him focus on this en route home.

By the time they arrive at the Lodge, boys and teachers alike have returned to the house for afternoon snack. During snack time the focus may initially be on school activities but it is likely to gradually change to plans for after school activities and today to plans for week-end activities. Again it is a time when teachers and house staff are involved together to provide continuity between the two parts of the program. Today Chris' parents arrive at 3:00 p.m. It is a busy time with many activities. This seems to be true every day, but even more so on Fridays.

In spite of a few spits of snow and continued cloudiness it is warm enough outside for most of the boys to be involved in a game of touch football on the flat area. A physical outlet for the energy accumulated during the more sedentary part of the school day seems beneficial for most. Adults and boys alike are involved. The structure, combined with an opportunity for the boys to learn and improve both physical and social skills, is important. As team members, they learn to cooperate with others, even with those that they do not necessarily like. This evening there will be an opportunity for some of the boys to be involved in a more individualized physical activity, roller skating. The roller rink in Denver provides them with an opportunity to compare their behaviors with "normal" peers, as well as an opportunity to interact with girls in a supervised setting. Staff knows that incoming phone calls from girls tend to increase in the days immediately following the skating activity.

While most of the boys are involved in the football game, Sally takes those who have difficulty with the skills involved in this particular activity over by the administration building to ride their bikes on the sloping driveway and sidewalk there.

As the dinner hour approaches the transition period is once again facilitated by the group coming together in the living room prior to entering the dining area. Tonight at the end of the dinner hour, Pete reads off the list of those who will be going skating. When Sally, Todd, and Kenny went downtown earlier they selected a video movie for this evening. Many boys, on admission, complain about the infrequency of television viewing during the week-days. However, those not attending study hall rapidly learn to get involved in a variety of alternate activities. In fact, tonight several choose to play Foosball and other games rather than watch the video. While the movie is playing, Sally moves from one younger boy to another with the nail clippers. Last evening she caught up on giving the younger boys shampoos so that they wouldn't be interrupted on a week-end evening. Some ask what activities are being planned for the week-end. As yet, no firm plans have been made and Sally suggests that a couple of boys might want to help organize a Saturday afternoon activity. Saturday morning will be devoted to a general cleanup both of yard and house. Jim comments that with luck there will be enough snow on the ground in the morning to preclude much yard work.

Between some boys being gone on visits and others at the skating rink, there are only thirteen here for evening snack tonight. Irwin has asked to make the snack this evening. A couple of the others volunteer to help him. Following the snack, while some of the older boys are helping clean up the dining and kitchen area under Mark's supervision, Sally and the younger boys head for the back bedroom.

She supervises teeth brushing, washing up, showers for a couple, and changing to pajamas. Before they are tucked in for the night, Sally reads them a story. A couple of the older boys wander back for story time. So long as they are able to enjoy the activity they may choose to include themselves. Knowing that bedtimes are difficult for Kenny, Sally suggests some quiet time with her in the rocking chair tonight after the others are tucked in. The room is darkened. Voices are lowered. She rocks Kenny for ten minutes and then quietly tucks him in and returns to the living room.

There too lights are being dimmed and voices are being lowered. Some of the boys continue to watch T.V. Others are taking showers or baths. Sally heads for the kitchen to make herself a cup of tea. Stan comes in and asks to join her. They sit at the kitchen table quietly conversing about some of Stan's hopes and dreams for the future. As opposed to school nights when it is lights out at 9:30 or 10:00, dependent on age, tonight there will be more leeway in bedtime. However, as Sally and Stan are talking in the dining room, Mark periodically goes from room to room upstairs, chatting about today's accomplishments and tomorrow's plans. He spends extra time with those whom he saw little of during the day. His presence in the upstairs provides a sense of safety. Near bedtime as children move from room to room and in and out of the bathrooms, as they face their fears and feelings of being alone, the potential for sex play is greater. The presence of an adult decreases both the intensity of their underlying feelings and the likelihood of the overt behaviors.

It is 10:30 p.m. As Pete enters the living room with the six boys who accompanied him to Denver, he reminds them to keep their voices lowered as they get ready for bed. Once again, he and Mark make the rounds of the bedrooms, supervising, interacting with the boys as they ready themselves for the night. Once everyone is in bed, Pete, Mark, and Sally share a final few minutes talking about how the day went for various of the residents and making preliminary plans for tomorrow. It is a time for clarification and communication to take place. Tyler, the night staff person, joins them before Mark and Sally leave. Tyler will be awake, doing various chores such as laundry and some food preparation for breakfast as well as randomly checking on the boys throughout the night. Pete will be sleeping in the small office, available during the night to meet either the physical or psychological needs of the boys. ∎

Guide for Parents

In residential treatment the milieu is the core program. Parents should feel comfortable with the day to day living situations to which their child will be exposed. Insist on having a full understanding of the

Here are some questions to help you.

1. Are daily caretaking routines congruent with the philosophy?

2. Do child care staff and residents seem comfortable in their interactions with one another?

3. Is the milieu chaotic or is there adequate structure to provide a sense of safety?

4. Is the disciplinary structure rigid or is it flexible enough to meet the needs of children with different types of problems and differing personality characteristics? Do the disciplinary measures used seem to promote growth and change or are they punitive in nature? Is there uniformity between different staff as to disciplinary techniques?

5. Are any of the disciplinary or therapeutic techniques in conflict with your family values or beliefs?

Conclusion

The milieu is the heart and soul of a residential treatment program. It is within the living environment that residents confront their fears and their weaknesses. It is here that they learn to recognize their strengths and experience satisfaction. In this setting they achieve the gains necessary for post-discharge success.

Adults involved in their lives may, by their actions, either reinforce the child's pathology or help him experience new modes of adult-child interactions. Some centers ask child care staff to take a neutral stance in their dealings with residents. That seems to be the essence of custodial care. In those settings, there are few opportunities and little encouragement for close relationships. In residential treatment facilities, on the other hand, every adult-child interaction throughout the day is viewed as having the potential for being therapeutic. The child is involved in therapy throughout all of his waking hours.

Notes and Elaborations

pg. 142 Psychological defenses usually start out as our minds attempts to help us cope with reality, reduce anxiety, or keep us safe;

however, through time the very defense which was once helpful may become a problem in and of itself. An example would be Beth (Chapter 1) whose avoidance of males initially was an attempt to provide physical safety but subsequently became a barrier to forming new, healthier interpersonal relationships.

pg. 146 Behaviorists frequently use isolation of the child from others as a disciplinary technique. They see misbehaviors as misguided attempts to gain attention; if the child gets less attention for a specific behavior he is more likely to stop the behavior. Proponents of attachment theory, on the other hand, will see negative behaviors as an attempt on the child's part to keep adults psychologically distanced; therefore, they will increase adult contact when the child behaves negatively. In general, those who support attachment theory will perceive a child who is out of control as being fearful of their own power and that isolation will only serve to increase that fear rather than diminish it.

pg. 149 In general disturbed children behave in extremely provocative ways. They are at increased risk for physical abuse at the hands of adults if the latter do not have, immediately at hand, skills for handling the behavioral disturbances in a more positive manner.

C O N T E N T S

Education

Kenny's Case   185
The Educational Program as a Reflection of
     Philosophical Base   190
Why Should this Child Be Going to School?   191
When Is a Child Ready to Go to School?   192
How Is a Child Expected to Behave in School?   194
What is the Child Expected to Learn in School?   195
What Makes Forest Heights Lodge School Unique?   197
School Structure   202
     Teaching Staff   202
     Curriculum   203
     Materials   203
     Individualization and Groupings   203
     School Reports   205
Relationship between School Staff and Parents   205
The Use of the Public School Setting   206
Case Example   207
Guide for Parents   209
Conclusion   209
Notes and Elaborations   210

C H A P T E R 6

Primary Contributor Carol Benedict

Education

Ken ran back over to the Lodge with a big smile on his face. "Sally, guess what! I'm going to public school this year." Sally's response was, "Great!" She started thinking about all the school related changes Ken had made since he had come to the Lodge a little over a year ago.

His parents had hoped Ken would be ready to start on-grounds school in September, about two months after admission. However, he had made it clear that he was not ready to make a commitment to working in school at that time. Given his history and behaviors in the house, staff was not surprised that it would take longer to help Kenny trust adults enough to have energy available for academic learning.

The Summers had been very anxious about his being out of school after the regular school year had started. They were concerned that he was going to fall further and further behind. Staff were feeling the pressure from Ken's parents. He surely must also feel under pressure to go and achieve well at school. Individual staff members gave each other support in not putting more pressure on Ken to be in school. Without giving him so much gratification that it would seem like a reward to be out of school, attempts were made to provide him with positive experiences while he remained in the Lodge during the school days.

Newer staff members were really surprised, as were Martha and John, when they saw Ken becoming more and more anxious about not being in school. For once anxiety about school was coming from within himself rather than being externally supplied. Glen, in particular, started confronting Ken about what he was going to do with his own mixed feelings. Was he going to keep up his stance of "If it's important to you, I'll show you that you can't make me do it" or was he going to help himself overcome his own anxiety about school by taking external support and working to make it go well for him?

By November, Ken was ready to make a firm commitment that he wanted to be in school and that he was ready to work while he was there. To everyone's surprise he consistently kept that commitment. Many other boys had problems following through once they started school. Although, as everyone expected, there were times when his behavior at school started to get out of control, a simple reminder that if he couldn't get himself calmed down, he could return to the Lodge and get help settling down worked for Ken. Many of the other boys were sent out from school for brief periods so that house staff could help them get things turned around. They could then return to school and be able to make it go well. Ken rarely needed this level of support.

Prior to starting in the on-grounds school, it was decided at a staffing that he should start out in Carol's classroom. Testing had indicated that although he had normal intelligence, he had many gaps in his knowledge. Carol wanted to determine how the gaps would affect his ability to perform at grade level. Since he was continuing to have more problems trusting women than men, it was also felt that he needed to have a woman teacher who could be both firm and supportive.

Although in his previous school he would have been entering fourth grade, Carol started him with third grade work. Initially Ken worked very slowly. He would approach each task with either a "Cinchy" or "This is stupid" comment. Fear of failure was obvious. He became verbally belligerent if he made an error, saying such things as "Fuck you, this is a shitty school." When Carol did not respond to his verbal baiting but still expected him to focus on his work, he would lapse into pouty, teary, whiny, baby behaviors. However, when she would verbally express his fears of failure for him—that he was unsure of himself, or that he was having trouble with his work and that she would help him—he would eventually sigh and return to work.

By spring, Ken was being incorporated into more and more of Fred's classes. The negative babyish and/or bullying behaviors were seldom seen in Fred's class. By March, the educational notes indicated marked positive changes. "Ken has made startling classroom behavioral changes and positive academic growth. He is able to smile, chuckle, and complain appropriately. He has dropped the pouty, naughty, negative behaviors that he showed in November. He can now ask for help appropriately and can quickly attack his work."

As Ken became more relaxed in the classroom and secure in his relationships with both male and female teachers, it became more and more apparent that under his charm and super vocabulary was an unsure learner who was constantly over-demanding of himself in terms of achievement. His own attempts to always achieve at the highest level would lead to increased levels of tension, fear, and anger. These feelings would trigger negative, controlling behaviors to cover the fact that he was down on himself.

During the remainder of the spring term, the school focus was on helping Ken enjoy his own level of school performance. A secondary focus was on his relationships with classmates. The problems seen in this area were similar to those seen in the academic learning.

Ken was immature in terms of knowledge of the world around him and of appropriate school behavior. His first responses would be meagre and as he tried to expand on them, obviously trying to make himself look good, he revealed little awareness of what he was really saying and how it fit in with the current conversation or situation. When peers responded in ways that indicated that his answers weren't making a lot of sense he would again either verbally attack them or would revert to babyish behaviors. However, it gradually became easier for Ken to accept the confronting of these behaviors. He learned to see how they were similar to his previous responses to academic expectations. The strengths that he had gained in learning more appropriate behavioral responses to his frustration and anxiety about his school performance could be used to help him overcome the problems in the social area.

In spite of his many gains in terms of academic achievement, behavioral control, and peer relationships at the on-grounds school, it was apparent that Ken's academic skills were more at a third grade level throughout the school year than at a fourth grade level. It was decided that the most legitimate goal would be to even out his skills at this level. This meant that when he returned to public school he would be a year behind grade level.[N]

Staff was firmly convinced that in the long run it would be much better for Ken to be a year behind in school, but to be academically near the top of his class, than for him to be at the grade level corresponding to his chronological age and to be struggling in the lower percentiles of the class for the remainder of his school years. Because they felt so strongly about this, they were able to help Ken accept the logic of this decision. For the first time in his life, Ken was feeling good about himself in relationship to school. He liked that feeling and wanted to keep it. He expressed concerns about how his parents might feel about his being a year behind in school. Relief was apparent when he learned that the teachers, administrative staff, and his therapist would be handling this area with his parents.

Staff believed that it was important that Ken have a positive public school experience prior to discharge. So many of his problem behaviors prior to admission had been intertwined with school achievement. Both Ken and his parents needed to know for certain that school could be an emotionally rewarding place for him and that he could perform without major behavioral problems there. If this could be achieved prior to discharge, then the main focus when he returned home could be on the parent-child relationships and changes in his behaviors there.

It was becoming more and more difficult to be able to provide a public school experience prior to discharge because funding sources in general seemed to feel that if a child could be in public school, he no longer had need of an in-patient residential program. It was difficult for them to see this as part of a continuum of building and consolidating strengths to the point that the child and family could maintain the gains after discharge. Ken's parents were willing and able to pay for the out of district tuition charged by the public school system. Staff were relieved that in Ken's case it was going to be possible for them to pursue the course that they were certain was best for him.

Prior to the start of the school year, Carol and Fred met with the principal of the local elementary school. They had had many such meetings with him in the past. The relationships between the Lodge teachers and the public school teachers were built on mutual trust and respect. As the principal heard more about Ken, he became more certain as to which teacher might be best for him. Carol had had previous contacts with one of the fourth grade teachers whom she greatly respected and she was hoping that the principal would place Ken in that teacher's room. However, Mr. Flagler mentioned that several of his teachers had complained that the Lodge always used the same teachers for their kids. Rather than the teachers who had had boys from Forest Heights placed with them complaining, it was the teachers who had not been used who were doing the complaining. He was quite certain that Mrs. Green, who had never had a boy from the Lodge in her class, would do very well with Ken and would be most interested in working with FHL staff.[N]

It was decided that at the onset of the school year, Ken would not be riding the school bus, but rather would be taken to and from school by staff members. This decision was made for several reasons. Ken had always had problems getting along with peers at school and it was felt that he needed the support of the more structured setting of the classroom initially rather than the less structured bus contacts. It was hoped that by Thanksgiving time he would be secure enough in his ability to have school go well for him that he would then be able to ride the bus. A second reason for the decision against his riding the bus was that in this way staff members would have some one-on-one time with Ken coming and going to and from school to review with him how things were going.

After Carol and Fred met with the classroom teacher, Mrs. Green, it was decided that Fred would meet with her and with Ken each week. Mrs. Green was told that staff wanted her to call if there were any

problems with Ken but that even without any major problems staff
thought that once weekly conferences would help Ken feel more secure
in the school setting. It was expected that Ken himself would be
involved in the conferences, as it was very important that he knew
exactly how others perceived him as doing. The teacher was willing to
go along with this approach although in the past she had rarely
included students in parent teacher conferences.

It was apparent that Ken was feeling considerable anxiety and
pressure to do well in public school. Child care staff and his therapist
continued to give him emotional support in terms of again dealing with
his own expectations for himself. Initially there were some problems
with Ken pushing, shoving and being louder than other students,
particularly during the less structured times between classes and
during the lunch hour and recess.

However, for the most part, Ken was able to keep his level of
anxiety and internal pressure at levels which could work for him rather
than against him. He used his energy to attack his work, master it and
succeed, rather than the pressure coming out explosively. One
exception occurred within the first month of school opening. Mrs.
Green was gone that day and there was a substitute teacher. Ken had a
difficult time at lunch. On the playground he got into an argument with
a classmate. In the afternoon, the substitute introduced an already
familiar math concept in a new way. Ken started to correct her. The
substitute confronted him and he verbally exploded, cussing at her
profusely. He was sent to the principal's office and Lodge staff were
notified.

Glen came to the school and met with Ken and the principal. It
had been Glen's intention to take Ken home with him for the
remainder of the school day. However, by the time he arrived in Mr.
Flagler's office, Ken was calm and was feeling very embarrassed by his
behavior. He was expressing this appropriately and, without anyone
else first suggesting it, was asking to return to the classroom so that he
could apologize. Mr. Flagler and Glen agreed that this was a good plan,
so the principal accompanied Ken back to his classroom, where he
apologized and resumed working on his assignments.

When Ken came home from school that day, he was afraid that
staff would be angry or disappointed with him for "blowing it." He was
reassured when they focused on how well he had done on turning the
situation around and on not letting it disrupt the remainder of his day.
"Maybe," he thought, "I will be able to make it in school. Maybe I can
do it."[N]

By Thanksgiving, Ken was riding the school bus. He was doing
well at the bus stop even though there were many children of varying
ages there. In October he had asked to join Scouts. His best friend at
school, Brent, belonged. This was another important step for Ken. He
needed to be in a variety of situations which gave him opportunities for

peer interactions. As he started working on earning badges, he selected areas in which he was truly interested.

As the end of the first semester approached, all of Ken's teachers were reporting positive experiences with him. He was doing slightly above average in terms of his academic work and was no longer having peer problems. In fact, there were beginning signs that he might emerge as a leader within the peer group. ∎

The Educational Program
as a Reflection of Philosophical Base

*"You can make me go to school
but you can't make me learn."*

Sam said that, and Sam was absolutely right.

Although the school program is a major part of the total residential treatment program at Forest Heights Lodge, it is not the primary component. Sam's response indicates that his primary problems relate to interpersonal relationships and to his perceptions of himself. For most of our boys, school has been a place where these underlying problems were acted out, not primarily a place for academic learning and growth. Therefore, at the Lodge the initial stages of treatment will focus on these issues. It is unrealistic to assume that just because of placement, the child will suddenly be open for academic growth.

Most children in residential treatment have a history of teacher-pupil interactions fraught with unusual hostility or a fading-into-the-woodwork compliance. Peer interactions may have been bullying, victimizing, or perhaps nonexistent. The child may have been the recipient of taunts or the object of ridicule.

Academic achievement has usually been erratic, delayed, and highly idiosyncratic. Our boys have felt like a failure both at home and at school. The whole process of getting up and subjecting themselves to this daily nightmare has led them to constant conflict around learning issues. Sam was certainly right. We can make children go to school. We cannot make them learn.

To help our children change this failing pattern of school behavior and production at Forest Heights we start out by asking ourselves several basic questions:

1. Why should this child be going to school?

2. When is a child ready to go to school?

3. How is a child expected to behave in school?

4. What is the child expected to learn in school?

"Why is this child going to school?" The usual answer—to learn to read or to learn math or science—just doesn't carry much weight with most children in residential treatment. Outside the residential treatment setting, kids go to school because they are supposed to. That concept is a given. Kids go to school. Disturbed children come with that idea angrily churning within them. They have known repeated failure both academically and socially. In fact, for most, school problems are a primary factor in the decision for placement.

In the residential treatment setting it is necessary that the memory of an unhappy history be changed into the promise of a positive future—being like other kids and looking forward to being back in school "because kids go to school."

At Forest Heights we choose to initiate this process in a unique manner. At the beginning we say, "You can't go to school." The impact of adults making this decision for a child is dramatic. At first few children question it. The usual response is, "Ha, ha, ha, I don't have to go to school," as if they have pulled off something on the adult world around them.[N]

We are not doing this just to create a paradoxical situation. We do this because we truly believe the child is not ready for school. However, we do recognize that with this decision we have eliminated a power struggle and have cleared the deck for a fresh start when the child does start school.

We realize that this child has just gone through the trauma of leaving his family and former school structure. Even though he may have been miserable in those settings, they were familiar to him. He knew the ground rules. In his new residence he is the stranger, knowing neither the adults nor the rest of the children. His old behaviors do not bring the same results. He cannot predict who is going to do what. He needs time to observe the routine with few demands made upon him. He needs time to absorb the atmosphere of care and trust between children and staff.

Because he is out of school, there are no expectations for academic achievement for him to fight about. The issues that come up will be those around daily living behaviors. At the same time our ultimate intent with every boy is that he will eventually go to school. He must, to accomplish what he came here to do. He must, to replace past failures with self confidence. He must, to prepare himself for his return to a community school setting. Most importantly, he must, to learn to believe that he is like other kids.

But in the beginning it is therapeutic for him to be out of school. He can begin, slowly, to experience small changes in himself. His tantrums and out-of-control behavior are handled with firm external control. No one is afraid of him. His bizarre behaviors do not distance adults. Gradually, he becomes aware of the fun other boys are having. Tentatively he joins in activities. He may go on a camping trip or skiing for a day. He may be a winner in a taco-eating contest or listen to another resident plan his birthday menu. He begins to expect to be involved in his new world. He is more co-operative with adults. He begins to feel more worthwhile. He not only sees other kids having fun, he begins to have fun himself.

The business of not being in school and of apparently just having fun can be difficult for parents and other adults to understand. Wasn't this child placed here to "work on his problems" and "catch up in school?" How can he work on problems if he is having fun skiing? How can he ever catch up in school if he isn't even in school?

Our staff help parents voice these concerns, while, at the same time, we are pointing out the growth that the child is making during this period. We see the fun activities as times the child is exhibiting appropriate behavior controls and having positive interactions with his environment. We explain how we use this time to help a child change his view of himself from a "can't do" or "won't do" individual to a child who can have some fun times with those around him. We point out that the child is learning to trust that these adults are not going to ask him to do something he can't do and that they will stick through the good times and the not so good times. Since our teachers are involved in these activities too, the child is also learning to trust them. The new child sees teachers working with, and playing with, children in non-school activities and realizes that teachers are interested in the whole child, not just his four page theme or a math assignment.

Slowly, the glow of not being in school begins to wear off, and the first questions begin. "Why don't kids have to go to school here?" Since all the other boys are going to school each morning, and no new child can avoid that realization for long, the question then becomes more pointed, "Why am I not going to school?" The calm answer is, "You are not ready yet."

When?

At this point we are moving on to the second question. "When is a child ready to go to school?" At first, boys usually ask vague questions about when kids generally are ready to go to school here. The answers are equally general. We tell him to relax and settle in. We tell him that he needs to get to know people here and feel safe, and, above all, we tell him not to worry about school. Finally, the question becomes personalized, "When will I be ready to go to school?"

This will lead to a discussion of how school was for him before he came to the Lodge, why he even wants to go to school, what he wants from this new school setting, and what he thinks he needs to work on in order to make school be different this time than it was before. All of these are serious issues for the child to own up to and to struggle with. Until now he has been able to make these the problems that his parents and the school seemed responsible for because they "made" him go to school.

This time, because he has said he wants to go to school, these are now his very own problems to be aware of and to work toward solving before he is truly ready. If he is successful in defining the problems, school can be devoted primarily to learning issues and only secondarily aimed at pointing out when the old personal issues are getting in the way of his being an active, aggressive learner.

An important event has happened with the new child by now. Before he came to Forest Heights Lodge, he was in school because he was made to be there. Now he has been out of school because we have said that he must be. To regain control over his life, he must convince us not only that he wants to be in school, but also that he is ready to be in school. Our job is focused on helping the child answer the question, "Why do you want to be in school?" When he can answer this question he will be ready to start in our on grounds school.

William has decided that he wants to start school. Why?

"I want to go to school, Carol."

"Are you sure you do?"

"Yeah. I'm ready for school. I don't want to get behind more."

"Oh."

"Really, I like math lots."

"I think you've been thinking about school."

"Yes, I really want in. I'm ready."

"Well, have you been thinking about how it was before?"

"It wasn't so good."

"Why don't you think about what you want to do differently this time and get back to me?"

This step in treatment is crucial. It establishes an alliance between child and teacher as to why the student is in school— because he has asked to be there. It helps him define clearly what he wants help in working on to make school a positive experience for him. The stage is being set for teachers and child care workers alike to help him with what he wants, rather than making him do something he does not want to be doing.

Over and over again, behaviors will be identified as needing to be stopped or changed because they are frustrating his capability to be in, and stay in, school. It is his responsibility now to work on these changes because he has decided for himself what he wants to do— go to school.[N]

How?

How is the child expected to behave in school? Since each child is introduced to school individually, the question concerning how he is expected to behave in school is relatively easy to define. School is ongoing. Classes are in progress. Standards have been set. The momentum is not just teacher imposed, but group modeled and supported. Each child is expected to be working "with" his teacher, not "against" him.

Each child's schedule is initially individualized. It may be decided that the new student's school schedule will be a one to one basis for thirty minutes, because that is as long as he can maintain contact with reality or as long as he can stay focused on an academic task. Or it may be decided that he will be in one particular subject only, because the teaching staff believe that that setting is the one where he has the most likelihood of being successful. Whatever the limitations on his schedule, while he is in school he is expected to behave like a learner, like the other boys.

Each child enters school with a set of behaviors that have kept him from learning. Before he begins school, while he is deciding that he wants to go and we are deciding whether he is ready, he identifies what it was that he thinks has caused him trouble and what he wants help changing. Whenever our teachers see those problematic behaviors emerging, they identify them for the child in a non-judgmental way. They offer alternatives to that behavior. The expectation is that the child wants to stop and wants to be able to respond in a different way. If the child does not align himself with the teacher during this confrontation, then he may not stay in school, because he is not doing what he said he wanted to do—learn to have school go well for him.

The teacher is not going to back away from expectations. To do so would be to let the child down. It would be helping the child continue in his old behavior after he had clearly told us that he wanted help in changing. We are always subtly saying to our boys that we respect them in their struggle to change, that we respect them enough to engage in nose to nose interchanges over and over again because their growth is worth both their struggles and ours.

Each addition to his school day becomes a reward, seen as indicative of growth. Each time he experiences his own power and achievement in one area, he has more energy and confidence available to extend himself even further. Eventually he will be structured into a full school day's program.

Our school has a record of being able to help children change their school failure pattern into a success pattern because we are different from most other schools in terms of staffing, groupings, and in terms of expectations of behavior and performance.

Performance is the foundation of our school program. Our general philosophy of supporting health rather than pathology continues from the living situation to the school setting. The tone of the classroom is serious, while at the same time it is alive with various interactions. It uses individualized confronting without losing track of the basic educational function. It is gratifying in a genuine way.

In the residence in the morning, the focus is on getting ready for the day. If it is a school day, the emphasis is on getting ready for school. Rooms are tidied. The child is helped to make his personal appearance appropriate for going to school and working. This enforces the expectation that school is an important event. An adult may say, "I don't think Carl is ready for school. His room is messy; he's wearing shorts on this cold, rainy day; and he had a tough time getting to breakfast. I'm keeping him here until he is really ready for school." This reinforces the expectation around school. One is expected to plan and prepare for school.

A large part of the school struggle will center on helping the youngster separate living issues from school issues, while still seeing how they may correlate one with the other. When he becomes overwhelmed by living issues, school performance will change in concrete ways. It cannot be denied that the youngster is having a bad day in school because of something inside himself. It is not that the math is too hard. The answer to the literature question is right there in the materials. He can, in fact, write a paragraph with ten sentences. But he cannot do any of these tasks while he is ruminating about whatever it is that is going on in his head.

It is at this point that the child needs to leave school. He deserves help in solving the internal conflict. Child care staff will help him sort through his thoughts, and the smoke screen of "school problems" can be dropped. When he returns to school freed from the interference of personal dynamics, he has energy available to devote to learning.

What?

The fourth, and final, question we outlined was, "What is he expected to learn?" For each child, the answer to what he is expected to learn in school will be different. One may need to learn how to learn in a group, another, how to ask for and accept help in appropriate ways. A third may need a new image of himself as able to learn, rather than the old picture of himself as retarded or so hopelessly handicapped by his craziness that he cannot function the way other children do. Others may need to come to grips with learning disabilities, understanding their strengths and weaknesses. All need to develop effective work and learning habits. Finally, they need to grow in academic areas.

The question of what the child will learn usually has a three pronged answer. First, the child will learn how to learn. This will involve giving up all sorts of old behaviors that kept him from working with teachers and peers. Usually, he will have identified some of these behaviors during the decision making process prior to entering school. Others will become painfully apparent within a few weeks of beginning school. The behaviors that emerge after school entrance may be those that are most difficult for the child to acknowledge or those that have been most effective in keeping people distanced.

Success with his academic work will lead the student to a position of greater trust in his teacher. This in turn leads the child to be able at least to take a peek at some of the behaviors his teacher is pointing out, behaviors that interfere with his feeling good about himself.

Secondly, each child will learn to understand more clearly his own ability to learn. With more and more distracting behaviors under control, the next awareness that both the child and the teacher will gain is a clearer picture of the child's learning style and the presence or absence of serious learning difficulties. Remembering that we want to work with the whole child, not just the academic learner, this clearer picture of learning abilities can give insights into how the child may be approaching and understanding, or misunderstanding, the whole world. Teachers work closely with child care staff, sharing their classroom observations and testings and suggesting how these affect the child's performance in the daily living situation.

The motor-mouthed child with the slightly skewed vocabulary and off the wall comments may be recognized as a child with word finding problems, who has difficulty both in processing auditory input and in verbalizing his own thoughts. Then, rather than just interrupting or confronting the less desirable behaviors, all staff are in a position to take a helpful role in facilitating communication with this youngster.

At this point the child, too, gains insight into the complexity of his own self. Instead of feeling like a nothing, he begins to be aware of more and more facets of himself. Through his experiences in school, each child, along with the adults who work with him, gains a better understanding of how he is functioning on multiple levels. With acceptance of his uniqueness, they mutually adopt the positive expectation that he can and will grow, learn and change.

Thirdly, the school will teach the child academic subjects. A youngster comes to us as a third grader or seventh grader with letter or number grades, but before he begins school here we need much more specific information. We need to know what he knows, what he does not know, and what he needs to begin learning.

Testing prior to school entrance will give us a rough idea of what grade levels to start working at, but far more specific is the information that will be gained by teacher observation and actual classroom work with the child. The teacher will be able to sense the child's shallow understanding of concepts, ideas that the child seems aware of but with just surface knowledge. The teacher will also note lack of firm grasp of earlier concepts and processes that in turn make current learning appear to be slow or confused. We must allow time in our scheduling for a steady reteaching in any areas that are not at an almost automatic level of recall.

If these needs are met, the child will ultimately be able to perform outside the residential school in a much less restrictive environment. Academic, behavioral and social goals as they apply to the classroom setting are established for each child. These school goals become part of the total treatment plan for each individual child.

We have now answered the four basic questions around school. Why? He is there because he asked to be. When? He is ready when he can identify what he wants help on changing so that school can be a successful learning experience for him. How? He is expected to behave like the other boys who are already in the program. What? He is expected to learn the skills that will ultimately enable him to learn in the less restrictive environment of the public school.

What Makes Forest Heights Lodge School Unique?

Having our own school allows maximum freedom in designing learning activities to meet each child's needs. Some educational needs are best met in the academic classroom. Others, such as self-care skills, must be taught in the living setting under the supervision of the child care staff. In our setting, a child moves into school for math and reading skills, to the house for the basic living skills, back to school for woodshop, social studies, science, or arts and crafts, and then to the house for physical education. Each child's schedule can easily be changed as his needs change.

That the school is on-grounds and that its program is fully under the control of Lodge staff is most important. Teachers are hired by and employed solely by Forest Heights Lodge. We do not use teachers from the public school system to staff our on-grounds school. This means that our teachers are part of the overall treatment program. They do not see themselves as only responsible for the boys when they are in school. They see themslves as a part of the treatment team. There are no problems with divided loyalty, with having to answer to two administrative structures.

The school is part of a total residential treatment program for boys who have had serious problems with family, school, and peers. There has to be a re-education process for the child in all of these areas. Our school must do something different and positive to change the failure patterns the children bring with them. Our philosophy concerning school staffing, curriculum, groupings, and expectations of behavior and performance accounts for school success both here and following the termination of in-patient treatment.

The first step in planning an effective school program for each child is knowing the child. This involves more than an understanding of his developmental and academic history. It involves living with the child, seeing him not just as an academic learner, but as a whole person. Therefore our teachers are also child care workers.

Parenting is a 24 hour a day process at the Lodge. Both teaching and child care staffs include male and female members. The person seeking a teaching role must also be a parenting person. He or she must be willing and able to do the daily caretaking, the cleaning up, the disciplining, and the housekeeping in the residence before he can define himself explicitly as a teacher. All teachers are required to begin their employment as child care workers. Even after becoming teachers they still function as child care workers one afternoon and night of each week, and during the usual school vacation times and the non-school hours of the summer months.

Because of the importance of knowing and being able to take care of the whole child, our teachers begin each day's work in the residence rather than in the school. It is the responsibility of the entire staff to help the boys get their day started, and themselves, their rooms, and the residence in order. Only then are staff and boys ready to go to school.

A teacher may begin his day by joining in breakfast, helping a child make his bed, seeing that the younger boys brush their teeth or supervising the daily chores. Working with the boys in these ways brings intimacy to the relationship. Teaching staff are better able to begin planning what school subjects a boy will function well in, what materials will be best for him, and what approaches are most likely to lead to success.

Just as school goals are only part of the treatment plan, so too is school only a part of the child's day. Although the purpose of our school is not to account for a specific number of hours a day, a schedule is posted and expected to be followed. Individual educational plans are formulated as a result of considerable contact with the student within both the school setting and the living situation.

The schedule notes who is working with what teacher and on what content. Our school program is a kind of umbrella where boys, teachers, and materials come together for the purpose of learning new skills. Teachers do not babysit an out-of-control boy or one who refuses to cooperate. That child is sent out because those behaviors need to be resolved in the residence. School is thus maintained as a place for learning. Once the child has regained self-control or has realigned himself in a cooperative stance he returns to school. Children are allowed to flow in and out of school with the immediate support of those caretaking adults whom the child trusts. When the child is in school, he is expected to be dealing with learning issues. He cannot do that efficiently when he is out of control or thinking bizarrely. At those times he needs to be in the residence. When the child can actually be successful during the periods of time that he is in school, he proves to himself that he can function like other kids. These periods become models for him to strive for in his total living pattern.

This does not mean that our classes are conflict-free. It does mean that teachers identify what they see going on, provide alternatives and help a child to perform the best he can. The frustrations of learning are identified, laughed at, and cried over. The expectation is that the child will allow the teacher to help him through the frustrating times. Sometimes on his own a child will acknowledge that he is not working because he cannot until he settles an internal problem. Other times the teacher, realizing the internal conflict, asks the child to return to the house until he can settle the problem. The expectation is that children and adults will separate out personal and school issues, laying aside the personal while in the classroom setting.

Expectation is the key concept. Once a child has made a commitment to begin school and, together with house and school staff, has worked out what kind of help he needs to change his old school patterns, then he is expected to be working on these issues when he is in school.

Example: Peter sits quietly, head bent over his math book, finger moving along the printed words, paper nicely headed and dated. Fifteen minutes later he presents the same picture. He has asked no questions, disturbed no one. In fact, he is doing nothing. Unless he can work with the teacher in breaking that pattern, he may not stay in school.

"Peter, you've been sitting there for fifteen minutes. I don't see any work done on your paper. Do you need help?

"No, I'm thinking." Five minutes more go by and still nothing has been written down.

"Can I help you start?"

"No, I'm starting."

Peter copies a problem, but his teacher notices that he has miscopied it. She sits by him and says, "Peter, you miscopied this. Something is the matter this morning. What's up?"

"Nothing."

"Do you want to work on this with me?"

"No."

Peter is sent out of school, back to the residence. The teacher calls the child care workers and describes what has happened. Obviously, something is keeping Peter from school work. He needs to return to the residence to get in touch with his conflict. When he is in school he needs to be able to concentrate on learning.

The interactions between teachers, Peter and caregivers are the cornerstone of our residential school. The child care staff will help Peter to vent his frustration about school and teachers, or his anger at having to pay attention to something outside of himself, or perhaps his rage at having to allow someone else to be in control of him. Or the block may be something personal having really nothing to do with school at all. He will receive support from child care staff in identifying and resolving the problem. Until that is done Peter will not be available for academic learning.

Peter will be led back over what it was that he said he wanted in school and what he thought he needed help with. All kinds of feelings may come up and be dealt with in a way that allows Peter to get past this incident and back into the flow of the day. He may return to class in five minutes, an hour, or perhaps not until the next day. Whenever it is, it will be a clean start for him. Any needed support is given. Teaching staff are glad to have him back ready to learn. A child care worker may walk him back to school to make his return easier or to help him say what he wants to his teacher.

The child care worker may call to inform the teacher that the student isn't going to make it back to school at all today and ask if the three of them can get together after school. In any event, Peter sees both the residential and school staff working together to help him get what he wants—the breaking of old patterns and the learning of new ones. As he becomes more adept at recognizing why he cannot work and allowing his teacher to help him, he is sent from school less frequently.

"I almost blew it this morning. It was really hard," is an exciting statement from a child who just won a battle and is feeling a sweet sense of mastery. As children see their school day being lengthened, and as they are sent back to the house less frequently, they sense their growth and begin to realize that they may really be able to successfully return to public school someday.

The teacher must be so aware of each student in his class that he can sense and reflect to the student what is going wrong with either behavior or academic work and intervene at the very earliest level of behavior. In this way, the child is more likely to accept the reflection without excessive defensiveness. It is then more likely that the boy will be able to take the teacher's lead and avoid escalation to a point necessitating physical removal from school.

Example: Stan checked his assignment sheet and turned to page 145 as noted on his assignment. He looked over the page and asked for help on the next to the last problem. Fred assured him that he would receive help when he got to that problem. Several minutes later Stan asked to go to the bathroom. When he came back, he couldn't find his math book.

Fred commented that Stan seemed to be having a hard time getting started. Stan avoided eye contact and began chewing his pencil. On the way to look for his book in the supply area, Stan bumped into another boy and yelled, "Look out!" Fred observed that he thought Stan was angry at him for not helping him on that math problem. As he made the observation, he helped Stan sit down and find the right page.

Again, Stan avoided eye contact. This time the teacher asked if he wanted to work on this problem of completing the page. Stan nodded, then blurted, "I get so worried about hard problems, I just can't think. I just have to do them first." Fred agreed to help him then. Together, they did the difficult problem first, and Stan then went on to complete his assignment successfully.

Without the early observation that Stan was having difficulty getting started, his teacher might have reacted quite differently to his "Look out!" outburst, and a long interaction might have taken place over that behavior rather than over getting started in math. The incident could have resulted in Stan's being sent out of school rather than in the positive completion of the assignment.

A particular student may be having an unusually difficult day, needing many redirections from the teacher. Other students are expected to tolerate this. In fact, frequently they do not. Some of the students may want the disturbing child removed from school. Others may seem to be egging him on, while still others may be thoughtfully watching, or even attending to their tasks. Actually, most other students are seldom far from the same problems themselves and should be learning from these observations. Instead, however, their agitation and discomfort may escalate, and intense confrontations may take place about what is going on with the entire group. This kind of problem must be dealt with in the classroom, for it is a classroom dynamic, not an individual one.

However, the teacher must retain flexibility to deal with every situation for the greatest advantage to the whole group. What he opts for one day may not be the next day's choice. The teacher's arbitrary choice may be: send the child out of school; ignore the behavior; use whatever tactics usually calm this particular child; or use the opportunity to help the other boys express themselves. The teacher can keep the classroom alive and dynamic by not getting caught in a strict "if this, then that" trap. Our school has been accused of being either "rigidly flexible" or "flexibly rigid." We hope the accusation is correct. A great advantage of having a small population is that we are allowed flexibility in managing specific situations while always remaining within the framework of our basic philosophy.

School Structure

Teaching staff:

The first qualification of a teacher here is that he be able to reparent children. The importance of his knowing and being comfortable with the whole child was discussed earlier. Beyond that ability, our teachers need additional knowledge and skills. They must have a firm knowledge of child growth and development, learning theory, and teaching techniques that pertain to the regular classroom. In addition they must be trained in the identification and teaching of children with specific learning problems, problems which interfere with school performance. Skill in only one of these areas is not enough.

A teacher who is aware only of normal development cannot readily identify or accept the areas of growth that for some reason are underdeveloped or maldeveloped. Further, identification of these areas is not enough. The problems must not only be recognized, but they must be remediated. Accepted does not mean excused. It means acceptance of the child as a valued person who deserves a structured plan to encourage growth. Understanding learning theory and teaching techniques as they pertain to the regular classroom is only a first step in this program.

Just as these children exhibit exaggerated tendencies or characteristics found in other children, our teachers' interpretation of theory and techniques needs to be exaggerated. This is necessary to magnify the learning steps and then break them down into the smallest segments possible. It is only with success in the very smallest steps that these children learn to extend themselves—to allow themselves the luxury of trying and failing and still feeling okay about themselves. Then they can try again and, this time or the next, be successful.

Our intention is to help our boys not be so different that they are unacceptable. We want to help them become more like other children. Although our teachers are skilled in child care and reparenting, in the classroom they maintain a role model much like any other academic school. They are neither buddies nor therapists. They are teachers immersed in helping each child attack his academic goals.

Curriculum:

To help the child find success as a learner, the school curriculum must be both flexible enough and complete enough to meet the variable needs of each student. Educational assessment pinpoints what the child knows and what he does not know. It identifies how he can most easily learn what he needs to learn. Harry may be a whiz in math but unable to express himself in written work. Joe's limited and concrete vocabulary may be curtailing his ability to comprehend what he reads in all subject areas. We are constantly assessing a child's learning and providing him with the materials and adult guidance that he needs.

To the extent of each child's ability to learn, he is offered a basic curriculum: language arts, math, science, social studies, arts and crafts and shop. Our goal is that he be able to return to public school at age appropriate level if at all possible and perform successfully.

Materials:

Because it is our usual goal to return these children to various public school programs, the materials used must ultimately lead to the child's being familiar with and able to handle the kinds of materials he will be asked to use when he enters public school. While these materials may be adapted to his specific unique needs at the beginning of his school experience, as he extends his school day and his classes, the materials become more and more standard.

A wide range of materials to teach any particular skill is needed to match various students' learning styles, strengths, and weaknesses. Failure to grasp a concept or process should lead both teacher and child to understand more clearly where the hitch is and try again with a different format. We are prepared to try again and again.

Thus, the child sees the adult as being aligned with him to gain his goal. After many of these kinds of experiences, the child begins to fear failure less and to be more accepting of looking for alternate routes to the goal. He also begins to accept himself and his uniqueness in a more positive way. His sense of personal worth grows proportionately.

Individualization and Groupings:

Children may be scheduled for individual teaching sessions, by age level groups, skill groups or in spontaneous, ever changing activity groups.

Individualization of math and language arts assignments is especially important in setting expectations for the maximum benefit of each boy. The student is accepted at whatever level he presents himself. He learns that what makes him feel good at school is putting forth his best effort. Working through and completing his own assignments is rewarding. While each child obviously knows at what level others are working, the basic competition is with himself, getting more correct than the day before, working faster than the week before, or understanding concepts with less difficulty than the month before.

Whether the child is working on a one-to-one basis with a teacher or in a small group setting, each child works at his own level and at his own pace. Each child is successful or "had a good day" if he has completed whatever work he was assigned. Within this concept Tom, age 11, struggling with second grade reading and completing his task, is just as secure in his sense of worth as Irwin, also 11, who is finishing his fifth grade reading series. We find that this tends to eliminate much of the "Ha, ha I'm ahead of you" talk that goes on in many schools. In fact, the other boys learn to appreciate how hard Tom is having to work. They become not only more compassionate, but also more grateful for their own accomplishments.

Although individualization is important for structuring succcess into each child's program, we also must help him gain the skills and processes that he needs to move out of our setting into a non-treatment school setting. Our staff must be knowledgeable of other less restrictive settings, being aware of both the materials used and the behaviors common in these classrooms. This is done by frequent contact with local public school personnel, continuing review of current literature and sometimes by taking relevant courses. Planning that may be very special at the beginning of a child's school program changes bit by bit to make his program as non-different as possible.

Some groups are made up of children of about the same age. Recognizing that they need practice learning with peers, even troubled peers, we teach science, social studies, crafts and shop within this type of group setting. Because performance abilities vary widely in each grouping, it is the responsibility of the teacher to structure the class with the burden of presentation on himself. A child's reading skills should not keep him from gaining this information or hands-on experience.

Periodically, several children will need to learn the same skill, and they will be pulled together into a group. This might involve practicing cursive writing, pre-test tutoring for a social studies chapter test, or punctuation practice. These classes are widely flexible and scheduled only until the specific need is met.

Spontaneous selective planned groupings occur whenever some particular event, activity, or experience is available in which certain children and teachers want to be involved. It might be training for a local foot race, learning how to use a particular tool, or locating and studying new materials to prepare for a field trip to a museum. These groups are spontaneous in the same sense that our schedule is planned to be flexible enough to include them as the specific needs arise.

School Reports:

School reports and conferences around them are an important tool for encouraging progress. The goals in academic, social, and behavior skills are thoughtfully planned and written so that there is maximum likelihood the child will attain the goal. He knows that the report goes into his file and that all the staff read it. A child often asks, "May I make a copy for my parents?" He may ask for a particular staff member or for his parents to be at his conference with his teachers.

Parents, child care staff, or clinical staff may initiate a request to be present. We want communication to be as open as possible. Often our boys ask, "What did you tell my parents?" Our answer is, "You tell me. You know." We can say this with assurance because we know that the child knows exactly what is in his school report. We further know that if we are relating to the child each day in an open and sensitive manner, there are no surprises to be found in any child's school reports or heard at conferences.

The reports become a cooperative effort between teachers and boys. Together they review progress in behavior and skills for a certain period of time and set goals for the next period. It is startling how close the students' and teachers' goals usually are. When there is a significant difference, this can be used as an important tool for growth and change. Has the teacher overlooked something that is on the child's agenda? Is the child avoiding something that the teacher thinks he is ready to tackle? Clarification of these issues may include house staff as well. Together the team help the child decide what he wants to work on and how he wants adults around him to help within the framework of the longer range goals that have been set for him. Again, the important concept is the alliance that is developed with the child. He is an active part of the educational process not a passive, or passive aggressive, recipient of it.

Relationship between School Staff and Parents

Naturally, most parents are greatly concerned about how their child is doing in school. Many, for the first time in their child's school career, no longer dread meeting with teachers but rather look forward to these contacts because they find them helpful rather than blaming of either the child or themselves. We want to share all of the information we gain about how a child learns and where his strengths and weaknesses are. Then parents too can begin to see their son in a more understanding way. Our growing knowledge of his abilities or disabilities may help them accept why this child was so difficult to live with. Knowing that a boy, in his own thinking process, confuses what he sees helps explain the fears and rages of earlier years.

We want to invite parents to be part of the school program as well as part of the living program. It is one thing for a teacher to describe Ralph's struggle with phonics and spelling to his parents. It is quite another for them to sit in a language arts class and watch his intense concentration while he is wrestling with his spelling lesson. A visit to the classroom can also show parents growth and production that the child may not display in any other setting. Hank's father was amazed when he saw and heard Hank read a story to his teacher. He would not even read billboards to his family. Teachers telling his father he could read has no reality. Hearing his son read in the classroom does.

The Use of the Public School Setting

Even though a student is consistently functioning well in our on-grounds school, both he and we may have the uneasy, nagging question as to whether or not he can make it in a less restrictive school setting. To answer that question we may place our residents in the local public school system, at their appropriate level from kindergarten to twelfth grade, while they are still in residence here, with full support from our staff and the residential setting. The pressure on the boy is intense. Parents, staff, and the child himself are ready for the step but each is apprehensive. They ask themselves, "Will the other kids pick on him as a crazy kid?" "How will he act?" "Can he successfully do the schoolwork?"

With good reason, our boys have developed a reputation with the staffs of the local schools as being productive and less trouble than some of the students not in residential treatment. This reputation rests solidly on the close relationship and frequent contacts we have always had with the public classroom teachers. Their vital role in this child's treatment is to treat him as they would any other student in their classroom. At the same time, we do ask the classroom teachers to observe this child's behaviors carefully, especially in areas that posed problems for the child in the past. Both of these expectations are consistently supported during the weekly conferences held with the boy and his teacher or counselor. Such conferences are always held when a student starts public school. The frequency may be decreased as child, teacher, and Lodge staff all recognize consistency in the student's production and acceptable school behaviors.

When our residents first enter public school, we find that they put tremendous energy into succeeding. Initially it is quite common for their in-residence behaviors to regress. By the time they come home from school in the afternoon they have sometimes exhausted their potential for controlling their own behaviors. However, with the Lodge staff's emotional support during this period of regression, it usually does not take long for the student to regroup and have energy available for continued growth in the residence as well as in the public school environment.

On occasion, we have placed students in public school prematurely. This has not happened often, but it has occurred. When it does, it is important that adults take responsibility for the premature decision. We acknowledge that both child and staff thought the child was ready but that it is apparent that that was more wish than reality. However, the adults must assume responsibility for the ultimate decision around public school placement. At the same time additional information has been gained about what the child and Lodge teaching staff need to work on together to insure success when the child does eventually return to the public school setting.

Although we believe that virtually all of our boys who are returning to non-specialized programs in the public school systems in their home communities, and most who are returning to more specialized programs, could benefit from public school experience in Evergreen prior to discharge, it is not always possible to implement this goal. Funding sources frequently will not pay for the public school experience.

When a youngster has successfully attended public school prior to discharge, this information is shared with the child's home school. Parents are less nervous about the child's fragility. The home school is less nervous about having the former student return. Most importantly, the child has proven to himself that the changes he has made in the residential setting are solid and transferable to other settings. With the help of child care workers and the Lodge teaching staff, he is more aware of what he has to do to make the transition from the Lodge to home school.

Case Example

The following description of Todd's school entrance illustrates some of the issues we have been discussing.

When Todd first came to the Lodge at age ten, he was always running, just running. His speech was not understandable. He did not consistently use the same sound for any object. He required nearly constant supervision by staff to insure his safety. On each shift a child care worker was designated to give him that specific attention. Rituals and fears consumed his life. At the same time, he had controlled the lives of those around him by those rituals, fears, and his inordinate energy level.

Months passed before Todd indicated that he wanted to go to school. Alice, a child care worker, had subtly given him the message that she would really like to be in school with him. His biggest desire was to be able to read the words in his books that Alice had been reading to him. His biggest fear was that he would not be able to learn, that he would experience another failure.

Considering our first two issues in education, we came to these answers. "Why is this child in school?" The answer: he and Alice had asked to be in school.

"When will he be ready for school?" The answer: when he could work with a teacher. We planned his school schedule to allow Alice to be with him, feeling that his trust and security with her would allow him to begin to trust his teacher. At the same time he had to be able to work with a teacher, rather than with Alice.

Initially his school schedule was a ten minute period in the classroom with his teacher. He sat on Alice's lap and worked with the teacher. Gradually, he moved to the table with Alice sitting behind him. The ten minute period became fifteen and then thirty. Alice moved from the classroom to waiting on the porch. Soon Todd was placed in a group of three. Alice walked him to school. She waited for him at the fence where he could see her. He became eager to be first into the classroom and was excited about learning, channeling his excessive energy into achieving. In that school year he moved from beginning reading to reading on a fourth grade level. His language development was keeping pace too, to the point that once when he considered an assignment unfair he accused the teacher, "You're stealing my childhood!"

Todd himself pushed for constant clarification of the third educational issue of how he was expected to behave in school. He would ask, "Is this okay?" or, "Is this goofy?" His energy level stayed in high gear as did his expectations of himself. At times he became utterly frustrated with himself and his teacher, unable to meet his own expectations.

The fourth educational issue, "What will this child learn in school?" was easily solved for Todd. He had to learn everything a child learns about the world around him plus the usual elementary school subjects, and he whole-heartedly wanted to. A primary task for the teacher initially was to assign small segments that he could digest quickly, avoiding frustration and feelings of failure as much as possible for he was certainly gorging to make up for years of lost time.

Ultimately his school days smoothed out for him. Two and a half years after admission and prior to his discharge from the Lodge, he successfully attended a regular fifth grade class in the public school system, behaving in class like the other fifth graders.

Why are children willing to endure all this pain of learning how to succeed in school? The answer is simple, but sometimes difficult to achieve. Our boys want desperately to be like other children. School is one of the chief areas where a child can concretely measure his okayness.

Because most children entering residential treatment have had numerous school related problems, parents usually have many questions about the school program. Basically, the questions fall into two categories: "What will my child learn in your school program?" and "What will be different so that he can be successful?" These are important questions. Although there are no right or wrong answers to the following, the responses should help you determine whether or not the school program at any given center might be adequate for meeting your child's needs.

1. How do educational needs fit into the basic philosophy of the treatment facility?

2. Is there an on-grounds school or do all children attend public school?

3. If there is no on-grounds school program, how are conflicts between school and facility in the areas of basic philosophy and expectations for children resolved?

4. If there is an on-grounds school, who selects and hires the teachers? Again, if the teachers are employees of the school district, how are conflicts between the expectations, needs and interests of district and the treatment center resolved?

5. Do the educational assessments include identification of the strengths and weaknesses of the child's learning style?

6. If there is an on-grounds school, are there opportunities for students to attend public school prior to discharge? How is it determined which children attend the on-grounds school and which attend public school? What kind of relationship does the treatment facility have with the schools in the area?

7. How will you know about school progress? Can you observe your child in the classroom?

8. Does each student have an individualized educational plan?

Conclusion

The educational component of the child's treatment greatly influences both the short term and long term outcome. Most children entering residential treatment have had marked problems in school. The problems may have been in the area of academic acheivement or they may have been in the area of behavioral control or social interactions. Commonly they have occurred in all three areas.

The core issues in the child's overall treatment are frequently highlighted in the school setting. Here, as everywhere else in the program, there needs to be congruency with the overall treatment philosophy and attention to detail. The child's learning style, strengths and weaknesses affect not only his academic achievement but his response to the total demands of his environment. They impact on his day to day functioning. Knowledge about these areas aids adults in better understanding ways to help this child grow and change in all areas of his life.

School performance is a major link joining the child's past experiences with his treatment experiences and setting the stage for continued success post discharge. School is a place where children readily see themselves in comparison with others. It provides an obvious area for the child to perceive himself as capable of change or as permanently damaged.

Notes and Elaborations

pg. 187 Because of the severity of both learning and behavioral problems in our residents, it is not uncommon for them to be functioning at below grade level. As they develop new levels of behavioral control and gain in academic skills they may make up some of the delays. Some will even out their skills in the major academic areas a year or so behind grade level; others, especially those with learning disabilities, will finish treatment with skills at varying grade levels. Members of the former group usually re-enter public school attending regular classes while those in the latter group are more likely to re-enter public school utilizing special education classes for those subjects in which they have particular learning difficulties.

pg. 188 We realize that sometimes relationships between treatment centers and public school personnel are strained. FHL has been very fortunate in that, in general, we have enjoyed excellent relationships with the public schools in our community. In the past we have had principals of local schools on our Board of Trustees. This, obviously, has helped. We have tried to develop one primary contact person in each of the schools. However, the most critical factor has probably been that our staff have made clear that we expect to be available to the public school teachers and to work with them to insure that enrollment of our residents is a positive experience for everyone.

pg. 189 We have purposefully chosen to include the same public school incident in several different chapters to demonstrate

the importance of child care, educational, and therapy staff
members responding to an incident in ways that are philosophically congruent with one another.

pg. 191 Many residential centers will start students in school immediately. What is done to help the young person be successful in this area of his life, how school coordinates with the other aspects of the treatment program, and how it reflects the overall treatment philosophy are all more important issues than school attendance per se.

pg. 193 A common question from parents is, "What if a child never asks to go to school?" In the over 30 years that Forest Heights has been existent we have not had this situation arise. Just as when we supportively help the prospective resident identify what he wants changed in his life as he makes a commitment to coming to our treatment program we find that milieu and teaching staff together can help him identify the school related areas that have interferred with his being successful. The key ingredient seems to be that he has started to experience success in the milieu so that he now sees change as a real possibility.

C O N T E N T S

Working with Families

Kenny's Case   213
Working with Families as a Reflection of Philosophy   222
Beginning Steps in Family Work   226
    Obtaining Information about the Family   227
    Strengthening Alliances   228
    Separation Interview   228
    Keeping in Touch   229
    Boundaries between Program and Family   230
    Identifying Family Dynamics   231
    Re-establishing Fun in the Family   232
Family Work during the Middle Phase of Treatment   233
    Family Education Weekends   234
    Visits to the Lodge   235
    Including Families in Treatment Planning   236
    Crises as a Time for Strengthening Family Ties   236
    Consistency Between Home and Milieu   237
Family Work during the Final Phase of Treatment   238
    Working with Families when Adoptive Placement
        Is the Discharge Plan   239
Guide for Parents   242
Conclusion   242
Notes and Elaborations   243

Working With Families

Family work with the Summers began during the pre-placement period both at the Lodge and at their home. The development of trust between Lodge staff and family members was emphasized during these contacts. It is important that Kenny see both sets of meaningful adults in his life respectful of each other. He must not feel that he is caught between two warring factions. Nor would it be helpful if he could pit parents against staff or vice versa. However, it is openly recognized with both Kenny and his parents that many children try to divide family and staff. It is the adults' responsibility to keep the lines of communication open so that such manipulations
cannot be successful. It is further recognized that although there may well be disagreements between staff and parents, such conflicts do not have to be harmful to relationships or interfere with the child's treatment. In fact, Kenny, like most of the other boys who live at the Lodge, needs to learn that people can resolve disagreements without someone having to be the winner and someone else the loser.

Martha and John knew they would be expected to be involved in family therapy along with Kenny during his stay at the Lodge. Therefore, they were a little surprised when they found that the emphasis during their first visit would not be on problem areas but rather on having fun with their son.

The plan was for them to arrive early Saturday morning. Initially they would spend some time with Kenny at the Lodge. Then in the afternoon Kenny would go with them for an outing, returning to the Lodge for the night. The following day Russ would meet with them in the morning, and it was quite likely that they and Kenny would then go off for a two day outing. In setting up the visit, Glen emphasized the importance of Kenny and his parents being able to have a good time together. The focus on family problems would come later. Glen also stressed that even though Kenny had asked for many new things during his telephone conversations, it was important that the family not come laden down with gifts.

In spite of their anxiety, that first week-end together went very well. Before Kenny and his parents left the Lodge on Saturday, Glen met briefly with them. He again stressed the importance of their having a good time together. Glen asked Kenny if he would be able to do this. Kenny was certain he could. Glen commented that if either Kenny or his parents thought that the visit was becoming too difficult or filled with hassles it was okay for either parent or child to decide to cut it short and come back early. They could still try again the following day.

The Summers had decided to get some sandwiches for a picnic and then go swimming at the local recreation center since this was one of Kenny's favorite activities. Everything went so well that they wished that they could spend a longer time together. That night John commented to Martha that he had felt shortchanged having to take Kenny back when they were having such a good time together. He said that in the past he had usually felt cheated when he had to continue an outing with Kenny when things weren't going well. Martha was relieved to hear this. She had thought that she was the only one who had these feelings during difficult times with Kenny.

The following day the parents met briefly with Russ, who summarized how things had been going with Kenny and answered their questions. Although an additional weekend visit was set up for later in the fall, and there was talk of Kenny coming home for a brief visit at Christmas, it was decided that the best time to start family therapy, per se, would be when Sarah had her semester break in January.

Again, before Kenny left with his parents for an overnight visit in Denver, Russ met with him along with the parents. First they discussed each person's perception of the visit of the day before. Everyone agreed that it had gone very well and each had wished that the three of them could have spent the entire week-end together without Kenny having to return to the Lodge Saturday night. Kenny made a commitment to work on having things go as well on the two day outing. Parents and child were again advised that if things were not going well it was okay for the visit to be cut short.

In January the whole family agreed to come to Evergreen for some intensive family work over a period of several days. It had already been decided that Vee, the Medical Director, would be Kenny's individual therapist. She and Russ would be co-therapists for the family sessions.

During the first session each family member was asked to draw a picture of their family. Although each drawing was done in a unique way, each one depicted Martha and John as primarily relating to each other by talking about the children. Prior to Kenny coming to the Lodge most communications had been about him and his problems. Interestingly, everyone observed that recently J.J. had had some problems. He had lost his job and moved back home. Now Martha and John were focusing their communications on issues relating to him.

During the several days of work with the family John, and Martha were asked to look at their own relationship and make some decisions about how to fill the void created in their communications patterns with Kenny away from home. Some of this work was done with the children present. Some was done with John and Martha alone. Both realized that they were not comfortable with their present relationship, but had been hesitant to say anything about the discomfort.

During the family sessions, the older children continually highlighted family dynamics. Because of their own stage of development—being both at home part time and separate from other family members part time—this was especially easy for them. Each had a strong investment in clarifying the changing relationship with parent figures as they became more independent. A variety of techniques was used to help members share more about themselves.

Considerable time was spent having the parents share information about relationships with their parents as they were growing up. The message that Martha had received most consistently from her mother was that she must always be "nice" and try to please others. A second message was that she should never show anger as that wasn't "proper" for well bred young ladies. She was most surprised when she heard that her husband and children were upset that she didn't let others know when she was angry. Because of this, they were never certain when they were pleasing or displeasing her. Martha started to look at how her own desire to be "good" and "proper" to please her own mother affected her feelings of self-esteem when her children were not always "good" and "proper."

Both therapists supported her in sharing information and feelings. At the same time they confronted her about taking responsibility for the choices she was making as an adult.

John Sr. was quite surprised that he was able to share many of his feelings. He had always viewed himself as somewhat of a loner—someone who didn't need, or want, to share much of himself with others. However, he found that as Martha talked about her childhood, a lot of his old memories resurfaced. As he saw how logical her behaviors seemed once he heard her view of her growing up years he became eager to explore his own past.

He had always thought that psychiatry was a bunch of

"mumbo-jumbo" that didn't have any relationship to common sense. As an engineer, he had great trust in things that could be observed and a great respect for logic. Now he started to see that psychotherapy also stressed these areas, just in a different manner. He realized that Russ was able to put him at ease because he, too, shared a lot of his thoughts and feelings. As J.J. and Sarah talked about their observations of how Martha's behavior affected them, Russ kept drawing John into the conversation.

John started talking of his perception of himself as the person in the family charged with the ultimate responsibility for all family members. Yet he saw himself as usually having to work through another person, Martha, whom he saw as the center of family functioning. He realized that that was how he also saw his own father and mother—the latter right in the midst of everything and the former the power in the background.

He had resented the fact that his dad never had time to do things with him. Even more, he realized that he was still angry because his father had died when John was 14. Subsequently he had to quickly become the "man of the family." He hadn't had either the time or money for much fun during his high school years.

In spite of his father having worked hard all of his life, he had been able to set aside little money. During the war years it was easy for John, as a high school student, to get jobs to help out at home. Every bit of money that he was able to make during these years went to supplement the family income. Following high school, John had continued to help out financially at home by getting a full time job. He felt he had no choices until his younger sisters were out of high school.

When the Korean war started, John enlisted in the Navy. While he was in service he realized that he had a real talent for seeing how things worked, how they ran. After the war was over, he decided to go to college on the G.I. Bill. He worked hard at the university. The academic learning did not come easily for him, but the more practical applications did. During his sophomore year he and Martha met on a blind date. He was immediately impressed by her. She seemed self-assured and always seemed to know the right thing to do in any social situation.

Although she was a senior, she was several years younger than he. They became engaged six months after they started dating. They married a year later. John thought they should wait until he graduated, but Martha had a full time job teaching and they were able to manage financially on her salary and his GI Bill benefits. They continued to help his mom financially as well.

John had been so pleased when John Jr. was born. He made plans about all they would do together as soon as J.J. was a little older. However, like his own dad, as family responsibilities grew John worked more and more hours. Professionally, it was important in those early years to always be available for extra work. It wasn't hard for him to do this because he enjoyed his work and was good at it.

However, as the years passed by, he realized that he, too, had been "too busy" to do the things he had planned to do with J.J. A year before Kenny's birth John realized that his son was nearly the same age that he had been when his own dad had died and that he and J.J. had a similar relationship. He tried to schedule more time to be with J.J. However it seemed that every time John had time, J.J. was more interested in being off with friends his own age. Usually when J.J. wanted time with his dad, John was in the midst of an engineering project.

John reminisced about his hopes and dreams when he found out that he and Martha were going to have a third child. He had so hoped it would be another boy. Now that he had his own business, he had more flexibility in scheduling. Again, he started dreaming of being able to have an ideal father-son relationship, one that he felt he had not previously experienced either as a son or as a father. Oh, the happiness he had felt when Kenneth was born.

As he talked about his early years, John found that the inner anger he frequently experienced was dissipating. However, it was being replaced by a deep sadness. He was really surprised when J.J. moved over closer to him and reached out. J.J. started talking about the things he had always wanted to do with his dad.

Subsequently Russ helped John focus on activities that he had particularly looked forward to doing with Kenny and the latter was then asked to select two or three that he thought he would enjoy.

As the family sessions continued it became apparent that it was difficult for any member of the Summer family, other than Kenny, to express anger very directly. A commitment was made by both parents to continue to address this area in their own relationship.

By the end of the four days everyone in the family was feeling emotionally closer to one another. Each was ambivalent about the sessions coming to a close.

Everyone concurred that one of the areas that Martha needed to address was being able to be firm in her expectations with Kenny without being afraid of what would happen if she showed anger or if Kenny became angry. It was agreed that she would return to Evergreen to "live in" at the Lodge for several days in March.

Sally, Kenny, and several of the other boys greeted Martha at the plane. Throughout her stay she was to be with Sally, the child care worker with whom Kenny had formed the closest relationship. Whether or not Kenny was involved, Martha would join in the activities in which Sally was engaged. Sometimes it seemed easier for her to accurately observe and learn from Sally's interactions with boys other than her own son.

Martha noted that some of the residents seemed to best control their own behaviors when they were in physical proximity of male staff members. It was as though just being near someone who could physically restrain them helped them to be able to control themselves. She now realized that maybe that was why Kenny had done better around John. She also observed that Mark would frequently comment that he sure would be glad when a particular boy felt comfortable enough and sure enough of himself that he could handle himself with Sally without any male intervention.

The supportive interactions between male and female staff members were obvious. Sally had no difficulty bringing a boy who was starting to escalate his behaviors to one of the male staff on shift saying "_____ is having a hard time right now. I think it might be easier for him if he stays close to you." Male staff members responded as though this were a routine request. They didn't imply that Sally herself should be able to take care of the situation, nor did they usually lecture or actively confront the boy involved. Mark or Pete usually just went on with whatever he was doing, quietly involving the youth in the activity. Martha was surprised that even when staff had a difficult time with some of the boys, they didn't seem to hold grudges. The focus usually seemed to be on how to have things go well.

Martha observed that in general Kenny was minding her better than he had when he was home at Christmas. Anytime he started being belligerent with her, one of the staff would say, "Kenny, what did your mom say?" After his response they would make a comment such as, "Well, then what should you be doing?" For the most part, Kenny would subsequently comply with the request. Occasionally, he would pursue an argument. Sometimes his points were sound. Sometimes they were not. Staff seemed to accept or reject the arguments dependent on their validity. At the same time, they would teach him how to make his point without arguing.

At the end of her visit, Martha was hoping that a time could be set up for John to come and spend some time "living in." She thought that it would be helpful for him to learn alternative ways to discipline. She had noted that John seemed to vary between overindulgence and anger in dealing with Kenny's difficult behaviors.

In June Kenny was to go home for a week. John came to the Lodge two days early. Prior to taking Kenny home for the visit, he would work with one of the male staff members, Rob. John had been thinking a lot about the family sessions in January and how the focus had been on feelings. He was surprised both at how angry Rob sometimes seemed to be with the boys, yet how gentle and supportive he was in helping them express their own feelings. Later he asked Kenny if Rob ever got really angry with him. His son's response surprised him. "Sure, if he thinks I'm not helping myself he gets mad."

Vee met with John and Kenny prior to their departure from the Lodge and they talked about several areas of change for each of them to work on during the visit. During a therapy session goals were identified for each family member to work on throughout the visit. A telephone contact was agreed upon for mid-way during the visit. Vee would talk with both parents and Kenny and find out how the week was going.

It was a good thing that the telephone appointment had been arranged. John and Martha were wondering if a week's visit was just too long for them and for Kenny. Everything had gone well the first three days, but the day prior to the telephone call it all seemed to fall apart. Kenny had been angry when told that he couldn't go on an outing with the neighbor children. From then on he wouldn't do anything his parents asked of him. At dinner he had challenged every rule. Bedtime had been a hassle as had the early morning. Both Martha and John were thinking, "Nothing has really changed. He's the same old Kenny, always into 'you can't make me.'"

First John and Martha talked to Vee on the telephone expressing their frustration. They were wondering if they should bring Kenny back to the Lodge today. Vee assured them that this would be an acceptable alternative, but that she wanted to talk with Kenny before a decision was made. She asked that he be put on the phone and that they let her talk with him privately for a few minutes. Then she would want to talk to all three of them together. When Kenny was put on the line, he became very defensive about his behavior. Vee interrupted him:

Vee: Ken, how did you feel when your folks said that you couldn't go to the amusement park with your friends?

Ken: I was really mad; they never let me.......

Vee: (interrupting again) We're not talking about ever and never right now. I was talking about how you felt yesterday.

Ken: MAD!

Vee: **Of course,** most kids get angry when adults say no. That makes sense. How have you been showing them that you were angry?

Ken: Well, if they won't let me do what I want, I won't do what they want!

Vee: That's how most people feel when they are caught in that kind of situation. Let me ask you something though. Is it working out well for you right now? Are you having a good visit right now?

Ken: No.

Vee: Right! Do you think that it is working out well for your folks right now? Are they enjoying the visit?

Ken: No-o-o-o.

Vee: Right! You know it's okay for you to be angry about not getting to go with your friends, but the important thing is that right now things aren't turning out well for either you or your parents. That's really too bad. I know that there are lots of times at the Lodge when staff tell you "no" and I can remember when you used to have tantrums whenever that happened. But I know that you've learned other ways to let staff know when you are angry or frustrated.

Ken: (interrupting) But this was my only chance to go with the kids......

Vee: Ah, so you weren't just angry. You were really feeling cheated and left out too. I bet that made you start wondering how many other things you had been left out of while you have been here at the Lodge.

Ken: (again interrupting) I sometimes wonder if they will want to invite me ever again.

Vee: You need to talk with your folks about those feelings too. They already know that you are angry and by now they are angry also, but I wonder if they know about how cheated you feel. I know that they would understand that because they have told me how cheated they have felt when they see some of the neighborhood kids and their parents having fun times together and you and they aren't together or aren't able to have fun times. You know, your mom and dad were telling me that the reason you couldn't go yesterday was because it was the only time when all of you—your dad, your mom, your brother, your sister and yourself—could be together during the visit home. Do you see how when you felt cheated you made sure that everyone else knew exactly how you felt? How do you think everyone in the family felt last night?

Ken: (quietly) Cheated.

Vee: Right. You felt cheated because you weren't with your friends. Your parents felt cheated of the good family time that they had looked forward to and I'm sure that your brother and sister felt cheated also. That's the way it goes in families. If one person feels he has lost he sets it up so the whole family loses. Now, what I need to know is whether or not you want to cheat yourself and your parents out of having a chance to have some good times during the rest of your visit? Can you turn things around or do you need to come back to the Lodge?

Ken: I want to stay here.

Vee: Good. I'm glad you want to stay, but the issue is can you turn things around?

Ken: Yes.

Vee: Are you sure?

Ken: I'm sure.

Vee: Well, okay, but I don't know if your parents are still too angry. I don't know if they think that there is any chance that you can all have fun together on this visit or not. If they don't, then I think you'd better come back to the Lodge early, because nothing you try then will work for you. Let's talk with them and see what they think.

After the parents got back on the line, Vee helped Kenny tell them about his feelings of always being left out with peers in the neighborhood and his feelings of having been cheated when they said he couldn't go on the outing. John had spontaneously said, "Kenny, so many times I've felt cheated out of having fun times with you. I feel like you don't even just leave us out. A lot of the time you push us out!"

Vee: (interrupting) John, do you like that feeling?

John: (adamantly) No!

Vee: Ken, what did your dad say—does he like it when you push him away? when you act like you don't care how he feels or what he thinks?

Ken: He doesn't like it.

Vee: Right. You and your dad are really a lot alike aren't you? John, Martha—Ken has told me that he doesn't want to cheat either himself or the two of you out of a chance for some fun times during the next few days. I need to know how you feel about it. Are you willing to see if you can get things turned around or are you still so angry and upset that you think you can't do your part in helping it to go well?

Both parents agreed to give it another try for the rest of the day and evening. Vee said she would to call again the next day and see how things were going.

Kenny and his parents were able to have some good close times for the remainder of the visit. At the end of the visit everyone felt very good about the fact that when things were not going well they had been able to turn things around and subsequently have a good time. That's what John and Martha had always felt they had been able to do with the other children, move from difficult times back to a more comfortable mode of interacting. Now there was beginning hope that they and Kenny could form a similar relationship. ∎

Working with Families
as a Reflection of Philosophy

A child entering residential treatment has strong emotional ties, whether positive or negative, to his family. Regardless of where the youngster will be living after he leaves the facility, the family will continue to directly or indirectly influence his emotional life. Even in cases where there has been a severing of the legal parent-child relationship, the child carries with him into his new family or living setting the genetic, cultural, religious, ethnic, social, and emotional influences of his birth family and the experiences he had with them.

A family gives the child a personal history. In turn, the child gives the family a future. The family teaches the child certain values and beliefs. The child carries these via family traditions and life choices into the future.

Usually the family provides the training ground for the child to learn how to relate to others, solve differences, share, express feelings, give and receive, be vulnerable, take risks, and trust. For some reason the child entering residential treatment has not been able to learn these skills within the family setting. In the treatment setting, this child not only needs to fill in these gaps in learning but he also needs to resolve or rework the effect of not having accomplished these developmental tasks in a timely manner within his own family framework. Only with the support and permission of the family is the child free to resolve the past and move forward with positive change.

At the same time, the family is suffering. The parents have recognized that they are unable to provide for their child's needs within the family setting. Out-of-home placement is necessary. Parents need to resolve their pain and anger, their hurt and frustration, in order to grow in a compatible way with their child. A major overall treatment goal for children in residential care is that when the child is ready for discharge he will be ready to grow and develop in a family milieu that is prepared to have him and provide for him. To maximize the potential of both child and parents, family work is an integral part of the treatment process.

The treatment philosophy always encompasses the facility's view of the family's significance within the treatment process. This is done either by openly acknowledging the family's importance and addressing ways to utilize its power, or it is done by omission, thus signifying that little emphasis is placed on the power of family relationships.

It is our contention that for all the potential power of our treatment milieu, it cannot begin to counteract the power the family has over its child if there is head-on confrontation between the two. It is not enough to neutralize the family. Its power must be used to enhance that of the milieu and become part of it. Even with very disturbed parents or disrupted family systems, treatment is seldom successful if the parents are in opposition. The underlying goal of all of our work with families is to utilize their power in a way that facilitates the treatment process.

"How can we make the family our ally?" is a question that is asked repeatedly during all stages of treatment. With some families it is a simple task. With others, particularly when the placement is involuntary, it is a greater challenge.

On occasion a court, a social service agency or a school district mandates a family to place their child at Forest Heights. However, because we control our own intake, we can still build an alliance with a family in this situation.

> **Example:** Ron, age 11, had been in a juvenile detention center on several occasions. He had a history of antisocial acting out when not closely supervised. Pre-referral psychological testing revealed that Ron was quite anxious and had many underlying fears. His acting out behaviors seemed to reflect his attempts at coping with these underlying feelings. The judge had ordered placement in a treatment facility.
>
> Ron's parents were quite hostile and defensive when they contacted Forest Heights. Emotional support for their frustrations in dealing both with their child and with the system was given. It was acknowledged that they probably felt they had little control in this situation. Russ pointed out that they did have a choice, however, about placing their child at the Lodge. In fact, we would not admit Ron unless the family wanted him here. First, they were entitled to know what we thought we could do in terms of treating their son and what involvement we would expect of them as parents. They may not have had a choice about placing Ron in a treatment facility but, as far as we were concerned, they had a choice about placing him at Forest Heights. Russ made it clear that we were unwilling to treat Ron unless the parents committed themselves to becoming part of the treatment team. By giving the parents a choice, we re-empowered them, thereby reducing their hostility and defensivenesss, which had greatly escalated as they felt they were losing control not only over their son, but over their lives as a whole.

As noted in an earlier chapter, at Forest Heights the underlying goal of our work with families is to initially use the power of the family to enhance the power of the milieu and subsequently to utilize the power of the milieu to strengthen family ties. This work starts with the early alliance building during the pre-placement period, continues with family involvement in overall case planning during the in-patient treatment process, and concludes with the implementation of post-discharge plans.

> **Example:** Alex had 10 placements between ages 8 and 12 when he was referred to the Lodge. His father had abandoned the family when Alex was 2. There had been no contact with him since. Mother had voluntarily relinquished her parental rights to Alex and his younger sisters three years ago, after they had been in fostercare for a year. Adoption plans were made for the sisters, but Alex had so many problems that he could not currently benefit from a family placement. He had already experienced an adoptive disruption and several group care placements. His behaviors seemed to indicate unresolved separation issues.
>
> Following review of the case materials, it was decided that the home visitor should try to meet with Alex's birthmother and see if she could give Alex permission to make use of therapy and eventually develop new family relationships. This was done. It was clear that she cared about Alex but did not anticipate ever being able to parent him on a day to day basis. In addition to a face to face meeting with Alex and the home visitor, the birthmother, Sharon, was asked to send a letter to Alex following his admission again conveying the permission.
>
> While Alex was an in-patient, it became apparent that there were many gaps in his own knowledge of his life history, and that social service records did not adequately answer his questions. Attempts made to track down other relatives were unsuccessful.
>
> However, about two years after admission a letter from Alex's paternal grandmother arrived asking for information about him. She had obtained his address from Sharon. Alex answered her letter and through subsequent communications was able to fill in the gaps in his personal history. Although there was no birth family member able to parent him on a day to day basis, family members provided him with the

information necessary for helping him understand how his past related to the present. As they realized that they were unable to meet his parenting needs, they again gave him permission to form new family connections after discharge from the Lodge. Although

they were no longer legally related to him, as the only family he knew they continued to be powerful influences in his life.

Our philosophical approach to treatment is based on the conviction that true change occurs only in the context of interpersonal relationships based on trust and attachment. This belief is evident not only in our treatment of the boys, but hopefully also in our interactions with their parents. We want to develop a strong alliance based on mutual trust and understanding. We recognize that the stronger the relationship between Forest Heights staff and family members, the greater the potential for a positive treatment outcome.

We believe that there are certain decisions which must always remain with the family. Although we may work with the parents on clarification of these issues, we do not challenge the family's role as the primary decision maker in the following areas:

1. whether or not they want their child at the Lodge

2. whether or not the parents stay married

3. the number of children they choose to parent

4. the child's religious orientation

5. the family's basic values and beliefs

6. where they live

During the pre-placement process, while the family is making the decision about placing their child at the Lodge, our philosophy and treatment approach are explained. We believe that our program will be effective only if it makes sense to the family and only if they are actively included in the treatment process. Just because the parents are themselves having difficulty meeting the needs of their child does not mean that they are not able to make decisions about his care. We want them to be fully aware of our program when they commit to it. They join the team voluntarily. This initial step is the beginning of a working alliance which must continue to develop throughout the child's placement.

Parental love for the child is not questioned. The fact that they cannot have him at home now does not mean that they don't care or that they can't make decisions on his behalf. If the family is made to feel impotent they are not as helpful to the child and to the overall treatment. If the family is recognized as doing the best they can in difficult circumstances and as having an important part in their child's progress, they can be stronger partners on the treatment team. The role of the family is accepted and acknowledged as important. How they express their caring and power may be challenged, but never the primacy of their position.

At the time of admission we respect the fact that the family knows more about their child than anyone else. In return, we ask the family to trust that the staff has had more experience in working with emotionally disturbed children. Our treatment principles are shared with the parents before placement so they actively agree to the Lodge's treatment approach. This opens the door for their learning new ways of handling their child. The techniques are simple and clear. The mystery is removed so we can work together. This builds trust.

We have seen that both Kenny's length of stay at Forest Heights and his treatment outcome were favorably influenced by the strong alliance between his family and the staff. In this case, the ease with which this relationship occurred was primarily a reflection of the parents' ability to form close trusting relationships with others. In spite of some obvious unresolved issues on the part of each parent, it was not necessary to overcome major barriers to developing a strong sense of mutual respect. Kenny's parents were open to help and Lodge staff recognized and validated their importance in their son's life.

Beginning Steps in Family Work

It is the mutual concern for the child that becomes the foundation for the relationship between treatment staff and family. The parents are not merely turning their son over to us "to fix." We need their assistance from the beginning of the pre-placement process until discharge. This supportive involvement of the family frees the child to establish the necessary attachments with the staff and to have energy available for growth in the therapeutic milieu of the Lodge.

During the first phase of the treatment process, the emphasis in family work is on strengthening the alliance initiated during the first contacts and on gathering information about the child and family. We are working on identifying, rather than changing, family dynamics.

Throughout the entire treatment process there will be an ongoing assessment of the family's ability to care for their child. Since the family system is probably the most dysfunctional and disturbed at the time of placment, it is difficult prior to admission to have a solid assessment of the parents' long range capacities. Some families cannot manage certain children. Some children have so many problems no family could handle them. Therefore, throughout treatment there is an ongoing question, "Can this child return home and have his needs met?" Although this is seen as the outcome of choice, it is not always possible. The decision must be made considering both the best interests of the child and the family as a whole. In situations where the child cannot return home, the family and treatment center must work together to select the best alternative for the child. Throughout the beginning and middle phases of treatment, data is gathered to make the best decision by the last phase of treatment.

Obtaining Information about the Family

Gathering information continues from the first pre-placement conference through to discharge and follow-up. In the beginning, information gathered is mostly on family history and emotional climate in the family. During the child's stay in residence, the nature of the information changes in emphasis from past history to current observations and reports on how new methods of handling difficult situations are working for them.

The genogram traces the family including several generations through time. This pictorial representation of a family helps elicit family patterns in such a way that they can be more clearly identified. (See Figure 1 for the genogram of the Summer family.)

This is also a time to be alert to the impact of placement on various family members, particularly siblings. Some questions in our minds are "Will another child become the recipient of the focus in the family with no real change in managing the family more effectively? Which one is the most vulnerable? What are the emotional forces separate from any biological component that contribute to this child in this nuclear family having emotional problems? How does the family see the problem? Do either set of grandparents play into the problem? How? How might placement affect the marital relationship? Where are the supports for this family during the placement process?" This information becomes one piece of the puzzle we put together as we better our understanding of the child.

The Eco-map reveals the external forces and pressures on the family that are supportive or draining of emotional energy. (see Fig. 2 for Summer family Eco-Map). As with the genogram, parents and a staff member complete the Eco-map together. As the information is pictorially arranged on the paper often family members draw their own conclusions and begin to understand their situation in a new way that enables them to be more objective about themselves and their child. They become more aware both of areas of stress and friction and of sources of support and strength.

Direct observations are a necessary complement to the reporting by the family. This too is an ongoing information gathering process which begins during the pre-placment visits and continues throughout the placement.

Strengthening Alliances

Throughout treatment, strengthening the alliance between our staff and the parents is an ongoing focus. The family empowers the Lodge to take charge of their child. Forest Heights, at the same time, recognizes the power of the family as an expert about their child, his past, and the primary relationships in his life.

The extended pre-placement home visit provides an opportunity for building an alliance and establishing trust so that we can cooperate in treatment. We are not attempting to take charge. We are wanting to learn more about the family and their child. We are wanting to provide emotional support for both child and parents during this difficult time in their lives.

We recognize that the family has suffered in the placement decision process. Placing their child requires parents to come to terms with the severity of the problems and the necessity of his leaving the family to get help. Family members may react to this painful experience in a variety of ways, including distancing, blaming others, self blame, guilt, etc. To maximize the chances of the child successfully returning home, the underlying pain, anger, sense of failure and rejection need to be addressed in the course of treatment. Parents, too, are deserving of emotional nurturance. Support for the family as a whole is therapeutically important. It is then easier for them both to remain in contact with their child and to perceive his changes during the treatment process as positive strivings toward more harmonious family functioning.

Separation Interview

The separation interview is a key point in the placement process. It is the moment the family leaves their child in the care of the Lodge. This is a traumatic time for the family, a time of crisis. Those family members experiencing the separation together have a bond, a memory, a sharing of an intense emotional experience. The more accepting each family member can be about the placement, the easier it is for the child to remain a part of the family while living at the Lodge and visiting at home.

During the separation interview loyalty issues are discussed. As we saw in Chapter 3, the child's fears about his parents not loving him in the future or his not loving them are addressed. The family gives the child permission to be actively involved at the Lodge while reassuring him that they will not desert him. At this time each family member is given an opportunity to express his or her feelings about the child's leaving and, as always, is helped to do so if necessary. Fears, hopes, anger, loss, frustration, and sadness are all shared. The child can hear that he will be missed and worried about. Lodge staff have modeled for parents and child alike the importance of open communication about difficult emotions. In this way we have set the stage for the nature of future family interventions.

At the end of the interview, after the child has left with a child care worker, parents are reassured that their son will be cared for and that he will someday come home. They are reminded of the many important tasks that may have been neglected because of all the time and energy taken by the problems of the child. Now is their time to make some life changes and to focus on addressing some of the other parental and family needs. No one person should be the center of the family and dominate all of its time and energy. The basic message is, "Because it is now our responsibility to take care of your son, you have the opportunity to meet the needs of other family members including yourselves."

Keeping in Touch

Children who come to the Lodge have a great need to maintain their ties with home. Between visits, telephone calls and letters are very important. They assist the child in working through the intense feelings about the separation, reassure him that he has not been deserted, and increase his awareness of the trust between family and Lodge. Parents are given suggestions as to ways to facilitate the child's adjustment during the early placement period. (see Fig. 3)

Suggestions for Parents

• Ask questions that show that you are interested.......

  "Have you gone fishing (skiing, hiking) yet?"

  "Who is your roommate?"

• Give information that keeps the child current on what is happening at home. Send pictures. The child should not be surprised about changes at home.......

  "We painted the living room."

"The Smith's dog had puppies."

"We fenced the back yard."

- Share the family recreational activies but do not overemphasize this.......

"We had a good time camping last week-end. We sure are looking forward to when you can enjoy activities with us."

- Speak of the missing child but always include your trust of the Lodge. The child should become aware that you are willing to have the pain of his being away because he is getting what he needs.......

"I really miss you, but I am glad that you are getting the help you need."

- Keep contact frequent and consistent. Cards, brief notes, pictures, etc are helpful. Frequent (one or two times a week) is better than lengthy, less frequent contact.

The separation is difficult for both child and parent. Parents may contact a designated staff member any time they want to know how their son is doing. They are assured that they will be contacted by staff if an emergency situation with their child arises.

Boundaries between Program and Family

Just as important as establishing a working alliance with the family is setting appropriate boundaries between the program and the family. Parents need to know how their child is doing. They need enough information to feel comfortable with the separation and the lack of day to day contact with their son. At the same time it is important that their child not have to deal with his family around each and every incident in his life at the Lodge. The child needs to feel enough safety and security in the treatment milieu to confront himself and try new ways of relating to others in an effort to function on a higher level. He cannot achieve this level of security if the parents demonstrate a lack of trust by insisting that each aspect of his life at the Lodge be fully discussed with them.

The boundaries provide limits to the involvement, to the details shared, and the type of contact. They are dynamic in nature and are likely to alter over the course of treatment as the needs of the child and family change. There are situations when it is essential for the Lodge to take charge and change the nature or frequency of the contact. Too much, too little, overinvolved, underinvolved, are examples of situations when staff would attempt to open or close the dividing line between Lodge and family. These boundaries are managed by the person in charge of contact with the family and by staff members at the beginning and end of visits.

Immediately after placement, responding to inquiries of the parents is delicate. If staff say that child is doing well, the parents may believe that we are being judgmental of them, and that there is really nothing wrong with their son. On the other hand, if details of misbehaviors are given, they may panic and fear either that the child will be prematurely discharged because of his behaviors or that he cannot tolerate the separation from them. It is safer to say things like, "We are beginning to understand what it was like to live with him." This validates the family and provides a protective boundary for the child and the Lodge in the early period of placement.

Respect and support for the family increases the flexibility in the working alliance. Nurturing the family and building trust reduce the likelihood of their interpreting limit setting as rejection. This attitude also minimizes the chances of a request for increased contact being interpreted as a reprimand. It is sometimes necessary in order to keep the alliance to direct a parent to only one administrative staff member. This allows the alliance to continue but removes the impact one step from the child's environment. It prevents a too permeable boundary with too many staff members.

Identifying Family Dynamics

Family dynamics are demonstrated by the parents both during contacts with the child and with the treatment staff. Parents will re-enact their usual patterns of interpersonal relationships in their ongoing contacts with various staff members. Having a good alliance includes the assurance that we will help both the parents and their son become aware of, and change, behaviors that work against healthy family functioning.

> **Example:** Carl was a member of a family where "let's you and him fight" was a common pattern. His parents, Vivian and Ben, divorced two years ago. The pre-divorce hassles and strife continued with frequent battles centering on the parenting of Carl and his two sisters. Carl's emotional problems served to keep the parents in close communication. However, they continued to disagree about the source of the problems and how to manage his behaviors.
>
> During the pre-placement contacts the parental discord was evident. However, both parents agreed on placement at Forest Heights. Within weeks of placement it was apparent that the family dysfunction

would be reflected in the contacts with Forest Heights. In all telephone contacts with his parents, Carl complained about being unfairly treated. Both parents called staff members daily with complaints. However, they continued to disagree about a solution. It was apparent that the family had few skills in conflict resolution. It was clear that Carl did not have parental permission to settle into the Lodge routine and develop trusting relationships with child care staff members.

At this juncture, both parents were asked to come meet with administrative staff. Family patterns were identified and it was reiterated that successful treatment could not take place without a firm alliance between parents and staff. Parental questions about Carl's complaints were answered, but it was made clear that Lodge staff were unwilling to discuss each day to day decision. It was necessary that both parents have some trust in the program.

This scenario occurs not infrequently. In most cases the parents, with supportive confrontation about their choices, will recommit to having their son at the Lodge and the stage will be set for learning alternate ways to resolve conflicts. However, in a few cases parents are either unable or unwilling to give up the pattern of family dysfunction. It is clear that their son will continue to be in the middle of conflicts between staff and parents. Since admission was based on everyone agreeing that this was an appropriate choice, and since this is no longer the case, we will facilitate the family in exercising their right to decide if they want their child to continue in placement at the Lodge. At the same time, we make clear the type of relationship that is necessary for continued treatment to occur. (See example in section on Parent Initiated Premature Discharges in Chapter 8.)

Re-establishing Fun in the Family

The emphasis with the family in the early part of placement is to communicate with their child and to start short visits. The purpose of these early visits is to have fun together. Even if they initially spend only an hour together the message is, "Enjoy being together again." Gradually the visits will increase in length as the child and family are able to manage being together in a new way.

Early on, family work is low key. The emphasis is on the child changing some behaviors and learning new ways of relating to people. He is helped to bring these changes from the milieu into the family during visits. In general, children change faster than adults. At the point that the parents see something different happening, they usually are ready to start working on changing their behavior to maintain the progress the child has made. This signifies the move to the middle phase of family work during which there is much more direct involvement with the parents. They are ready to try some of the things they have seen and heard about at the Lodge. They are hopeful and want to learn.

Family Work during the Middle Phase of Treatment

The act of placement often reduces anxiety in the family. However, this decrease in tension is only temporary. It does not reflect any fundamental change in the family's system of interacting. The lessened tension serves only to relax the family enough to try new ways of being with each other. However this flexibility is essential for more fundamental changes. When the family can have fun together even for a very short time, they are usually ready to expand on this positive experience and learn new ways of interacting with their child.

During the middle phase of treatment, work with the family parallels similar work with the child in residence. An alliance based on mutual trust has been developed and additional facts leading to a more accurate assessement have been ascertained. With the family the focus moves to changing the dynamics or emotional processes in the family. With both parents and child it is time to more actively confront resistances to change. We are working with the child to increase his capacity to handle himself appropriately in the family. Simultaneously we help the family develop the skills necessary for supporting and maintaining the changes their child will make during the treatment process. At the same time we help the family accept those conditions, such as learning disabilities, that are likely to persist.

During the middle phase of treatment information gathering is less on background data and more on current observations made by the parents during visits with their child. We learn how the child is behaving during home visits and how the environment might have already changed. At the same time we learn how realistic the family is with regard to expectations of their child. The more parents can deal with the situation as it really is, the greater will be their ability to provide for their young person's special needs.

Family sessions begin when the child is capable of behaving differently for the parents. The frequency of the sessions, of course, depends on how far away the family lives. With local families we provide the family work. When the family lives at a distance we suggest that they work with someone in their home community. Sometimes this is a therapist they worked with prior to the admission. Other times it is someone new to the family. Initially, the family, without the child in residential treatment, will work with this therapist. Prior to discharge, however, this child will join in the family sessions when he is at home on visits. All families meet with us for some aspects of family work at the Lodge before and after visits with their child and become increasingly involved with us as discharge approaches.[N]

Skill acquisition for the parents usually will be centered on emotional management, relationship skills, and conflict resolution. Parents may need to increase their ability to tolerate anxiety and other forms of emotional discomfort. This parallels similar work with the child in the milieu. Parents and child alike may need to learn new skills for handling emotional interactions. The greater their confidence in making more effective choices, the greater their ability to tolerate emotional discomfort. As each family member begins to look realistically at his choices more emotional tension can be tolerated. Acquisition of new skills reduces the tendency for the old automatic reactions. For example, an increase in parenting skills reduces feelings of helplessness, frustration, and anger and redirects a new hope towards the child. This change in attitude through support by the staff offers an alternative response and thus increases tolerance for tension.

In family therapy sessions we use a variety of techniques aimed at increasing the family's ability to meet the needs of all of its members and helping them function more effectively as a family unit. These techniques include: 1) working with expression of feelings; 2) modelling; 3) teaching new tools for parenting; 4) changing patterns of interaction; 5) reframing; 6) leaving power in the family.[N]

Family Education Week-ends

Virtually all of our families need to learn some new skills. We teach families parenting tools similar to those used by the child care workers. It is helpful to share our experiences with handling difficult situations. We need to be clear that we do not have all of the answers. We too are anxious about difficult situations and make mistakes, yet we are able to manage these unsettling dilemmas without feeling a sense of panic. This is a skill that we want to share with parents. Families who have had extensive experience with unsuccessful out-patient therapy may be more receptive to an educational approach than a "therapeutic" one. This approach is the most economical one in terms of time even for families who are very receptive to other forms of family therapy.

Once or twice a year parents are invited to come to the Lodge for a week-end to be involved in learning more about children in general, and more about working with disturbed children in particular. For some sessions all parents are involved. Other times parents are divided into groups since some of the areas we focus on relate more to post-discharge planning than others. During the family educational weekends we examine a variety of topics.

1. **Normal development:** We have found it helpful for parents to understand the normal developmental tasks of children. Most of our families need to learn to differentiate between behaviors indicative of normal development versus behaviors signifying underlying emotional problems. This understanding helps them become accepting of the less than perfect behaviors which are nonetheless expressive of normal development. Parents of all children need to have skills in managing conflict, anger, mild anxiety, mild depression, and testing of limits.

2. **Basic communication skills:** The principles of good communication including active listening, I messages and problem solving skills are taught.

3. **Supportive control:** Confrontation and discipline can come from either a pro-child or anti-child stance. It is important that our parents learn to confront and discipline in ways that enhance rather than further decrease the child's self esteem.

4. **School achievement:** Parents are concerned about academic skills and achievements. Because many of our residents have various learning disabilities, it is important that their parents understand not only the impact of these problems in the school setting, but also how perceptual strengths and weaknesses affect adjustment in the home. Parents of children who have been in residential treatment usually have extensive contact with school personnel. They need to be knowledgeable about current educational laws and may need emotional support in advocating to insure that their son's needs are being met.

5. **Attachment and separation issues:** Most of our residents have had difficulty forming normal attachments. Many experienced parental separations or losses even prior to admission to our program. Their parents need to be knowledgeable about both of these areas of psychological development.

Visits to the Lodge

Families come to the Lodge for visits in the milieu, scheduled family sessions, case consultations with the staff, and to pick up and return their child from visits. The informal contacts with staff around visits provide an opportunity for staff and parents to chat and get a sense of each other as unique individuals. Being at the Lodge even for a few minutes at a time gives parents a sense of what happens here.

Distance does not remove the need for alliance building. For families coming from a distance, contacts are usually more concentrated and intensive. They come for several days and have a variety of meetings with staff. They may take their child off grounds for fun times as well as visiting on grounds. They will have a variety of opportunities for observing their son in the living situation, possibly at school, with peers, and with his therapist.

In addition, a parent might be invited to spend several days in the milieu. This may occur either during the middle or final phases of the treatment process. The parent has an opportunity to see some of the discipline, parenting, and communication principles in action. The parent has an opportunity to practice their new parenting skills in a supportive environment. For the child, sharing his parent with other children can simulate sibling issues, thereby highlighting an area for staff, parents, and child to work on together. Seeing his parent in the milieu working toward the goal of his coming home, the resident knows that he is not the only one making an effort.

Sometimes staff meet with our families in their homes. This might occur either in the local area or in distant cities. Occasionally, the staff person is in the area primarily for another purpose. Other times a clinician might travel specifically to work with the family and their child in their home. This may occur to insure that a visit goes well. It might occur as part of pre-discharge planning. It may occur as part of the transfer of behavioral changes from the Lodge milieu to the family setting. Such contacts may occur either during the middle or final phases of treatment dependent upon the child's issues, the family, and the availability of a staff member.

Including Families in Treatment Planning

Throughout the child's stay at the Lodge, parents are invited to participate in their son's staffings. Most parents do not attend every staffing, but hopefully all will attend at least one. When present, they actively contribute taking their turn in adding information and observations. They are encouraged to either agree or disagree with staff members' remarks about the child's progress. They become part of the overall treatment planning. It is particularly important that they become active participants as we formulate discharge planning and post-discharge recommendations.

All staffings result in written treatment plans which are shared with parents, either during a discussion when they next come to visit their son or by sending them a copy. Occasionally the proceedings may be videotaped and the tape sent to the family's therapist in their home community for use during family therapy sessions.

Crises as a Time for Strengthening Family Ties

Just as a behavioral trauma provides a state of high arousal and the concomitant opportunity for bonding as the child releases tension, so too does a family trauma provide a similar opportunity for all family members to strengthen ties. Our treatment philosophy acknowledges the importance of events accompanied by intense emotional states in building and solidifying relationships. Because our long range goal is always to strengthen family relationships, we try to use all of the major events that occur in families, whether these be events accompanied by joy or those accompanying crises. An occurrence such as a birth, death, marriage or serious illness brings relatives together and renews the bonds. It is important that children in placement be allowed to participate in these important family events. If they are not ready to manage such a visit on their own, we prefer to send a staff member with them rather than have them miss out on an opportunity to share an experience which reaffirms their family membership.

Likewise, there are times during the treatment process when the child is experiencing a crisis and we will want to involve the parents with the objective of strengthening the parent-child relationship.

> **Example:** Robert had had difficulty accepting nurturing from his parents. His mother had always felt ineffective with him, rejected by him. After he had been at the Lodge for a year and a half, Robert was hospitalized one night with acute appendicitis. The parents were notified and came to the hospital. Initially it was clear that Robert looked to Alice, the child care worker, for reassurance and nurturing rather than to his mother. However, over the course of the next several hours Mother and Alice shared the emotional support of Robert. Alice used the power of her relationship with Robert to include his mother in the caretaking. Over the remainder of his hospitalization the parents stayed with him, cared for him, and Lodge staff took on more of a visiting role. Robert went home with his parents for a few days of convalescence after his discharge from the hosptial, prior to his return to the Lodge. During that crisis his relationship with his parents, particularly with his mother, changed. As he accepted Mother's nurturing she became more confident of her ability to parent him.

Consistency between Home and Milieu

It is unrealistic to expect that rules at home need to be the same as those at the Lodge. Following discharge, the child will find that home, school, and other settings have differing standards for appropriate behavior. He needs to be confident of his ability to meet varying expectations. He needs to learn that people he loves and cares about do not have to agree about everything. Individuals can have different opinions and continue to respect and care for each other.

However, there are some areas where consistency between the milieu and home are important. The basic attitudes toward appropriate and inappropriate behaviors and the acceptance of appropriate expression of feelings need to be consistent and not contradictory. There needs to be a consensus on what expectations are supportive of the change process. There should be agreement on the level of supervision and support the child needs and deserves.

Family Work during the Final Phase of Treatment

By the end of the middle phase of treatment changes in both the resident and in his parents are well underway and we are ready to focus on discharge planning. Once more, family and child treatment are parallel during the final phase of treatment. We center on consolidating the changes made by all family members. We will work more intensely on transferring the behavioral gains made during the treatment process from the Lodge setting to the family setting. We want to identify the point when the child can continue his work using out-patient, as opposed to residential, services. Discharge is not the end of change, nor indeed is it the end of treatment. The family becomes aware that progress must continue as the child matures.

During the final phase of the in-patient treatment process we work with the family on identifying appropriate post-placment services. We actively transfer positive behavioral gains and attachments from the in-patient staff to the parents.

Even though a return home is always being considered and evaluated, the family is not misled. If the decision is made that the child will be living other than at home with his family there is the further acceptance of either their own limitations or of his and a new sense of loss to deal with. Feelings of disappointment, rejection, anger, guilt, failure, etc. are aired and a commitment to a new relationship is made. What do parents and child want from each other? What is each prepared to give to other family members? The future is made more real and specific rather than a vague unknown. "How will it be to have parents visit wherever the child is? What would they like to do on the first visit? How often will the child come home?" A commitment to remain a family is reaffirmed even if they do not live together.

If the child is going home, the family is supported in their capacity to handle the child and the boy is supported in his ability to handle himself at home. Changes in relationships are reinforced and integrated. Specific planning with the family around discharge is based on looking at the facts. What progress has been made? What are the educational and emotional needs of the child? How can these best be met? What services do the parents need to arrange for in their home community? What can Lodge staff do to help?

In this reality-oriented planning, the family may again experience the loss of some hopes or dreams for their child. For example, parents may have to face the fact that their child will always have problems learning. The fact that he relates better is encouraging, but he is still, for example, two years behind academically. There is acknowledgment of his learning disability in arranging for the new school program.

At this point in treatment the family is again assuming more responsibility for their son. There will usually be longer visits with the child at home. At least an approximate discharge date is set several months in advance. Details of school, out-patient follow up treatment, social activities, etc. are arranged cooperatively by family and staff. The family is encouraged to discuss their fears and anxiety about taking full charge.

Parents may need help and support in understanding their child's feelings as he copes with discharge planning. Other family members may also have their own separation issues with Lodge staff. This period may be as difficult for the family as was the pre-placement period. No matter how much we plan, it is never enough to alleviate the terror the family may feel about having full responsibility for the child once more.

Working with Families when Adoptive Placement is the Discharge Plan

For those children without families, adoption is arranged whenever possible. Timing of selecting an adoptive family is critical. The child must have made enough changes that it is possible to identify the ongoing behaviors with which a family must be prepared to work. A clear picture of the youngster's long term psychological strengths and weaknesses must be evident. The child must have reached some sense of resolution around loss issues as they relate to his birth or previous foster or adoptive families so that he is emotionally free to invest in a new parent- child relationship.

Although it is difficult for him not to know where he is going when he leaves the Lodge, during most of the treatment process the emphasis will be on getting ready to be a family member. We ask the youngster to explore his own past history and behaviors as they relate to this. We encourage him to seek information from other boys who are anticipating return to their birth or adoptive families about the nature of most family life. We ask this child to trust that we will work with the agency legally responsible for him to insure that an adoptive family will be available for him when he is ready for discharge.

It is difficult to empower a family with whom the child has never lived. To facilitate this, we think that once a child meets a prospective adoptive family we should be prepared to move into pre-placement visits, rather than having an exceedingly long period of back and forth visits without the child actually moving.

We have learned that the goal prior to adoptive placement is to help the child make sufficient changes to enable him to live in a family setting, but not necessarily to have achieved all of the growth possible. It is important both to adoptive families and to the child that they achieve continued signs of growth and change soon after the move. This facilitates the claiming process. It says, "This is the right parent-child combination." It leads to further empowerment of the family. This is a critical issue for the child who has left a previous family and who in general has diminished trust both for a family's availability to him and for their power to meet his needs and keep him safe.

> **Example:** Eric was ready for placement in an adoptive family on discharge from the Lodge. Prior to his admission the emotional pain of unresolved separation issues prevented his forming new healthy parent child relationships in his therapeutic fosterhome. The focus in the milieu was on helping him again learn to trust adult caregivers, and subsequently to learn to trust his own abilities for behavioral control. In individual therapy he explored the depths of his emotional pain. "Why me? Why didn't I get born into a family that could and would love and take care of me?" He was helped to grieve fully for the family that never was, the primary source of his pain. Following this, he was ready to make a strong commitment to working in an adoptive family. The family selected lived several hundred miles from Forest Heights. The adoption agency responsible for the placement submitted several homestudies and Lodge staff was part of the selection process. Prior to Eric meeting them, the Jacksons sent a book with many pictures of their family and home. In addition the family worker sent a videotape of all family members interacting at home. For the first visit we asked that the parents come without the other children. It was important that their relationship be established as the primary one. They spent some time with Eric and various staff members at the Lodge the first day of the visit. The following day they and Eric went off skiing. This was an activity in which Eric excelled and one that the entire adoptive family enjoyed.

The next contact took place at the Jackson home five days later. Eric flew to their hometown for a four day visit. Eric had a lot of "homework" to accomplish during this visit. He was to learn more about each family member's likes and dislikes. He was to learn about family rules and expectations as well as about the disciplinary measures used in the Jackson home. He was to observe how family members showed affection for one another. Following that visit, Eric and his therapist talked about his perceptions of the family. It was acknowledged that "family building" is difficult work. He was asked if he was ready to make a commitment to working toward an adoptive placement. Meanwhile the family worker discussed the Jacksons' perceptions of Eric. Did they think he could fit into their family? Were they willing to commit themselves to working toward this end?

Once it was determined that everyone was committed to the placement, the Jacksons returned to the Lodge for another visit. This contact was scheduled for over spring break so that the two other Jackson children could come with them. Eric's therapist met with everyone in the family. Eric shared his Life Book with his new parents. They talked of the problems he had earlier in his placement and of the many gains he has made. They talked of possible problem areas in the future. Another visit to Eric's new home was scheduled and a date for the final move was set.

At the time of discharge the parents came once more to the Lodge. Sally and Rob both played active roles during this visit. They were the two staff members to whom Eric had the strongest attachments. Although they were sad that Eric would no longer be part of their lives, they were happy that he was ready to become a family member. When he first came to the Lodge they were uncertain as to whether or not he could make the kinds of attachments necessary to healthy family life. They and Eric shared their joint feelings of success with his new parents. When the therapist asked Sally if she hoped that Eric would learn to love his new parents even more than he had learned to love her she responded, "That's what I want for you more than anything else in the world ."

As parents, you are the most important adults in your child's life. Although you may be having difficulty helping your child overcome his problems, you will continue to be a decisive component in the change process. The following questions are meant to help you identify the role that a treatment program expects you to play in your child's life while he is in residence at the facility.

1. Philosophically, how does the facility view parents? other family members? Are you treated as though you are knowledgable about your child?

2. During initial contacts with the treatment center are you treated as part of the solution or only as part of the problem?

3. What types of contacts will you have with your child while at the treatment center? What types of contacts will you have with child care staff, with administrative staff, with teachers, with your child's therapist? Will you have opportunities to participate in the milieu at the facility? Will staff visit your home prior to, during, or after treatment? Does this facility provide any parent training?

4. Will you be expected to be an active participant in family therapy? If so, will the therapy be provided at the treatment center or external to the center? If the latter, what type of contacts will take place between the center staff and your therapist?

5. Are you planning to have your child return home after treatment or to make other plans for the remainder of his years prior to emancipation? How does this facility view your plan?

Conclusion

A critical component of our overall treatment program is the work done with the family. The goal of our staff is not to usurp the family's power or position in the child's life, but rather to strengthen and enhance family relationships. For a successful treatment outcome the changes that the child makes while an in-patient resident become the basis for continued growth and change post-discharge within the family setting.

The family is the primary facilitator of the child's overall growth process. Our staff will be a major influence for only a relatively short period of the child's life. Therefore, to be most effective, we work intensively with the child to make the changes necessary for successful life adjustment and we work intensively with the family to create a post-discharge environment that is supportive of continued growth in these areas of change.

Notes and Elaborations

pg. 234 Family therapy recommendations do not follow a predetermined regimen, but are individualized based on family dynamics, the nature of the child's problems, where the youngster will be living after discharge, where the family lives and resources available to them in their home community. Forest Heights staff involvement varies from the intensive family therapy services provided to Kenny's family at the Lodge to only working with the family on learning new communication and behavioral management techniques during the pre- and post-visit contacts, while someone in the home community does additional work with them.

pg. 234 Many adults have not learned how to identify or appropriately express their emotions; this may be a focus of family therapy. Some examples of this were given in the description of the four day family therapy session with Kenny's family. Staff members who work with families are expected to model supportive control techniques in their contacts with other family members. Parenting techniques are taught both during the family educational week-ends and during family therapy sessions. They may include communication techniques, environmental controls, behavior management and conflict resolution. Reframing, as described under supportive control techniques in Chapter 5, is used with adults as well as with children. No matter what interventions we utilize with families, we both recognize and support that they continue to have both the legal and moral right to make the final decisions about their families. We believe that it is our responsibility to clarify their choices and help them explore the possible long range effects of these choices, but the parents have the obligation of actually making decisions on their family's behalf.

C O N T E N T S

Individual and Group Therapy

Kenny's Case	245
Therapists and Consultants	256
Selecting Therapists to Work in Residential Care	256
The Therapist as a Consultant	257
The Therapist's Role Working Individually with the Child	259
Determining Readiness for Individual Therapy	262
Educational Component of Therapy	264
Confidentiality Boundaries	266
Therapeutic Modalities	267
Involvement of Line Staff in Therapy Hours	269
Involvement of Family in Therapy Sessions	270
Group Therapy	271
Case Example	273
Guide for Parents	275
Conclusion	275
Notes and Elaborations	275

Individual and Group Therapy

Of course, Kenny already knew Vee as she had done his admission physical and had checked him over after a fall from his bike. In mid-January she told Kenny that she would be seeing him on a regular basis and explained why staff believed that he was ready to be in individual therapy. She referred to comments that Kenny had made to Jules, the child psychiatrist, during his regular pre-staffing meeting with him in November. "When I saw Kenny this morning he had a lot of mixed feelings about starting school. He wants to go, but he is afraid that he will disappear if he 'gives in' and does what adults ask of him. At the same time he doesn't feel very good when he is doing just whatever he wants to do. His underlying fears seem to be related not just to fear of failure, but even more to annihilation fears. The ambivalence and his obvious anxiety are good prognostic signs. If the focus is kept on him and his choices I think that he will be able to make use of individual therapy. It's going to be important to not fall into control battles with him in therapy. He is going to try to set them up." Initially, Kenny was upset that Jules had shared his comments with the rest of staff.

Vee: Jules and everyone else on the staff share with each other important information about you and all of the boys. If we didn't how could we all know how to best help you? Was what you told Jules true?

Kenny: Of course it's true. Do you think I lie?

Vee: No, I just wanted to make certain that it's true. Sometimes people misunderstand what others say. I want to make certain that I check out how you feel about things. Do you think that how you feel is important?

Kenny: Yes.

Vee: So do I. I think that it is real important. I think that what you said tells us that you are ready to do some work in these areas. First, you told us that you were ready to do schoolwork and you certainly have kept that commitment. Carol told me that sometimes it is hard for you to follow through but that you've been really stubborn about it. Lots of times in the past your determination has worked against you. Now it's starting to work for you. Now, you are telling us that you're ready to look at some things in therapy and we believe you. I hope I can teach you some other ways to make that persistence work for you. I really like working with kids who are stubborn, because it's so neat once they get all of that energy working for instead of against themselves.

In this way, Vee was able to build an alliance with Kenny to work on some issues. At the same time she redefined what had previously been viewed as a negative trait as one that could be positive. Changes he had already made were identified. Although problem areas were listed, equal focus was placed on his strengths and the gains that he had already made.

During the two hours that Ken and Vee had together before his family came in late January, she completed structured activities that would help her better understand him. Kenny was easily frustrated when drawing. In this setting, as in school, he seemed to have high standards for himself and difficulty meeting his own expectations. His auditory memory was poor. It wasn't clear whether this was secondary to anxiety, distractibility or to some other cause. A specific fear of failure as well as a pervasive sense of fearfulness was apparent in his responses to the projective testing.

Kenny had a lot of questions about what would happen during the family sessions. He thought that all the time would be spent discussing his problems. Vee told him that they certainly would be talking about the problems he had had prior to coming to the Lodge and about the changes he had made since his admission. However, in addition, they would be trying to identify the areas that each of the other family members might need to work on. Parents, brother, sister, Russ, Vee, and Kenny himself would all have to work together on identifying problems and finding solutions. Boys at the Lodge were expected to work hard, but it was important that parents and siblings do their part as well.

During their first session after the family work in January,

Kenny expressed his surprise that so much time had been spent on others' problems. He looked a little disappointed as he talked of this. In the past family discussions had always centered on his difficulties.

Martha had brought Kenny's baby book and some of the family albums as requested. Vee had asked if she could keep them until Martha came in March. She wanted to use them in her individual sessions with Kenny. Over a period of time, Vee and Kenny reviewed these together. He was able to go back and share his perceptions of events and his feelings at the time. His memory was excellent. There were many opportunities to help him become more aware of his strengths and his vulnerabilities. He also gained some awareness of how his parents perceived him and his problems.

Feb 17 Therapy note: Kenny and I have been going through his baby book and the family albums that Martha brought when they came for the family sessions. I've been trying to help him understand further about his early relationships with family members. I've been focusing on the cyclic nature of the family interactions. He has been very interested in this activity. However, he tends to want to focus on who was at fault in various interactions. With some support however he is able to bypass that issue and put himself in other family members' shoes and express how they might have been feeling.

Vera Fahlberg, M.D.

A recurring focus of the sessions was the cyclical nature of family interactions. Kenny and Vee made many pictures representing interpersonal interactions. Kenny started to learn what he could do to help interrupt negative cycles. He was already utilizing these skills in school with Carol. Vee frequently would ask what he thought adults could do to make it easier for him to be successful. She would focus on what adults too could do to break the negative cycles. This made Kenny feel that everything wasn't his "fault", a feeling he had commonly had in the past. It became more and more apparent to both Kenny and his therapist that it was his expectations for himself, as opposed to others' expectations, that posed the major problem.

During Kenny's February staffing, it was decided that he was a good candidate for Attachment-Holding Therapy.[N] He had developed beginning trust for several staff members. He was young. He had a lot of confusion about his emotions. Underlying fear was frequently expressed as anger. Loneliness exploded as hostility toward others. Sad feelings were glossed over. Denial, minimization, and projection were prominent defenses. At the same time, there was an aura of neediness about him. In some circumstances he seemed to be able to make use of early levels of nurturance, enjoying activities usually reserved for younger children. It would be easy to make certain that the issues were coming from Kenny's agenda, rather than from an adult imposed routine. Although Attachment-Holding Therapy was not seen as critical for achievement of his long term treatment goals, using it would probably decrease the overall treatment time. Because of his particular issues, it was predictable that anger would be the primary emotion that he would focus on in the initial session. Since his parents had already experienced his extreme anger, but had seen little of his vulnerability, it was decided that the initial holding session would be done without the parents present. It would be more desirable to have them present for some of the subsequent sessions when he would, most likely, be demonstrating some of his underlying fears and other emotions more indicative of his vulnerabilities.

Vee's therapy log notes record the issues addressed during these sessions.

Mar 3 First Holding Session. Holders were Glen, Sally, Fred, and Mark. Initially, Kenny expressed his discomfort at being held by being very silly. Becoming indignant followed. Then came all of the expected "you're hurting me" statements. He followed the fairly predictable stages of moving toward anger. His projection of blame onto others and his tendency to focus on who's at fault were prominent. Initially when I avoided any talk of fault and reflected his underlying feelings, he became filled with rage. His anger was most directed at Sally and me. Verbal outbursts and physical resistance aimed at Sally were particularly vehement. Kenny was very surprised when he was told, "Good. You're doing such a good job of getting rid of all that anger that's been inside you. What a good job you're doing." For a few minutes he seemed so caught by the paradox that his initial anger subsided. However, it came back full force within five to ten minutes. As in other situations, Kenny seems to become most engaged when interactions are of high intensity. We'll have to work on gradually modifying this so he can respond equally well to interactions of more normal intensity. His persistence, good long term memory, and follow through on verbally made commitments were all praised.

We spent a lot of time talking about the choking episode in second grade. As we probed this incident in detail it became apparent that the underlying stimulus to the outburst was Kenny's feeling of inadequacy. He seemed relieved, rather than resistant, when he found that there was a logical explanation for his behavior. We connected this with observations of each of the holders about incidents that had some similarities. Glen was able to point out several recent occurrences when Kenny had similar feelings, would start to have an outburst, but would be able to take an adult's help in controlling his own behaviors more successfully. He seemed comforted by the reassurance that he really is changing and that additional change is anticipated. At the end of the session he spent a few minutes curled up on Sally's lap. He looked very relaxed as he left with Fred to return to the house.

Mar 5 Carol, Sally and I met briefly with Kenny today. Carol had noted that Kenny couldn't concentrate at all in school today. Since most of the boys concentrate so much better after a holding session she was puzzled. When she couldn't quickly identify the source of the problem she called me and we arranged to meet with Kenny right after lunch. After a quick check with Sally, who said Kenny had seemed more emotionally distant to her since she came on shift yesterday morning, we decided she too should meet with us. At the outset I wasn't certain if we would have to proceed to another holding or if the issue could be dealt with sitting up. We had holders "on call" if necessary.

In talking with Kenny and Sally together it became apparent that he was fearful of some form of retaliation for the amount of anger he had discharged toward her on Wednesday. Initially, he thought that surely he would be restricted from Thursday group. When he found that didn't happen he became hypervigilant, watching for Sally to express her disapproval in other ways. Again, when that didn't happen he felt so unsure of his relationship with her that he just avoided her. I told Kenny that I had really goofed it. Clearly, I had not gotten the message across that children are NEVER disciplined outside a session for anything they say or do during the session. We had made clear that adults are responsible during the session to insure that no one—neither child nor adult—is physically hurt. We had not made clear that adults would not later "get back at" the child for things said or done during the session. Kenny looked so relieved. However, during the discussion it was clear that he was embarrassed about what he had said to Sally— always a good sign. Again, we stressed the difference in expectations in the house, school, and public versus during a therapy session when we are trying to provide him with an opportunity to discharge those difficult feelings. At the end of the session he asked to return to school and complete his morning assignments. We set up an activity for him to be involved in with Sally later today.

I'll have to make certain that Martha understands that Kenny is in no way to be chastised after next week's session for anything he says or does during it. He needs to hear us tell her.

Mar 10 Sit up session with Kenny. We reviewed some of the observations each of us had about last week's holding session and our Friday meeting. His memory for more recent events seems to be improving. He could bring up an instance over the week-end when he was feeling like he wasn't "measuring up" and when he started to verbally lash out at David. He says he caught himself and stopped on his own. We talked about the upcoming session with Mom. It's clear that he has ambivalent feelings about her being in on a holding session. He seems to want to have an arena for discharging some feelings in a protected setting and with staff help, but he also seems fearful that Mom won't be able to "take it." I assured him that it is my responsibility to help her understand and to give her any support she needs. His responsibility is to be straight with her.

Mar 11 Holding session with Mom present. Other holders included Glen, Sally, and Carol. Kenny did not tap into nearly the same level of anger today. He seemed to move quickly from anger to underlying fears and worries about not measuring up. Martha seemed to feel she was responsible for Kenny's feelings. Much of the session focused on how people are responsible for their own feelings as well as their own actions. We talked about the fact that individuals who care about each other want to be helpful when loved ones are having a difficult time, but that it is disrespectful to try to rescue others from their own feelings. We shared with Mom the pictures Kenny and I had drawn of the family interaction cycles. We talked of ways that Martha could help interrupt the negative cycles. After we looked at some of the positive interactional cycles we agreed on some homework in this area for Kenny and his mom to work on during the rest of her visit.

Mar 14 Met with Martha before she left and we went over a variety of areas. She asked lots of questions about the interactions she had observed between child care staff and the boys. The questions reflected her close attention to what was going on. She was surprised at how fast staff switched from confronting to being close and nurturing and was really impressed at how staff members were supportive of and used each other to help the boys express their feelings more openly. She wondered if she and John would ever be able to do that. She is most anxious to have John come and spend a few days with one of the male staff members. She thinks it would be very beneficial to him.

Mar 17 My focus with Kenny today was on his relationships with women. How had he felt when mom and he were alone at home prior to coming to the Lodge? How had he felt with Sally and Alice when he first came? How had he learned to trust Sally and Alice to be able to take care of him when there wasn't a male around? And how had all the old feelings resurfaced when his mom and Sally were together? He was able to talk quite openly about his ambivalent feelings when his mom and Sally were together. Part of him was scared about how it might go. Part of him was happy that his mom was learning new ways to help him. At the same time he hated to give up the old ways of interacting with her. He, himself, brought up the fact that he had sometimes disobeyed Sally when his mom was there, not to find out what Sally would do ("I already know what she will do then"), but more to find out what his mom would do when Sally "took care of me." He seemed to be relieved that staff felt comfortable confronting Martha about how uncomfortable she was when they confronted the boys.

Mar 24 Third holding session with Kenny. This was a short session with a focus on happiness and fun. We did lots of "little kid" games. Ray and Glen participated. Ray always gets into these kinds of sessions—makes my work easier. Kenny seemed to enjoy it nearly as much as Ray.

There were occasions on which Ken didn't want to come to therapy. A couple of times, Rob had to physically accompany him to Vee's office. Kenny would come storming in, throw himself in a chair with arms folded and would say, "Damn you, Vee, I'm not going to talk to you. You can't make me talk." At those times, his therapist would respond, "Of course not, Kenny. If you don't want to talk today, that's okay. I've set aside this hour for you and we'll just sit here together." Sometimes, Vee would then do some paperwork. Usually after 15-20 minutes Kenny would start to physically relax. Vee would then comment that it looked like he was nearly ready to talk or to draw. Those were always good occasions to help Kenny recognize and talk about his angry feelings.

After one such occasion, she had Kenny draw a picture about anger—"either something that makes you angry, how you feel when you're angry, or anything that will give me an idea about you and anger." On this occasion, Kenny drew a very small picture of himself. He had arms but no hands. In the picture, he had a large mouth but no ears. Vee handed him a copy of the self-portrait he had done during their first therapy hour when he wasn't angry. He noted the differences and observed that when he was angry he felt small. He had trouble listening then. He only wanted to make certain that he was heard. He felt powerless to affect others. The anger would grow and grow inside. Responding to his fear that others would lash out at him in anger he would be aggressive first.

Kenny gradually became increasingly aware of the fact that when he was angry, he was afraid that others wouldn't listen to him. Via some joint sessions with his therapist and child care workers, he was able to start expressing his fears to those responsible for taking care of him on a day to day basis. They learned that when he started to lash out either verbally or physically, it was more helpful if they responded to his fears of not being heard or understood, rather than to his behavior per se. Once assured that they would take the time necessary to listen he was able to regain behavioral control.

In May, when Jules was again seeing Kenny for an evaluation prior to a staffing, he asked him about his thoughts about therapy. Kenny talked of his relief when he learned that Vee wasn't going to "give up" on him just because he was angry and refused to talk. However, he said the thing he liked best about talking with her was that she always shared what she was thinking and feeling and didn't just ask him to share.

252 *May 5* Kenny has been really struggling with "big" vs. "little" conflicts. He is very aware of the fact that many of his behaviors are babyish. He then gets embarrassssed but doesn't handle that feeling well and is likely to do "something stupid." He needs help when you think that there is even a chance that he might be embarrassed. It's sort of like when he used to lash out at others because he was afraid others would lash out at him. Once we focused in on his fears the aggressive behavior slowed down. If we can help him deal with his embarrassment around acting "like a baby" it will be helpful. He has decided that one thing that might help will be to be called Ken after his tenth birthday because to him Kenny sounds "babyish". I tried to help him see that there was a certain element of magical thinking in this but agreed that we would go along with it.

May 12 Had a holding session today. Ken rapidly moved into anger, projecting responsibility for his feelings onto others. However, he was able to move through this pretty fast and again tap into the well of underlying sadness and fears of not measuring up. He can realistically acknowledge, and exhibit pride in, the changes he has made. I used the birthday as sort of a milestone. We talked a lot about how things were going in his life near past birthday anniversaries. We pulled out the Lifeline we had drawn in one of our early therapy hours and re-examined many of the drawings he has made during therapy hours. I helped Ken remember how he used to be afraid that he would "just disappear" if he "gave in" and did what adults asked. We talked about his recent comments to Jules and about how maybe his fear of sharing is related to his fear of having nothing left for himself. I assured him that I would tell his parents about this and help them share their thoughts and feelings with him as this makes it easier for him to share with others. By the end of the session, he was looking at a pretty realistic timetable for continued goal achievement. No signs of the old pattern of bargaining—"but I PROMISE I'll NEVER _____ again."

Jun 13 Holding session with Dad as one of the holders. I told Ken that his Dad should not be left out of this aspect of his changing and growing. Mom had gotten to be in on a session and I thought Dad needed the opportunity as well to hear about how things had seemed to Ken in the past. As might be expected, Ken had to check out Dad's tolerance for the expression of anger. That didn't seem to pose much dilemma for Dad. It was when Ken started talking about his old fears, worries, and loneliness that Russ, who was one of the holders, had to really confront John. Dad keeps trying to cope with others' feelings on a cognitive basis—i.e. "You shouldn't feel that way. There's no logical reason." John seems to need permission from another man to acknowledge and express emotions. During the session we spent a lot of time talking about specific objectives for each family member to work on during the upcoming visit.

Ken is to work on being straight about feelings, and on following through on adult's requests. Dad is to focus on accepting others' feelings. We reviewed what he had learned about active listening during the family education weekend. Russ suggested that John review the handouts and added that many parents find it easier to first practice the communication skills with other adults. At the end of the session we had a conference call with Martha to discuss objectives for the visit. She is to work on being explicit about expectations for Ken (i.e. not saying, "Do you want to set the table?" when she means, "I want you to set the table," and is to follow through on requests/ expectations.

At the May staffing, the possibility of Ken attending public school in the fall had been raised. Carol believed that he could be successful, but knew that he still felt uncertain of his capabilities. It was recognized that again it would be important for Ken to want to go to public school enough that child care staff could be seen as helping him attain his goals, rather than it primarily being their goal. For that reason, it was decided that Vee would raise the possibility during therapy hours and would help Ken explore the pros and cons of the decision making. If he decided that he wanted to work toward that goal, she would help him formulate his goals for public school.

When Vee first asked Ken if he had given any thought to the possibility of public school the following year, he gave a quick, and adamant "No." Vee replied, "Oh, I just thought you might have, but it's okay that you haven't." She then moved on to another subject. Two weeks later, as she reviewed the treatment plan, she asked Ken about how he perceived his progress in the on-grounds school and about his own goals for discharge. The focus was on what further skills he needed to develop prior to going home. Ken identified as a primary goal "being able to make and keep friends." Although he no longer was antagonizing other boys, he continued to have difficulty getting along with anyone on a consistent basis. David was the resident he played with most consistently. Sometimes they got along quite well, but other times they seemed to provoke each others most negative behaviors. David's reactions to frustration and anger were very similar to Ken's—both would become stubbornly resistant, initially in a passive manner, but both could easily escalate to more active expressions of their emotions.

Vee and Ken spent considerable time during several therapy hours identifying ways that the latter could assess when his time with David was likely to turn out well for both of them, and times when it seemed to be destructive. Vee would identify what she wanted Ken to pay attention to during the following week—i.e. "If you are feeling down, is playing with David helpful? Does he make you feel better or do things get worse?" Ken developed an understanding of the dynamics of his relationship with David. He started paying attention to the same kinds of things in his relationships with others. Vee again brought up that at some point it was going to be important for Ken to find out how he did with peers who didn't have severe problems. At this point Ken responded, "Yeah, I've been thinking about public school, but I don't think I'm ready. I'd have to work too hard."

Subsequently, Ken and Vee talked extensively about his past and present fears of failure and about what skills he had learned about identifying his fears and asking for help. Again, she gave him therapy homework related to summer school. Again, the homework related to paying close attention to himself and to what worked out well for him and what didn't. Within a month, Ken was clearly experiencing more ambivalent feelings about going to public school in the fall. Although he readily talked of his fears of failure, there was a concomitant spark of excitement as he talked of the possibility. Vee assured him that he didn't have to hurry about making the decision. Mid-August would be soon enough. At school, the teachers continued to identify both his strengths and the areas he still needed to work on. They made no mention of the possibility of Ken going to public school.

In early August Ken stated that he wanted to consider the possibility of going to public school. At this point, Vee switched gears and said she certainly didn't want to pressure him into such a decision. Was he certain that it was he who wanted to work toward this or was he feeling pressure from her or from his parents? Ken stated, "No. I know that even if I do have trouble, I can turn things around. Things are different for me now. I know myself better. I can count more on myself."

Vee reminded him that a Lodge prerequisite for enrollment in public school was the student coming up with academic and behavioral goals which he would have to share with his current teachers, Carol and Russ. She suggested that he might want to talk with Glen about his perceptions of changes and get some input from him. Ken did this the following week. There was no procrastination. Clearly, he was making a commitment to himself to pursue the possibility. Within another week he had some ideas about goals. He discussed these with Vee. When she asked if he wanted her present when he talked to either Carol or Russ, he replied, "No—why would I need you? I can do it myself." High on his list of goals was, "I want to learn to make, and keep, friends with kids who don't get in trouble at school."

Once school started in the fall, the focus of most therapy sessions was on actively transferring the more positive behaviors Ken had acquired at the Lodge to the public school setting. Early in the school year he expressed concern about his choice since he was again being "sat" a lot when he wasn't in school. Vee supported him in dealing with his own expectations for himself, yet pointed out that maybe he was asking too much of himself too fast to have energy enough to do well both at school and at home. She reassured him that doing well behaviorally at school was the top priority. It was understandable that there would be some early regression at home. Soon it would become easier to do well in both places. Again, they focused on how he could keep his expectations for himself high enough that they would keep him striving without allowing them to become so high that he felt he was a failure. She pointed out that this was a skill that all successful individuals needed to master.

When Ken was in public school and in Scouts, much of the emphasis of the therapy sessions switched to peer interactions. Ken was encouraged to look at the ways that he handled feelings of frustration, anger, jealousy, and embarrassment with peers. He was asked to identify both times when things worked out well for him with peers and times when they did not. He and Vee especially looked at what qualities in Brent made him a good friend. They talked of how Ken might go about selecting friends in the future when he returned home.

As things evened out at school, Vee again switched the focus of the sessions. Now it would be on transferring skills from Lodge to home community and on identifying further skills he needed to acquire prior to and after leaving the Lodge. It was time to help Ken see that everything did not have to be perfect—all problems didn't have to be solved prior to discharge. Change and growth would be an ongoing process which would continue after discharge.

Nov 10 The focus of my session with Ken today was on his feelings about Mark leaving and Tom coming. I think that Mark's leaving has made Ken start to think about his own and others' feelings when he leaves. I'm certain that right after discharge his parents will get many of the same behaviors that Ken is directing toward Tom now. In talking with Ken, I get the impression that he is checking himself out as much as he is checking Tom out, i.e. "Can I start to hassle an adult and then stop myself?" I think he needs this verbalized for him with a statement such as, "Well, can you stop yourself or do you need my help?" If he needs staff help, provide it.

Vera Fahlberg, M.D.

As December approached, there was increased talk about discharge planning. It was decided that Linda would be doing the post-discharge work with Ken and his family. Therefore she started joining the therapy sessions after Christmas. Linda talked about her early observations of Ken and all the changes he had made. She asked what he had done in therapy to facilitate those changes? What had Vee done to help him? What did he still need help in? What did she need to know so that she could help his family understand his needs better? As the three of them discussed the answers to these questions, the therapeutic alliance was transferred from Vee to Linda. On the day of discharge both Linda and Vee met with Ken and his parents to outline the goals and expectations for the post-placement services. ∎

Therapists and Consultants

Although the distinguishing characteristic of residential treatment is the creation and enhancement of the milieu as the primary therapeutic modality, most treatment centers provide a variety of other formalized therapeutic interventions. In addition, many have consultants who provide a variety of ancillary services. In this chapter we will explore the various roles of therapists and consultants in residential treatment as well as the ways that individual and group therapy fit into the overall treatment program in our setting.

Selecting Therapists
to Work in Residential Care

At Forest Heights our consultants provide direct therapy to some residents as well as consultation on all. Therapist/consultant qualifications for employment at our facility include two critical factors. First, irrespective of the actual therapeutic modalities used, strategies and tactics must be supportive of the basic philosophy of treatment. Secondly, the therapist must recognize that as a team member he will not be the sole determinant of the treatment approach. He must be committed to the importance of the milieu in residential treatment.

The more varied the population of the treatment center, the greater is the need to have therapists with a range of expertise. Some residents will profit most from therapeutic interventions that follow the traditional psychodynamic approach, while others may need a more here-and-now oriented approach or a behavioral approach. We have been fortunate in that our three female and four male therapists come from differing backgrounds in terms of training. They vary in terms of their preferred therapeutic modalities as well.[N] However, because all support the basic philosophy of the Lodge, their individual strengths complement one another.

Therapists and/or consultants at residential centers provide a variety of services extending from the pre-placement period through the post-placement follow-up. The role of the therapist is likely to change throughout the course of treatment. At Forest Heights, during the initial stages of treatment therapists function primarily as consultants. Prior to admission, a clinician may provide input relating to decisions about intake. Early during the child's residence, consultants will be available to help formulate the therapeutic interventions that will occur in the milieu. Later one therapist will be selected to work with the child and his family both on an individual and family therapy basis. In the final phase of in-patient therapy, the therapist will help in discharge planning and in the selection of post-placement services. If the child lives the Denver area, his Lodge therapist may directly provide the post-placement follow up.

Our philosophical stance supports the notion that basic changes in the child occur in the context of the relationships he develops while in residential care. When a child is admitted to Forest Heights, we are acknowledging that the traditional out-patient relationship between child and therapist is insufficient for facilitating and maintaining adequate changes. We recognize that at this juncture he needs the more pervasive therapy that occurs within the milieu. The therapist functions as one part of the comprehensive treatment program. His importance lies in being part of the whole.

Because we perceive the primary therapeutic interventions as occurring in the day to day living situation, the child care workers are viewed as the dominant change agents. When seeing a child in either individual or group therapy a prime role of our therapists is to facilitate and support the changes occurring in the milieu. This takes place in a variety of ways. First and foremost, the therapist is supportive of child care staff and of the milieu therapy. Therapists facilitate the child's attachment to the child care givers. They do not attempt to become the primary attachment objects themselves. A major focus of therapy will be the issues that keep a child emotionally distanced from adult caregivers. What defenses has the child developed which interfere with developing trust for adults? keep him from taking nurture from them? keep him from developing reciprocal relationships? It is the therapist's role to enhance the effectiveness of the milieu by identifying these maladaptive defenses and reducing resistances to change.

Although we recognize that some treatment facilities utilize child care staff and/or their chief administrator as individual and family therapists, we have chosen not to do so. We believe that the roles of the child care staff and the therapists, while both important, each have unique components which do not lend themselves to blending of the functions.[N] Although we have found that most of our administrative staff can work effectively as individual therapists for our residents, we perceive a potential conflict of interest when the Executive Director acts as an individual therapist. The individual therapist must always advocate for his patient (client) and his family. The responsibility of the Executive Director is to advocate for the needs of the program as a whole. Sometimes these two sets of needs are in conflict.

The Therapist as a Consultant

At Forest Heights we ask that our therapists act as consultants to the child care staff. The child's behaviors in the living situation identify both his underlying needs and his perceptions of his world. The child's daily behaviors further clarify his defenses as adaptive or maladaptive. As treatment plans are outlined, consultants provide an interface between the child's needs and the day to day living situation. Utilizing their expertise in psychodynamics, they will help "decode" the child's day to day behaviors, identifying underlying needs, perceptions, and misperceptions particularly as they relate to adult-child relationships. Clinicians utilize their special areas of expertise as they help the child care staff devise strategies for meeting the child's needs and for providing healthy re-learning experiences in the residential setting. The child's primary therapist will not be the only one involved in this process. All of our consultants will likely have input into each resident's treatment planning.

Our therapists come from a variety of training backgrounds. Each provides a unique perspective. We believe that it is important that some of our clinicians have a medical background. Throughout the years, we have learned that a significant proportion of children in residential care have a variety of underlying medical conditions. Sometimes developmental or emotional problems are an integral component of the pathology. For example, those with Fragile X syndrome[N] demonstrate physical, learning, and behavioral problems. It is important that someone on the consulting staff have expertise in identifying such underlying conditions so that appropriate referrals for further diagnosis and treatment can be made. Since many of the children referred to our center have been on varying medications with diverse results, medical input as to the efficacy of differing drugs and their side effects is imperative.

Other times we need a clearer picture of the child's intellectual capabilities and of his underlying personality structure and defense system. In these situations the expertise of our child psychologist may provide the most helpful input. We also use his theoretical background in learning theory as we devise and implement specific behavior modification strategies. Or we may utilize the input of someone with a strong background in family systems theory to help us view a resident from that perspective. With our emphasis on a developmental approach to understanding and meeting a child's needs we need consultants with a strong background in both physical and psychological development.

Prior to admission a clinician may be asked to interview the child or perform some testing aimed at further clarifying the child's needs. Such an assessment usually attempts to help identify the child's underlying needs, his maladaptive defenses and the strength of his resistances to change. While administrative staff members usually spend time first with the family, the clinician's initial contact is likely to be directly with the child. His input, uncolored by the parent's perceptions, gives an additional insight into what may be going on with the child and may yield information crucial to the decision about admission.

During the first phase of the in-patient treatment process the focus is on building an alliance with the child and establishing the beginning attachments between the youth and child care staff. In general every-thing possible is going to be done to enhance this. All program components encourage the building of such relationships. It is likely that the child will not be in school during this phase of treatment. Likewise, it is uncommon for him to be involved in individual or group therapy. We actively try to heighten the frequency and intensity of interactions within the milieu. Other aspects of the overall program work to enhance these beginning attachments rather than compete with them. Therefore, the clinician's role during this phase of treatment is likely to be centered around helping child care staff better understand the child and devise strategies for the day to day interactions which encourage a sense of safety and security.

One of our child psychiatrists has the added role of interviewing each resident soon after admission and then at least once every six months. He is less involved in the living situation than our other therapists who usually spend considerable time in the milieu. Based on these intermittent contacts he brings a unique objectiveness to the treatment planning sessions. He identifies how well the program is succeeding in meeting the individual treatment goals for each child.

It is to be expected that when staff are dealing with difficult and demanding children, and sometimes with difficult and demanding families as well, that there will be times when staff members become very frustrated with either child or family. Thus, another major function of our consultants is to help staff discharge their feelings of frustration in ways that are not counter-productive to the overall treatment goals or strategies. At the same time the therapist continues to be an advocate for the child and family.

The Therapist's Role Working Individually with the Child

Although all staff are involved in the overall treatment of the child, there is a division of the work load. The child care staff work with the child primarily in terms of the here-and-now. On the other hand, the therapist provides a sense of continuity between past, present, and future. He provides a link between family, community, and treatment center. He helps the child see how issues being worked on in the residential setting relate to past life experiences and problems. At the same time he helps the youngster relate these same issues to the future when he will be asked to meet family, school, and community expectations.

It is during the middle and final phases of the treatment at the Lodge that individual and group therapy are most useful. In the middle step of treatment the focus is on skill building and behavioral control. During this stage individual therapy comes into its own in terms of helping the young person gain further understanding of himself, decrease resistances, and devise strategies for trying out new interpersonal skills. The emphasis on problem solving and conflict resolution is prominent in both individual therapy and in group therapy settings.

During this same middle period, a therapist is usually actively involved with the family, either at the Lodge or in their home community. During the final step of the residential treatment program the individual therapist plays a major role in devising the strategies for accomplishing the overall goal of transferring behavioral and emotional control achievements to the family setting.

Throughout the child's stay at Forest Heights each member of the overall treatment team—child care workers, teachers, therapists, administrators—will use the power of their varying relationships to further empower each other. Frequently a boy is willing to try a healthier form of adult-child interaction in the therapy setting where the overall demands are less. If he is successful in this setting, the therapist encourages him to explore this new mode of interaction with one child care staff member or one teacher. Subsequently the youngster is helped to generalize the more adaptive behavior to a variety of settings.

On the other hand, a resident may first disclose a particularly traumatic aspect of his past history, sexual or physical abuse for example, to a trusted child care staff member. It is that staff member's responsibility to insure that the information is transmitted to the boy's therapist. The child is likely to be given a choice as to how the information is transmitted—by the child care worker or the boy himself, etc.—but the information must be shared. In this way empowerment is a two way avenue with everyone utilizing the power of his relationship to enhance and strengthen other relationships.

Child care staff members in their interactions with the youngster encourage him to work through feelings about family with his therapist. This diminishes the likelihood that the child will get mixed messages. Redirecting talk of feelings about family to the therapist also decreases the child's potential for defusing strong feelings by talking with a variety of people on a non-intense basis rather than working with the same feelings in a more intense manner with one person, the therapist.

The therapist provides a feedback mechanism for the child. He interprets observations, both positive and negative, made by child care staff and those made by family, teachers, or others in the community. The therapist checks whether or not the child's perceptions of events are congruent with adult perceptions. If they are markedly different it is important that the therapist do further probing to find out how the child perceives his world, identifying misperceptions and confronting the child's denial and projection. At the same time, the therapist has an opportunity to determine which modes of interacting work best in decoding misperceptions and in confronting resistances. These modes can then be passed on to child care staff and to the family so that they too can facilitate more rapid change.

It is usual for disturbed families and/or disturbed children to see all relationships in terms of power. They view interpersonal interactions as attempts to control. They tend to see relationships, particularly those between authority figures and children, as conflicted, competitive, even adversarial. A major goal of therapy is to correct this misperception by re-defining the adult-child realtionship as a positive alliance of benefit to both child and adult. The therapist needs to model this reciprocity in interactions with child, line staff, and with parents.

Many of our residents have a variety of underlying fears which have a pronounced effect on their day to day adjustment. A frequent objective of individual therapy relates to clarification of these fears and helping the child overcome them. Both play therapy and art therapy are useful in helping the pre-adolescent child overcome both reasonable and unreasonable fears. The use of play materials may also be used in helping to determine the child's developmental levels and perceptions in a variety of circumstances.

We want the child in treatment to see the therapist as someone who will help him cope with day to day life. The therapist's role is not to protect the youngster from emotional pain nor to take sides, but to be supportive of attempts to cope with reality through building relationships and problem solving. Although the therapist may be supportive of the child's feelings about the demands placed upon him, at the same time he must be supportive of the overall expectations of the milieu.

In the final phase of treatment the therapist will be helping the child and his family focus on discharge planning and post-placement services. He will be helping both the young person and his parents identify the areas where there will need to be concerted effort for continued growth and change. Work will be done to actively transfer the behavioral gains made during the residential treatment to the less restrictive environment that the family and community will provide. The family will be advised about the levels of environmental support that their son will require to maintain changes and promote further psychological growth.

Readiness for individual therapy is decided as part of the staffing process. Both line staff and teaching staff will have input into determining both readiness and therapist selection. They are the ones who know the child best. They know his strengths and weaknesses both in terms of relationship building and in terms of learning new skills. Since each of our therapists tends to work in slightly different ways with the boys, it is important to do some matching of those strengths and weaknesses. We attempt to match our residents with a therapist in terms of the specific needs that each of the boys brings to treatment and the areas of expertise that each of the therapists brings to his or her approach to therapy. For example, we might select a therapist who uses art as a means of communication for the child whose preferred mode of learning is visual as opposed to auditory. Or, for the child with a history of multiple losses, a therapist who has worked extensively with grief counselling will be selected. We count on the child care staff whom the child most trusts to empower the therapist.

Although the Executive Director is responsible for assigning therapists, the Assistant Director usually plays a critical part in this decision and frequently plays a major role in empowering the therapist by explaining to the resident how he sees individual therapy as facilitating and hastening the overall treatment process.

Specific objectives for individual therapy will be outlined at the staffing. When the therapist starts seeing the child he will share these plans with the boy. In general, individual therapy is utilized to help the child understand how the past, present, and future relate to one another. The therapist will facilitate the resurfacing of emotions related to past events and will provide a safe environment for the ventilation of these frequently intense feelings. In therapy the child will gain further insight and understanding of his problems. In addition the therapist will help the child share his perceptions with his family and, in turn, understand how adults perceive interactions and how they may feel.

Some children in residential treatment may be ready to make use of individual therapy immediately upon placement. However, we find that most of our residents are not able to make use of formal psychotherapy until after they have had an opportunity to settle into the living situation and form beginning attachments to child care staff. Our residents usually perceive the initiation of individual therapy as a sign of overall treatment progress, just as they perceive enrollment in the on grounds school or movement to a less closely supervised bedroom as a sign of individual growth.

In general the more disturbed the child, the less likely he will be able to make use of individual therapy and the more important the interactions in the daily living situation become in terms of creating the environment which encourages change. Individual psychotherapy works best when the child is experiencing an optimum level of internal anxiety with regards to his psychological and behavioral disturbances. In general, the greater the level of psychological disturbance the further removed from the normal range is the level of anxiety. Either too little or too much internal anxiety leads to a decreased likelihood of changing the child's view of his own and others' behaviors.

A major goal of individual therapy is to help the child realistically view his choices and take more responsibility for his decisions. Obviously this becomes more important the older and the less disturbed the child is. A psychotic child cannot be held accountable for his own behavioral choices in the same way as the acting out child can be. With the psychotic child, the first therapeutic tasks are to entice the child to interact with the real world more frequently and to help him clarify the boundaries between fantasy and reality. These tasks are more easily accomplished in the daily living setting than in the therapist's office. The child's blurring of the boundaries between fantasy and reality are particularly evident as he plays and interacts with peers as well as with adults. Clearly the number of hours spent in the milieu exceeds the number of hours any child will spend in the more formal therapy setting. Therefore we want to maximize the impact that child care staff have in terms of being the primary change agents. We find that the combination of meeting dependency needs, emotional nurturing, and setting appropriate supportive limits provided by the child care workers is especially effective with the more disturbed individual.

With the psychotic child the therapist's role may well be that primarily of consultant to the child care staff in terms of decoding resistances and defenses, identifying underlying needs and developmental levels, and devising strategies for therapeutic interaction between line staff and child.

However, even with this child there may be times when some individual sessions will be scheduled early on. It is our belief that the majority of psychotic children have underlying perceptual problems which are secondary to some form of organicity. Usually, the goal of these early sessions will be to more thoroughly identify this particular child's modes of interacting with the environment and to try to identify the ways that he misperceives the world around him. Individual sessions may also further identify how and where the child is stuck in terms of psychological development. However, it is probably unrealistic to expect individual sessions with the psychotic child to do much in the way of changing the child's perceptions per se, nor is it likely that such sessions in and of themselves will meet the child's unmet psychological needs. For such children the milieu is the crucial aspect of the therapeutic program.

There are some children with behavioral problems, especially those behaviors which may be seen as precursors to the development of an antisocial personality, who again may not profit from individual therapy early on. Frequently these children have already had extensive out-patient therapy and they are able to interact in totally normal ways during therapy sessions. Their problems lie in their interactions with others when expectations are placed on them. It is then that their egocentricity, impulsivity, and problems accepting controls become highlighted. In general emotions are more intense during the interactions that occur in the milieu than in those that take place in formal therapy hours. It is in the situations accompanied by affective intensity that this child's pathology becomes evident. These youngsters usually have problems learning to trust adults. They have difficulty forming enough of an attachment to then incorporate the values of the primary attachment object. We believe that it is inappropriate for a therapist who usually sees the child in an artificial setting for a very limited number of hours a weeks to become this attachment object. Indeed, these youngsters may use the relationship with an individual therapist as a means of avoiding involvement in deeper relationships with adults with whom they live.

The child who is most likely to be seen in individual therapy immediately after placement is the one who already has a relationship with one of the staff therapists prior to his admission. He may have been seen in out patient therapy by this individual or he may have been seen for an extensive evaluation. In either case he has some level of relationship with this professional. It is the therapist's responsibility then to use the power of that relationship to empower the child care staff and that is the purpose of the early therapeutic encounters in the period soon after placement.

Occasionally, the new admission seems to exhibit just the right level of internal anxiety to be able to utilize more formalized pyschotherapuetic interventions. In such cases, he will be started in therapy soon after placment. The therapist will use this anxiety level to help the child look forward to the long range goal of returning home and make use of this discomfort in identifying the needed changes and in overcoming the resistances to change. Certainly, if the child is showing an appropriate level of separation anxiety it is much more difficult for him to, at the same time, keep up his denial system in other areas. Thus it is easier at that time than at other times to confront many of the child's maladaptive defenses.

Educational Component of Therapy

However, for most of our boys formalized therapy in either an individual or group setting will be postponed until they have developed some attachment to house staff and have started to identify with the expectations of the facility. It is precisely at this point that therapy may have the most value. At this time the child is usually showing more motivation toward change. He is getting enough positive feedback that he has some energy available for confronting internal resistances and looking at past failures and problems. It is then that individual therapy will help speed up the overall therapeutic process. During early therapy hours the therapist will work on identifying perceptual and intellectual strengths and weaknesses. Concomitantly, the therapist will be identifying both resistances and the modes of interacting that work best in reducing or overcoming them. He and the teaching staff will consult with each other about their findings and will formulate a plan for reconciling any differences in observations or opinions.

Both daily living staff and therapist may be involved in helping the child learn to identify, accept, and appropriately express feelings. At least initially in placement, the child care staff will probably observe inappropriate expressions of feelings on the part of the child.

For many disturbed children, since their behaviors tend to be objectional to adults, the focus has been on what they should not do. However, most of these children have few resources for developing more positive strategies for interacting with the environment. One of the therapist's roles is to help the child develop these strategies by actively teaching the child new ways of interacting. Initially this coaching may occur in the therapy sessions through role play or by the use of other therapeutic tactics, but later the therapist will want to encourage the child to extend these gains into the residential environment and practice them there.

Once the child has had an opportunity to try out these new modes of interacting in the somewhat protected setting of the residence, the therapist may again be involved in helping the child extend these interactions into the home or community environment. This transfer and extension process usually has to take place in a fairly direct way by: 1) identifying the new behaviors; 2) getting a commitment to try them outside the therapy setting; and 3) helping insure that the child has the opportunity to try them out and receive positive feedback for the change.

> **Example:** Troy has problems with change. He has trouble moving from one activity to another. Helping him with this has been an objective in his individual therapy. In that setting, he has experienced some success. He has made a verbal commitment to transfering this gain from the therapy setting to the school setting. Jay, his therapist, invites Carol, his teacher, to participate in part of a therapy session. Jay encourages Troy to tell Carol what he is working on and to ask for her help. Together, the three of them identify the times in the school setting that will provide Troy with opportunities to practice his newly acquired

skills. They will decide on how reminders might be given and on how feedback will be provided, both to Troy and to Jay.

Several weeks later when it is evident that Troy has been successful in transferring this achievement to the school setting, Jay will encourage him to make a commitment to work on transferring it to the milieu and will now involve one of the house staff in emotionally supporting Troy and in providing adequate feedback.

Confidentiality Boundaries

Confidentiality implies that some therapies, or some individuals, are more important than others. Residential treatment is based on the concept that all staff are involved in therapeutic encounters. Therefore confidentiality between the psychotherapist and child negates the basic premise of residential therapy. If the milieu as a whole, and the therapist as part of the overall environment, is to be successful in meeting the child's needs and facilitating positive changes the relationship between therapist and child can be neither exclusive nor can it be confidential with regards to other residential staff. To facilitate the building of trust and enhance relationships, attachment objects, whether they be child care workers or parents, must be included within the confidentiality boundaries. At Forest Heights the boundaries of confidentiality are extended from therapist-child or therapist-family to encompass the entire treatment staff, including child care staff, teachers, and administrative staff.[N]

To make the most of contacts with the child, information gleaned by the therapist is shared with child care staff. This enhances their effectiveness with the child. The child knows that what is discussed in therapy will be shared with all staff "because staff cannot help you if they don't know what is going on with you."

When we exclude line staff from knowledge about the child because it is "confidential" the message to the child is that the child care staff cannot be trusted with such material. Children may either interpret this to mean that the child care staff are too weak to deal with such material or that their own thoughts shared with the therapist are so "bad" that no one else can handle them. Neither interpretation is helpful in terms of empowering care givers. Again, to facilitate the effectiveness of the day to day interactions the therapist must share his findings and information interpreting the underlying significance in such a way that the staff's interactions become more therapeutic.

We have found that our residents will frequently use the extended confidentiality boundaries to their own benefit. If they are uncertain of the consequences of direct communication with an adult caregiver they may choose to share information with their therapist knowing that that individual is committed to facilitating the communication process. In such circumstances the therapist is quite likely to ask the child how he wants the information transmitted. Is the youngster asking for help in determining how best to directly approach the staff member? Does he want the therapist to invite the staff member to join them for a discussion of the problem? Although the resident knows that the information will be shared, he learns that he has choices about the context in which it is shared. Since the sharing of information is bilateral youth may on occasion utilize child care staff to help them convey messages to their psychotherapist.

Similarly, in our residental program empowerment is a two way street. Child care staff use the strength of their relationships with the child to initially empower the therapist who will be seeing the child on an individual basis. In turn, as the therapist's relationship with the child deepens he will utilize it to transfer the decreased resistances and the behavioral gains achieved during the therapy hours to the milieu. The strength of relationships is not static. It is constantly changing and fluctuating. It is important that all adults involved with the child in the residential setting maximize the potential of their individual relationships with the resident by extending the positive aspects of their rapport through empowering other staff.

Therapeutic Modalities

As we mentioned earlier our therapists come from a variety of differing backgrounds, disciplines, and experiences. Obviously the specific strategies and tactics each uses to overcome resistances to change and help the youngster learn new interpersonal skills, behaviors, and emotional control will vary from one therapist to another. The actual techniques used in therapy will depend to a great degree both on the child's developmental levels and problem areas and the therapist's training and orientation. However, all of our therapists will share similar goals and objectives in the treatment of children.

The modalities used will vary from being relatively non-directive, to experiential, to quite confrontational in a supportive manner. Indeed, our therapists may use markedly different therapeutic strategies at different times during the course of treating the child.

Although the therapist will want to enhance the acquisition of feelings of trust and safety, his primary goal will not center on these areas as they will be addressed extensively in the milieu. Therefore, the therapist is free to focus on other areas. One of the goals of individual therapy usually involves helping the child know more about himself. During this process, it is quite likely that there will be a resurfacing of emotions and opportunities for ventilation and resolution of these feelings will be provided.

Therapeutic Modalities
Used at Forest Heights

Reality therapy

Gestalt therapy

Art therapy

Play therapy

Behavior modification

Psychodynamically based insight therapy

Transactional analysis

Attachment-Holding Therapy

Family systems therapy

Different therapists will use differing specific tactics to encourage the ventilation, and subsequent resolution, of strong emotions. Strategies may include providing a safe environment for physical discharge of anger and hostility. Utilization of art or writing may achieve the same overall goals.

Many children in residential treatment have had many moves and/or losses. If this is the case, it is quite likely that the child is confused about his own background. We have found that a technique developed and primarily used by child welfare caseworkers is particularly helpful in such cases. This technique involves helping the child understand his past by reconstructing it through compilation of a Life Book. It is important that the therapist not only try to get as much factual information for the child with regards to his past, but that in the course of the compilation the therapist help the child recognize and come to at least beginning resolution of the feelings associated with past events.[N]

Denial and "forgetting" are common defenses for young children. When we are faced with trying to help children understand their past and how it affects their present behaviors, such defenses are maladaptive and need to be confronted. Pictures or other concrete reminders of the past, such as letters from past parent figures, help overcome the child's denial. As the therapist works with the child, both to gather factual information and to elicit emotional reactions to this information, feelings of attachment between therapist and child are likely to emerge.

In our treatment center it is quite likely that the therapist will want to involve the line staff in some of the therapy sessions. This helps the child to see that the real purpose of therapy is to help the child's daily life go more smoothly. The therapist is particularly likely to involve the child care staff whose interactions with the child most closely approach the interactions the child has with his own family or school.

Involvement of line staff in the therapy sessions helps to decrease the possibility of compartmentalizing or of trying to play the therapist and child care staff off one against the other. At times when the line staff is involved the therapist may well act as a coach for the child encouraging him to try out new ways of communicating or relating to adults and exploring alternatives in relationships. Usually this will occur after therapist and child have worked extensively together on these skills.

At times the therapist will ask one or more staff members to join the child or family in a therapy session so that staff can experience and recognize the underlying pain or conflict that child and family are experiencing and thus be more supportive of getting the conflicts resolved.

Although it is not uncommon for milieu staff to be involved in some of the therapy sessions where the focus is on increased self awareness, ventilation, and understanding how the past effects current functioning, it is almost certain that they will also be included in some of the therapy hours when the focus is on acquisition of new skills including improved behavioral and emotional control. Particularly when the youngster is learning more about successful problem solving and conflict resolution line staff members will be part of the therapy hours. Child care staff are always involved in the Attachment-Holding sessions.

For some, experiences in the living situation continue to tap into old unresolved feelings. Therapy hours may then center on recognition and resolution of these "old" issues. During the opportunities provided for ventilation, the child may not only be allowed, but encouraged, to utilize actions and words that are not generally acceptable within the milieu. When this occurs, it is particularly important that house staff be involved. In this way, they give support for making use of therapy, while helping the young person understand the boundaries between what is acceptable during the therapy hour and what is acceptable in the milieu. Therapist and child care staff together work with the boy toward clarification of these boundaries.

If a particular resistance has been broached in a therapy session and attempts have been made to start to overcome it, particularly if the child has committed himself to working on changing a particular behavior, it is important that this be conveyed to child care staff, both so that they can watch for changes and support such changes in the child, and also so that they can supportively confront the day to day resistances in this area by referring positively to the child's commitment made in therapy. For many children, this means that the child must observe direct contact between therapist and child care staff.

> **Example:** Alex's therapist invites Mark, one of the child care staff, to join them near the end of Alex's weekly therapy session. The therapist tells Mark, "Alex and I have been talking about his problems minding adults when they unexpectedly ask him to do something. Do you think that during this next week you could help him with this by asking him to do some tasks and reminding him of his commitment if he forgets?"

In this way the message that the therapist will help the child define goals while the child care staff help him attain them is clearly demonstrated. The further message of "we are all working together to help you" is given.

Involvement of Family in Therapy Sessions

Sometime prior to discharge, whether other family members are being seen in therapy at the Lodge or not, it is certain that the therapist will also involve the family in the child's therapy sessions. Again, this helps the child see that the primary goal of therapy is to facilitate other relationships not to promote exclusivity of relationship with the therapist. Family involvement is likely to be extensive both during the middle and the final stages of the treatment process. Family members will usually be involved at some time during Attachment-Holding Therapy.

The therapist plays a major role in helping the child transfer the gains made in the daily living situation into the family or community situation. He helps child and family deal with past feelings as well as helping them look ahead to the possibility of strong feelings in the future. The child is provided opportunities for sharing his past pain with parents. Parents are provided opportunities for sharing their old fears and worries with their son. The therapist helps all family members prepare for coping, in a non-pathological way, with future problems. Opportunities for joint problem solving and conflict resolution are provided. Family members learn to identify times they may need outside help and to see therapy as helpful and productive.

Obviously, milieu therapy per se is a form of group therapy. However, at Forest Heights we use a variety of other groupings to address additional aspects of the overall therapeutic process. In general, these groups are focused on skill acquisition. However, in addition, they provide opportunities for controlled supportive peer confrontation which may help overcome resistances to change. In all of the forms of group therapy, the adult leaders take an active role in deciding goals for the group and developing strategies for achievement of these goals. They also take a limit setting role, not allowing individual behaviors or peer confrontation to become destructive to any one individual or to the group as a whole. While we recognize the potential for positive confrontation in group therapy settings, we also realize that children with severe emotional problems will at some level act out their pathology in the group setting. The adults are responsible for insuring that the interactions are helpful, not counterproductive.

Thursday Group:
This group is comprised primarily of younger residents who are in the earlier stages of therapy. It is led by two female staff members, one a teacher and one a child care staff. The primary goal is to provide opportunities for children to experience the joys of a variety of play experiences in a non-competitive setting. Many of our boys are developmentally delayed when it comes to play skills. Because of their behavioral or emotional problems they did not have adequate opportunities to achieve the psychological growth afforded by early play experiences. The activities of this group are designed to provide these residents with occasions for observing non-Lodge adults and children interact in a variety of non-structured and semi-structured settings. Activities might involve playing in a park; going to the Stock Show; or being involved in holiday or party preparations. This latter type of situation would involve planning, shopping, and actual preparation as well as participating in the final activity.

While experiencing unearned gratification, the child has an opportunity to learn to identify and stay within limits in a public area, and to practice a variety of safety concerns which might include appropriate car behavior, interactions with strangers, etc. At the same time there are many learning experiences relating to practicing social skills such as making purchases, ordering food in a restaurant, asking directions, etc. as well as interacting with a limited number of peers.

Social Skills Group:
This has some similarity to the Thursday group but is for boys who are older. Again, the primary emphasis is on providing opportunities for the participants to practice their skills in a variety of social situations. Members of this group must be able to control impulses and be able to

focus on issues in a group setting. Skills focused on might include resisting peer pressure to be inappropriate, getting others to listen to his point of view, constructive resolution of disputes, or increased awareness of emotions in social situations and learning to express themselves appropriately.

Communication Group:
With the emotional support of adults they know well and live with, the participants of this group have an opportunity to learn more about listening to others, expressing themselves in ways that make it easier for others to hear them, and joint problem solving. In the group setting, they learn that others have similar feelings and concerns. They are provided with opportunities to offer help, advice, and support to one another, thus increasing their own feelings of self worth.

Movement Group:
Opportunities for engaging in physical activities in a non-competitive manner are provided. Participants are involved in a variety of physical movements, ranging from stretching to movements similar to those involved in dance. In this group gross motor movements are used to identify and overcome resistances. Youth who are inhibited in terms of exploring alternative ways of behaving and interacting with others frequently demonstrate this by inhibition of physical movement as well. Others who have problems controlling impulses likewise have problems maintaining adequate control over body movements. In spite of the attention being centered on only one small aspect of overall functioning, we find that, in general, resistance to change in this area is minimal. As the young person learns to either move more freely or under more control we find that he can frequently generalize this new skill into other areas of overall functioning.

Values and Sex Education Groups:
Usually there are three of these groups with boys divided among them based on age and stage of development. The purpose is to provide a regular, structured time for learning basic facts and for asking questions about these areas of development. The adult in charge helps identify knowledge gaps and provide accurate information. A variety of value laden topics and issues, ranging from sex education, to drug and alcohol use and abuse, to health care issues are discussed. As in some of the other group settings, the participants learn that other peers share their concerns, thoughts, and questions. At the same time, we let the boys know that these are areas of discussion to be shared with adults as well, including their parents.

A second focus of the group is on helping increase resident's awareness of what behaviors lead to their feeling better about themselves and their decisions and which behaviors lead to guilt feelings. We want them to learn to recognize that they have great control over the choices they make both in the here and now and in the future and that they ultimately will be responsible for helping themselves feel capable and worthwhile in terms of these choices.

Specific therapy issues groups:
On occasion we have had several boys who are working on similar areas in individual therapy. It sometimes makes sense to have them be seen together in a small group setting. For example, children who have experienced parental abandonment or abuse might be seen together in a group to explore the effects of these early life experiences as they resurface during adolescence. Again, we find that the boys who live together can help each other identify their own resistances to change as well as clarify how the experiences affect current behavioral functioning. The knowledge that others share similar experiences and feelings helps each individual feel less isolated and provides opportunities for positive sharing and support.

Case Example

The following case demonstrates how the composite of milieu, group and individual therapy is utilized to meet a specific child's overall therapeutic needs.

Victor, aged 12, prone to explosive behavioral outbursts was referred to Forest Heights primarily because he was initiating sexual interactions with younger boys in his fosterhome. Victor entered the fostercare system at age eight, ostensibly because of neglect and out-of-control behaviors. It was only after he was in a fosterhome that sexual abuse was suspected and subsequently confirmed. He had been brutally sodomized between the ages of 4 and 6 by mother's boyfriend. This same man had physically abused Victor's mother. Because of his problem behaviors, Victor has been in three different fosterhomes in the past three and a half years.

Throughout his stay at Forest Heights, therapists and consultants were involved in Victor's treatment in a variety of ways. Initially, they helped the house staff understand how the earlier sexual abuse, combined with maternal neglect in a variety of areas, interrupted the accomplishment of normal developmental tasks. Psychological testing helped identify Victor's perceptions of both male and female caretakers and helped identify his intellectual strengths and weaknesses. His underlying needs for protection, safety, and security were stressed. Consultants, administrative, and child care staff worked together to meet these early unmet needs.

Basically, there was a three pronged approach to Victor's therapy. Initially, the reparenting experiences held center stage. Subsequently, he was involved in group therapy experiences with the sexual abuse being a focus of attention. In this setting he gained information, learned more about himself and learned a variety of skills which helped overcome the effects of his earlier life experiences. Finally, he was involved in individual therapy aimed at helping him resolve his strong underlying feelings and changing his self-image.

STEP ONE: As with other children, the initial focus of treatment was on helping Victor form beginning attachments within the living situation. Undoubtedly his early life experiences led him to believe that adults are not trustworthy and have had a negative impact on his feelings of self-worth. He has not learned appropriate expression of underlying feelings. Interpersonal relationships with both adults and peers were exploitive in nature. These areas were treated in the course of the re-parenting experiences provided within the milieu.

Once Victor had experienced safety, security, and a sense of positive accomplishments within the daily living situation, he was involved in a variety of group therapy situations. Because he had missed out on many of the gratifications and learning experiences usually afforded to younger children, he was included in the Thursday Group as well as being in one of the Values and Sex Education groups.

STEP TWO: In addition however, since sexually abused children seem to be particularly responsive to group therapy, with other sexually abused residents Victor was included in a specifc therapy issues group. This was led by a female therapist. It was a time limited group with a structured format and specific goals which included providing opportunities for: further disclosure, learning how the sexual abuse impacted on his overall development, understanding his underlying perceptions and feelings. In addition, further sex education was provided as gaps in Victor's knowledge were identified. Communication and peer interaction skills were underlying themes in all of the group sessions.

STEP THREE: Once Victor's trust level for staff was reasonably secure and he had gained some further skills in emotional management and communication, he was seen in individual therapy by a male therapist. The female group therapist took an active role in transferring the trust and information she had gained to the male therapist. This was done with Victor present. In the individual therapy hours Victor had an opportunity to explore his fears, ventilate his anger, and develop an increasing sense of competency in asserting himself in age appropriate ways. The therapist chose to use Attachment-Holding Therapy to facilitate attainment of these goals. The female group therapist also participated in some of these sessions.

Victor's individual therapist, as well as other consultative and administrative staff, with the input of milieu staff, was involved in long-term planning with respect to where Victor would be placed after discharge. His therapist was actively involved in the process of transferring the gains to the post-placement setting. 25

Guide for Parents

Although out-patient therapy has been insufficient for meeting the therapeutic needs of your young person, most parents of children entering residential treatment are concerned about how all of their child's therapeutic needs will be met in the residential facility. Questions to be answered include:

1. Is individual therapy provided as part of the overall treatment? Is group therapy provided? If so what type of groups are there? Who provides the individual and group therapy? What are the qualifications of the therapist?

2. How is individual and/or group therapy integrated with milieu therapy?

3. How are decisions made about readiness for individual therapy? How are decisions made about selection of the therapist?

4. What contacts and input will parents have with the child's therapist?

5. Will the child have one therapist and the family another or will the same therapist be involved with both?

Conclusion

In residential treatment there is an opportunity to utilize a wide range of therapeutic groupings and strategies. These range from the milieu as a whole, to smaller therapy groups with specific goals, to individual therapy sessions which may at times involve other staff or family members. A comprehensive treatment facility can be flexible in structuring a variety of therapeutic maneuvers to best meet the individual needs of each resident.

Notes and Elaborations

pg. 247 There is likely to be considerable confusion about the term "holding therapy." Although holding is involved in both, there are distinct differences between Attachment Holding therapy and Rage Reduction therapy which also has prominent proponents in the Evergreen area. Special thanks to Dr. John Allen of the University of British Columbia in Vancouver B.C., Canada, for helping us formulate and implement the concepts of Attachment-Holding therapy as used at Forest Heights and for helping in writing the following explanation of the therapy process.

We have found Attachment-Holding therapy to be an efficient cost-effective way of resolving core issues in therapy. The results indicate that this method accelerates internalization and resolution of therapeutic issues. As few as three sessions can lead to significant progress in: 1. reducing destructive and inappropriate behaviors; 2. strengthening attachments to staff members and family alike; 3. increasing the ability to verbalize thoughts and feelings.

The youngster is usually seen once a week for an average of two hours. The therapist, child, parent(s), and one or more staff members are present. All participating parties are informed about the process in advance. The holders sit on a couch and chairs facing one another, while the child lies on his back, on cushions, across the holder's laps. The therapist takes the child's head comfortably in his hands, turning the youngster's face so that eye contact is easily maintained. The parents, one next to and one across from the therapist, hold the child's hands while other adults each hold a foot and ankle.

The purpose of this position is to provide a safe and protected space in which the child can express overwhelming emotions while maintaining eye contact. When the child is lying down and safely held, powerful emotions, thoughts, blocked memories and secrets tend to be expressed more freely. The holders take their cues from the child—when the child relaxes they relax their hold. If the child struggles and rages, they increase hand pressure only to a point sufficient for the child to push against without feeling dominated.

Therapist and holders alike strive to maintain a strong therapeutic alliance with the child. There are three ground rules: 1. the child will not be hurt; 2. the child can do or say anything he wants (the adult holders are responsible for insuring that no one is physically hurt by the child); 3. the therapist decides when it is time to end the session. Even during periods of physical resistance, the focus is on the child's strength, courage, persistence, etc.

In the horizontal position the therapist verbally engages the child, focusing on his strengths, struggles, and core issues. The therapeutic goals are to help the child 1. receive emotional support and nurturance while experiencing a wide range of intense emotions; 2. resurface repressed material; 3. put his thoughts, feelings, and desires into words; and 4. experience an end state of calmness and relaxation with significant adults after the period of affective arousal.

Although all feelings are given equal attention over the course of several sessions, any one session may focus primarily on one emotion. For example a child such as Kenny may use anger as a shield to protect against experiencing what he considers the more painful emotions, such as sadness or fear of abandonment. In this situation the anger might be the focus of one therapy encounter and the sadness or fear the focus of a subsequent session. Through conversation with the holders, with whom the child lives, he receives concrete feedback as to how internal struggles are externalized in day to day behaviors. The session frequently ends with a focus on a here-and-now task that moves an issue toward resolution.

The therapeutic process is not adversive. While being mindful of developmental issues, the therapist follows the lead of the child as opposed to controlling his thoughts. The younster is an active particpant. With emotional suport from caring people he struggles with intrapsychic issues. In this way he attains a sense of accomplishment which in turn leads to increased self-esteem and more energy for continued growth and change in the milieu.

pg. 256 As we mentioned in the first chapter, a variety of techniques can be utilized in either re-education or insight oriented therapy. One therapist may have more experience and skill in utilizing behavior modification, another in using art therapy, another in facilitating experiential techniques, such as gestalt therapy.

pg. 257 The child care worker acts primarily in a parental role, placing expectations for the performance of daily routines and obeying limits and providing emotional nurturing. Child care workers are responsible for the group as a whole as well as each individual within it. The individual therapist, on the other hand, is not involved in the daily living routines or limit setting in general. While understanding the needs of the group as a whole, the therapist will primarily be an advocate for the individual child and his needs.

pg. 258 Fragile X syndrome is a pervasive developmental disorder that comes about secondary to a chromosomal abnormality. Males are more likely to be affected than females. Although those affected have many of the signs and symptoms of childhood autism, there are some differences.

pg. 266 We realize that our views about the most useful confidentiality boundaries are not necessarily shared by other mental health professionals; however, we have tried to explain why we believe as we do and what we do to implement our beliefs.

278   pg. 268 A Lifebook provides not only a chronology of the child's life but also addresses the youngster's emotions about these events. Pictures of the significant people in the child's life are frequently an important component. A complete description of life story books is provided by Ryan and Walker in *Making Life Story Books* published by the British Agencies for Adoption and Fostering in 1985. A less complete description is included in Vera Fahlberg's *Putting the Pieces Together: Helping Children When They Must Move* available from the National Resource Center for Special Needs Adoption.

C O N T E N T S

Discharge Planning and Follow-up

Kenny's Case   281
Discharge Planning and its Relationship to Philosophy   285
Criteria for Successful Discharge   286
      The Child's Involvement in Treatment and
         Discharge Planning   290
Premature Discharge   291
      Treatment Center Initiated Premature Discharges   292
      Parent Initiated Premature Discharges   293
Re-admission Policy   296
The Discharge Process   297
      Discharge as a Time of Grieving   297
      Focusing on the Future   298
      The Going Away Party   299
Preparing Family and Community for the Child's Return   300
Post Discharge Treatment   301
Guide for Parents   302
Conclusion   303
Notes and Elaborations   304

Primary Contributors Linda Clefisch and Vera Fahlberg

Discharge Planning and Follow-Up

The Summers came to Evergreen for several days in November and sat in on Ken's staffing. Early on in the fall he had had some problems keeping it together after school. By now he seemed to be using less energy to keep things going well at school. His reserves were sufficient to help him maintain his behavior after school as well. Scouts was going relatively well. He had gone through a period of not wanting to work on his badges and of wanting to give up scouting. With minimal supportive confrontation he had decided to keep with it at least until he left the Lodge.

The central question addressed at the November staffing was "When should discharge take place?" Ken had made many gains, but he continued to need considerable adult support to make use of the gains. Should he stay until the end of the school year and have more time to consolidate the gains? Or should he be discharged in January and consolidate the gains within his own family living situation? There were pros and cons to each course of action. John and Martha were ambivalent. They wanted Ken home but they didn't want to do anything to jeopardize the gains he had made.

A variety of alternatives was explored. It was finally decided that Ken would be discharged in January and that Linda would fly to his home once a month for one to two days. She would be available to work with Ken and his parents on behavioral issues at home and would also be available to work with his teachers. Although this kind of planning was rarely implemented with adolescents, there were many advantages to it with grade school children.

In spite of John and Martha's basic confidence in Dr. Jorgenson, they were concerned that he and Ken did not currently have an alliance. They were unwilling to cut themselves off from the Lodge personnel, who had become very close to them during the treatment process. Both John and Martha talked openly about their fears and worries about their abilities to cope with Ken on a day to day basis. They wanted assurance that Lodge staff would be available on a regular basis.

There was considerable discussion. Finally agreement was reached. The goal of early post-placement services would be to further consolidate the gains in treatment. It made sense to have Lodge personnel involved. The longer range goal was that as Linda went to their home on a monthly basis she would start meeting with the Summers and with Dr. Jorgenson together. Gradually the case would be transferred back to him.

Ken had some difficulties during his visit over Christmas vacation. When he returned he was acting out more at the Lodge. Some of the newer staff were questioning whether or not he was really ready for discharge. Glen reassured the family, Ken, and child care staff that this was a common pattern as discharge time approached.

Glen and Vee worked together on helping Ken express his own ambivalence about going home. He was excited and happy about his pending discharge. He was also scared—was it going to work out okay or would it all go back to being the way it had been before he came to the Lodge? He was sad about leaving staff members that he had learned to trust and love. He was sad about leaving friends at the Lodge, at public school, and at Scouts. The more he talked about his feelings, however, the stronger his desire to go home became.

From Christmas until the time of discharge Linda joined Ken and Vee in their weekly therapy hours. She needed to gain an intimate knowledge of Ken's current strengths and weaknesses. Empowerment by Ken's current therapist to continue the work at home was necessary. It was most easily accomplished by their having joint sessions.

The schedule for the first post-placement visit was dictated by the fact that through the years Lodge staff had noted that three weeks seemed to be long enough for the child and family to get down to the real issues posed by again living together on a twenty-four hour a day basis. Yet it was short enough that child and family were unlikely to already be firmly locked into non-helpful patterns of interacting.

Linda arrived in the late afternoon so that she was with the family for dinner and the evening. As they were eating she noted how changed the atmosphere was from the first time she had come. She commented to Ken about specific behavioral changes. She also commented to the parents about the changes she was seeing in them. Martha seemed more sure of herself. She was much less tentative and guarded when she made requests of Ken. Ken, obviously, did not always like her requests, but he demonstrated his frustration with pouting and stomping his feet as he did as she asked. These were certainly much more age-appropriate demonstrations of frustration than Ken had shown prior to placement.

The main at-home problem seemed to occur at bedtime. Ken was slow to get ready for bed and frequently got up right after he went to bed. For Ken, fears and worries had always been most prominent at bedtime. He was prone to feelings of loneliness at this time of day. Ken was able to recognize that at bedtime many of his old thoughts and feelings seemed to resurface. Both John and Martha became aware of the fact that because of his severe bedtime problems in the past, they tended to become more anxious as Ken's bedtime approached. Alternative ways for both Ken and his parents to handle their feelings were identified.

Both Ken and his parents brought up the fact that there continued to be problems with peers in the neighborhood. A pattern emerged. One of his friends would do something that irritated Ken. Ken would then threaten to tattle. A verbal battle would ensue and Ken would then act out in some way and the neighbor children would tattle on him. For years, Ken's position in the neighborhood had been that of the "naughty child"—the "acter outer"—for the others. In structured situations Ken was able to control his own behaviors and be more socially acceptable. In the unstructured neighborhood activities, peers were still able to hook him into doing the acting out. As Ken and Linda looked at the specifics of the interactions she observed, Ken became aware of the points in the interactions when he had options about his behaviors and together they explored a variety of alternative choices.

During her visit, it was also apparent to Linda that when Ken did choose to disengage from the group and to involve himself in some other activities, Martha would become anxious about his being left out of the group. This cycle of interactions was pointed out to the parents. Martha was reminded how this situation might tap into her own issues. It was important that she learn to identify which problems were hers and which were Ken's. Linda observed that all of the parents in the neighborhood subtly invited the children to tattle. She also observed that Martha's communications with her about John and Ken had a tattling quality about them. This was pointed out as something both parents needed to work on.

Happily, school was going quite well. Linda again met with Mr.Torres, the principal, and sat in on Ken's class for a while prior to recess. As she left she had an opportunity to observe Ken with classmates on the playground. Everyone reported that there had been no major incidents.

When Linda arrived four weeks later, things were no longer going so smoothly. Both John and Martha were wondering if it had been a poor decision to have Ken come home in January rather than at the end of the school year. Again, Linda had come in the afternoon. The focus of the family session that evening was on Ken's escalating behaviors. When disciplined by being sat, he was throwing things. He was sometimes avoiding routine requests, such as getting ready for bed, and he was hassling about most everything. Ken did not deny these behaviors when his parents brought them up.

Linda: Do you agree, Ken, that these are problem areas now?

Ken: Yeah.

Linda: You know, Ken, I saw you be able to mind your mom when she asked you to help bring in the groceries. You weren't hassling then. After dinner when you were asked to help clear the table and you started hassling, you were able to stop as soon as I commented on what you were doing. It didn't look like it was very difficult for you to turn it around, was it?

Ken: No.

Linda: I wonder why it is that when I am here you are able to do things without a big hassle, but when I'm not here, it is more difficult for you to switch gears. Do you have any ideas?

In this way, the problem was identified as Ken's. While support for positive behavior was given, at the same time the assumption was made that Ken needed help in some way to change his behavior. Likewise, it was supposed that he was capable of accepting that help and of changing.

Later in the evening after Ken had gone to bed, Linda talked with both John and Martha. She had brought along some of the pictures they had drawn during the first family sessions fourteen months previously. The parents and Linda reviewed the pictures and the notes Russ and Vee had made about the family dynamics. John and Martha were encouraged to identify which areas they saw as problems at present. Which things did they think had changed? What things were they unwilling to change? Martha brought up the fact that she thought that she was again starting to use Ken and any problems he had as a bridge for talking directly with John. It was decided that this problem area would be mentioned when they all met the following day with Dr. Jorgenson to begin the transfer of the case back to him for ongoing treatment.

The following morning, Linda again spent some time in the classroom. During the morning recess she and Ken had a conference with the teacher who brought up two problem areas. Ken was talking in class when he should be listening. Frequently his voice was too loud or his behavioral reactions were too intense for the situation. Again, Ken agreed that these were problem areas. Non-verbal cues were agreed upon so that the teacher could help him become more aware of when the behaviors were occurring. She agreed to mark a chart for him so that he would have feedback on how he was doing on interrupting himself in these behaviors after she had given him the cue.

In the afternoon, John, Martha, Ken, and Linda all met with Dr. Jorgenson at his office. He had received copies of the treatment plans while Ken was in placement at the Lodge and had, with the family's permission, also received the summaries of the family therapy sessions. In addition a copy of the videotape of the final family therapy session with Linda and Vee when Ken had been discharged was shared with him.

Linda brought up the current areas of concern that she was working on with Ken and with John and Martha. Because of her strong relationship with all three family members, she had no hesitation about doing this with them in the room. All three family members committed to working with Dr. Jorgenson around these areas. It was agreed that he would see them on a weekly basis for a while. Linda would return for one last visit in another month's time and would meet with all of them for a joint session then.

Discharge Planning and Its
Relationship to Philosophy

The goal of all efforts in residential treatment is preparation of the child and his family for life outside the treatment facility. Discharge planning is the culmination of weeks, months, sometimes years of effort on the part of the child, family and staff. The optimum in discharge planning occurs when parents, child and center staff all agree that the goals of placement have been achieved and there is no longer a need for the child to remain in residential treatment.

In this final phase of the treatment process at Forest Heights we once again look to the philosophy to guide our efforts. Three features of our philosophy are particularly important in terms of discharge planning. Our emphasis on relationships and our belief that the gains of those relationships are transferable dictate much of our behavior at the time of discharge. The alliance with the parents and child enhances joint decision making as we approach discharge planning. Finally, our commitment to creativity and flexibility in meeting the needs of our residents allows us wide latitude in individualizing post discharge services to best meet the needs of a particular child and his family.

Discharge planning starts during the pre-admission contacts and continues throughout the treatment process. Just as joint decision making is important when a child enters our facility, we believe in utilizing everyone's input in determining when the child is ready to leave the Lodge and where he will go at that time. Parents, having the ultimate legal and emotional responsibility for their child, make the final decisions. Simultaneously, however, treatment center staff are making their assessments and recommendations.[N]

Criteria for Successful Discharge

How will we know when the child is ready for discharge? How will we know when the family is ready for the child's discharge? Will the two happen at the same time? Certainly, our goal is always to facilitate this as the long term prognosis is much better when child, family, and treatment facility agree on discharge readiness. However, in general, it is more difficult to get this agreement than it was to get agreement on the need for residential treatment.

During the development of the initial treatment plan, discharge criteria are identified. These are reviewed at each subsequent staffing. Sometimes during the course of treatment they need to be modified or totally revamped as additional knowledge about the child and family comes to light.

In determining timing of discharge the question is not, "Has the child reached his full potential?" Rather, the critical issue is, "Has he made sufficient progress to assume that he can continue to improve outside the treatment facility?"

Treatment goal setting is a dynamic, not static, process. At the outset of the treatment process, an attempt is made to formulate realistic long term goals. These become the focus of treatment. In initial contacts with the family, we attempt to define what has to change for the child and family to be successful in living together. As problem areas are outlined, the initial goals of therapy are formulated. History taking sessions help parents identify the specific behaviors or concerns that led them to seek out-of-home placement. The child's strengths and weaknesses as well as their own are examined. During the course of the child's treatment, the family works to develop strengths in meeting the challenges of parenting their particular child. Child and family concentrate on interacting in a more positive way, becoming aware of positive changes in their interactional patterns.

For treatment and post-discharge planning to be successful, the agendas of all family members have to be identified, clarified, and acknowledged. This is an ongoing process throughout treatment. Prior to admission, the home visitor explores with various family members their current thinking about long term planning for the child. Most times the parents' goal is to have their son be able to return home. Sometimes it is learned that the parents' goal is to have the child be able to go to a boarding school after treatment. Occasionally a sibling expresses the desire that their brother never return home.

During this pre-placement visit, we try to identify the child's agenda for treatment as well. Children are prone to magical as well as realistic thinking. Both types of thought processes have considerable influence over the child's behaviors. Sometimes a child is looking forward to returning to the home community to seek revenge. Other times he exhibits a healthier "I'll show them I can make it" attitude. Sometimes the child has decided that under no circumstances will he return to his home school. No matter what the subsequent discharge plan is, at some point these early thoughts and wishes of all family members must be addressed.

Hidden agendas have their maximum impact at the time of discharge. If parents have decided that the goal of treatment is that their son be able to attend a private school, and the boy has decided that for him the only worthwhile goal of treatment is to return home, no post-placement plan has a chance of success without some form of problem solving and conflict resolution taking place between parent and child prior to the discharge.

Throughout the child's residence at the Lodge, we work toward developing and strengthening attachments, helping the boy gain control over his own behaviors, and increasing skill levels in terms of personal, academic, and social growth. Ideally, the child consolidates and internalizes the gains made during the treatment process prior to discharge. Now it is time to switch from acquisition of new skills to transferring these bonds and the fruits of the re-education process. If he, and we, have been successful in our endeavors, the resident will be able to use the gains he has made during treatment as the foundation for further growth and adaptation post-discharge. This has been the emphasis during the final stage of therapy.

At Forest Heights discharge planning usually centers around achievement in these three distinct areas: 1) adult-child relationships 2) behavioral control and 3) skill acquisition. It is important to look in some detail at these three areas and see how they influence the planning for discharge and post-placement services.

1. **Adult-child relationships:** We have repeatedly stressed how important we believe relationships are in terms of change. The essence of our treatment philosophy is the development of such attachments. One of the measures of a child's readiness for discharge rests on his not only having developed a strong attachment to a staff member, but on that relationship being strong enough to influence the boy's behaviors in other relationships. He is now capable of transferring the attachment to other adults. Especially for adolescents, the power of relationships must be maximized, as essentially all adult power is dependent upon the strength of the adult-adolescent

relationship. Once a youth has a strong relationship with an adult, each member of the relationship can use that power to influence the other.

When a boy is admitted to Forest Heights we ask the parents to use the strength of their relationships to empower Lodge staff. In preparation for discharge we ask Lodge staff to re-empower the parents. Usually this is an ongoing process during parent visits. However, near the time of discharge it is always important that child care staff and therapist actively transfer the attachment to those who will take on their roles subsequently. When the child was admitted we accepted that the parents knew their child better than anyone else. Now we ask them to accept that, at this moment in time, we know their child better than anyone. It is their turn to learn from the expertise we have gained while being part of their son's day-to-day life and, more importantly, part of the change process.

2. **The development of internalized behavioral controls:** Most boys come to us unable to control their own behaviors. As was noted in the discussion of the three phases of treatment in the Milieu chapter, a child needs to learn to trust first that others will take care of him, secondly that others can and will control him, and finally that he can trust himself in terms of self-control.

Until a boy has learned some measure of behavioral self-control, it will be difficult for him to do well in a home and school setting. Although it is usual for those environments to provide external controls for a younger child, it is much less common for them to be in a position of providing ongoing external behavioral controls for the adolescent. This is a major factor in readiness for discharge.

The child should have minimized constant control battles with adults and have experienced how it feels to be in control of his own impulses and life in a positive way. It is certainly preferable if he can be in control of completing his work in school and behaviorally maintaining himself with minimal adult intervention. However, this is not always achieved prior to discharge.

The level of care recommended in the follow-up plan is dependent in large measure upon the degree to which self-control has been achieved. How much, if any, adult intervention is necessary for the resident to maintain a reasonable level of behavioral control? A child who continues to need adults to physically restrain him when he's angry would obviously need a more structured daily living setting than the child who has learned to express his feelings in a more appropriate manner. Other youth who do not need physical control for maintenance of self control but who are still dependent upon knowing that an adult is readily available will continue to need more adult supervision than others of their age. Those who need only adult verbal reminders will need less adult supervision.

3. **Skill acquisition:** The area of skill acquisition is less a determinant of the child's readiness for discharge than the other two factors. It is, however, the primary determinant of the nature of post-placement supportive services.

At the time of admission, we acknowledge that a major aspect of treatment must be aimed at helping families reorganize in a way that encourages the child to play a healthier, more appropriate role in the family system. The final test of success in this area will occur when the child returns home. When they are living together on a day-to-day basis, can both youth and parents maintain the healthier roles they have learned while apart? In general, our boys and their families will need continued encouragement and external help to maintain newly acquired skills and continue to grow and change in skill areas.

We find that many parents of disturbed children need considerable support themselves when the child returns home. Because they have not shared, on a daily basis, months and even years of their child's life, their expectations for what is normal for someone their son's age may be unrealistic. They may need encouragement as they practice the newly learned modes of conflict resolution. They will quite likely need continued counselling in ways to supportively confront problem behaviors so that they avoid falling back into old patterns of negative interactions.

After discharge our residents may need special help in school in terms of skill acquisition in the academic areas, necessitating placement in special educational programs. They may need supportive aid in terms of expanding and perfecting socialization skills. This may include plans for being involved in structured activities with peers. It may mean being involved in some form of group or individual therapy which provides a forum for the youth to examine alternative modes of interacting and problem solving with peers. They and their families may need ongoing counseling in terms of understanding reasonable expectations of each other and in cooperative problem solving.

In assessing the areas of skill development, it is necessary to not only examine the child's strengths and weaknesses in the seven skill areas, but also the parental strengths and weaknesses, particularly in the areas of emotional management, relationship skills, and conflict resolution. It is the combination of child and adult strengths and weaknesses in these areas that will determine the outcome of their living together. We must balance this combination of strengths and weaknesses against the resources available within the home community. The availability of special school programs, recreation programs, structured activities, support groups, and therapy must all be determined. Some communities have more alternatives than others. The extended home visit prior to admission provides an opportunity for a beginning assessment of the variety of community services available for post placement support. As we approach discharge planning, these services must be explored in more depth. This will help staff, family, and child decide whether placement at home or in an alternative setting is the best option.

The Child's Involvement in Treatment and Discharge Planning

At Forest Heights the child is part of the placement decision process. During the extended home visit he has input in defining the long range goals of treatment. He makes a commitment to change at the time of admission. Throughout his stay he is included in ongoing discussions about what he has already accomplished and what goals remain in preparing for discharge.

During each child's staffings, strengths are discussed as well as the areas on which the child needs to continue to work. Staff must evaluate the child's ability to change as well as the child's motivation to have things different in his life. Although we are responsible for creating the environment that facilitates change, we must realize that no matter how much the parents or we, as professionals, want things to be different for a child, it is his responsibility and commitment to change that determine whether or not he makes use of the opportunities provided him. We need to continually evaluate the child's choices and how they relate to our goals.

Indeed, someone goes through the treatment plans with both the child and his family, usually separately. Occasionally, early in the course of treatment it is decided that reviewing the treatment plans with the child will not be helpful until a stronger alliance has been achieved. A listing of current goals and objectives is in the front of each child's log. Staff refer to these and discuss them with the children during the middle and final phases of treatment.

In addition, the child's therapist periodically discusses the treatment plans with the child. The treatment plan may be discussed immediately prior to a staffing to learn how the child himself views his progress toward attaining the various goals and objectives. He is frequently consulted about his perception of the need for additional objectives. In this way, the therapist tries to clarify what the child's agenda might be.

Following a child's staffing the therapist again is quite likely to discuss comments made by various staff members, letting the resident know how adults see his progress and what the recommendations are for future interventions or additional objectives. In reviewing treatment plans the discussion naturally leads to discharge planning. Where does the child sees himself as going, and when?

Our boys frequently ask staff members, their therapist, and their family when each thinks he will be ready for discharge. Staff members tend to focus with the boys on the gains he has made and the areas he still needs to work on. Therapists may do the same, but, usually in addition, try to get the young person to identify how he will know when he is ready to leave and when he thinks that will occur. Parents take varying approaches in responding to their child's questions about discharge. Their responses frequently reflect their own thinking about how the decision is made. This is useful information for the clinicians to have.

The older boys, as they are well into the middle phase of treatment or in the final phase, may be asked if they want to participate in their own staffings. In general, this is an indication that staff have seen many gains and that we are expecting the youth to take more responsibility for his own actions and for the treatment planning process. If the youth participates, the staffing is videotaped and the therapist reviews the tape with the resident. We do this because we have found that our boys tend to hear only part of what is said during the staffings. We want to make certain that they are clear about how others perceive their progress.

In all of these ways, we attempt to make the resident an active part of the treatment planning and implementation process. We expect him to have an ongoing sense of how he is doing and what he continues to need to accomplish prior to discharge. We can frequently help him assess his rate of change as well and set realistic goals around discharge timing. Surprises, as they relate to discharges, are not helpful to child, family, or staff.

Premature Discharge

Although ideally discharge takes place after the treatment goals and objectives have all been met, this is not the reality in all cases. There are times when discharge takes place prematurely. This may happen for a variety of reasons. Such discharges may be initiated by either treatment center staff or by parents.

Planned, but premature, discharge may occur with children who for various reasons are not responding to our treatment program. Assessments before admission will eliminate some of the children who are not likely to be helped by our treatment program. Occasionally, however, it is only after admission that a resident demonstrates certain behaviors or problems that would have precluded admission had we known of them before, or that we become aware that our treatment is not going to be successful.

For example, if a youngster becomes a chronic runner, we know we have difficulty containing him long enough to treat him. Or, it might become apparent that the child has a character disorder. In those cases, it is our responsibility to help the family find a resource that follows a treatment model that better addresses his needs.

Infrequently a boy admitted with problem behaviors subsequently develops symptoms indicative of adolescent onset psychosis which can better be treated initially in a hospital setting. On the other hand, we are not able to provide as well for the psychological and social needs of those whose pathology reflects primary adolescent developmental conflicts as opposed to those teens who have early unmet developmental needs.

Occasionally a child who has been in residence for some time no longer responds to our treatment process. In such cases, if we cannot modify our program to better meet his needs, we discuss the lack of progress with the parents and offer our services in helping them find an alternative treatment program that better meets their son's needs.

There are children who after a certain period of time "learn the system" of an institution. They learn ways of responding to adults and acquire the ability to either avoid or engage exclusively in patterns of interaction which do not promote growth and change. Again, we try to be flexible and modify our treatment program to interrupt the child's resistance to change, but sometimes we are unsuccessful in this. In spite of not achieving the treatment goals, we have facilitated all of the change that the child is capable of at that time within our program. In such situations a change of environment may be absolutely necessary for any continued growth to occur.

A difficult situation occurs when a child makes attachments and learns to trust others' control but does not, or cannot, make the shift to trust of self. We see this in a small but significant number of children, who have previously been diagnosed as "unattached" children. We continue to struggle with ways to identify such children at an earlier stage of treatment and ways to successfully implement continued growth and change in these children. At present, however, we sometimes have to acknowledge our seeming inability to help that young person bridge the gap from trust of control by others to trust of self. Usually these children, for whatever reason, fear growing up. Dependency upon others seems preferable. When we are unsuccessful with such a child we try to focus with him on recognizing behaviors indicative of dependency vs. independency struggle, making certain that he is aware of those behaviors indicative of continued growth. He may, at some point in the future, be able to make better use of skills he has been exposed to but not incorporated while in our program.

In all of these instances of center initiated premature discharge planning, we have recognized that our facility is not able to fully meet the child's therapeutic needs and it is our responsibility to help the family locate more appropriate services and then to work with child, family, and the new service providers to facilitate the transfer process.

Parent Initiated Premature Discharges

There are also situations that may lead to parents withdrawing their son from our program before the treatment goals have been achieved.

Sometimes soon after admission it becomes obvious that the parents are not ready for the child to be away from home. The parents are unable to empower staff to care for the child. In expressing their feelings about the separation process it is not uncommon for the newly admitted child in his initial telephone, letter or personal contacts with parents to work on the latters' feelings of guilt. Children sometimes say, "You've got to get me out of this place. I didn't know what it would really be like." For placement to be successful the parents have to be able to again reaffirm the decision for placement. Sometimes, particularly if parents are wavering in the decision making process, it is necessary to have them come, meet with staff, and make a decision about the child remaining or leaving. They then meet with the child, either to facilitate premature discharge or to reinforce the previous decision and to once again verbalize support of the Lodge program. If the latter is done, the child is usually able to settle in and start work on the issues at hand. Some youth cannot do this until they first check out their own power with the parents, and the strength of the parents' convictions about where they need to be.

Occasionally the parents' own ambivalence about the separation and placement is so strong that they cannot follow through with the decision for placement. In such cases, it is important that Lodge staff acknowledge both the child's need for treatment and the fact that treatment at our facility cannot be successful without the parents' commitment and support. We may try to help the parents explore alternatives within their home community that would allow the child to remain living at home, while utilizing supportive resources and in-home interventions. The reality is that usually these alternatives have been previously exhausted. However, in re-exploring options, the parent once again has to take responsibility for making a decision about discharge or supporting the child's out- of-home placement. If the parent decides on premature discharge, we will express our concern about the decision but also our hope that it can work out well for both child and family.

> **Example:** Ned's parents decided four weeks after his placement that they had made a "mistake" in placing him at the Lodge. Ned was writing them daily letters telling them of his sadness and expressing his strong desire to leave. He made promises to "be good and do well at school if only I can come home." He commented frequently, "I've learned my lesson."
>
> The parents have had difficulty accepting the severity of Ned's problems and have always believed that he could "shape up" if only he chose to do so. Lodge staff see Ned as in need of residential treatment. In spite of exercising considerable control over his parents' emotions and behaviors, he exhibits little control over his own behaviors and seems to have little recognition of his underlying feelings of fear and anxiety.
>
> The parents have decided to take Ned home, place him in a private school, get a tutor, and provide out-patient therapy. Lodge staff's message to Ned will be: "We know that you really miss your family. We recognize that you think you made a mistake in coming here. You think that you can control your behaviors once you leave. We too wish that you could do that. Understanding your feelings and changing behaviors has always been difficult for you and we think that you still need help in this area. I guess that we have a difference of opinion about this. We sure hope that you are right and that things can work out well for you at home. That was our goal when you came here—to help make that possible—and it is still our goal and yours."

In this way we acknowledge that the real goal of placement was successful discharge, rather than placment per se. We give the child permission to do well at home and, indeed, acknowledge that it is acceptable for him and his family to "prove us wrong."

Sometimes, later in the treatment process the parents, aware of the child's current strengths and weaknesses, decide that both the child and the entire family unit have changed enough to be able to integrate the child back into the home. Staff at the Lodge might not believe that the child has completed treatment, but the family has seen enough change to feel capable of again parenting the child in the home environment. The parents alone may have made this decision or it may be that both parents and child will decide that enough gains have been made that the child should be able to live at home successfully. Again, if staff do not agree, we will certainly point out to parents, and possibly to their son as well, what our areas of concern are. If parents decide to proceed with discharge planning, we acknowledge our differences in perception of readiness while recognizing that everyone concerned desires the same goal—successful reintegration into the family. We will do everything possible in terms of helping the family with post-placement planning that is supportive of this shared goal.

Our discharge plans in such cases are dual in nature. First we outline our primary recommendation for continued in-patient treatment, identifying why we are advocating this by identifying what we see as still needing to be accomplished. Secondly we outline the recommendations for post-placment support given the fact that the family has decided against our primary recommendation. Again, we recognize that unless both family and child believe that something positive is to be gained from continued placement, and that the positives can and will outweigh the negatives, it is unlikely that we can be successful in continuing to facilitate growth and change. Although we may believe that child and family are wrong, we do not want to become invested in proving them wrong. In fact, we would much prefer that they prove us wrong by being successful post discharge.

Sometimes funding agencies make independent decisions about discharge timing. When either insurance companies or public agencies are funding a placement, we want parents to understand that our contract for treatment is with them as the legal parent, not with any agency or company. We will work to provide the third party payor with information about the child's progress as required, but we must always keep clear that our recommendations and those of funding sources will not necessarily coincide. Sometimes such funding sources decide to terminate payments prior to achievement of the treatment goals. In that case, again, we want to make certain that the parents understand what our recommendations are with regards to ongoing treatment.

We also recognize that it is the parents who will have to make the determining decision when the insurance company and ourselves do not agree about length of treatment. Again, our post-discharge treatment plans may have to acknowledge the difference of opinion by stating what our primary recommendations are—i.e. continued placement, identifying specific reasons, and goals to be accomplished—and, given the reality of premature discharge, our alternative recommendations for post-discharge planning and treatment. Although both child and family may be aware that continued in-patient treatment is desirable, we can help them focus on the positive changes that they have made and help them utilize community resources in the most effective way possible.

With every premature discharge, whether initiated by ourselves or the parents, we can acknowledge that we all have the same long term goal—that the child can be successful in his post-placement adjustment. At the same time, we acknowledge that different people may have differing opinions about what is necessary to insure that this comes about.

Re-Admission Policy

Our basic policy is one of no re-admission after discharge. In general, we adopt the position that unless we state that a child is ready to leave and will not come back to the Lodge to live, we are not empowering the child and family to be successful. We may thereby undercut the commitment to having it work at home. If the child's adjustment at home is inadequate he can usually move to a less restrictive environment than residential care. Resources may include private school, group homes, foster care.

However, on occasion we have made exceptions to our no re-admission rule. In the past these situations have included:

1. Children with certain organic problems such as autism or Fragile X syndrome have returned for short periods of time to recharge and revitalize. These are children who are never "cured". Because of their organicity, as they reach new developmental levels they may demonstrate increased problems. They need help integrating new levels of development, regaining behavioral control, and indeed may need added help in attaining new skills to cope with their changing situation. Both child and family may profit from periodic recharging. The child's brief return offers respite for the parents while the child is working on integrating the new developmental steps.

2. When the family initiated discharge with magical thinking that if their family were back together it would be okay. All efforts to dissuade their thinking have failed. Discharging the child to his family may act as a heavy jolt of reality that there is more work to be done. At that point the family is ready to return and begin dealing with what needs to be done for a successful return home. In these cases a short discharge allows family and Lodge to re-clarify common objectives.

Trial discharges are carefully set up so that the child's return to residence is not seen as a failure but as a step toward success. The message is that the discharge provided an opportunity to learn more about current parent-child relationships and current behavioral problems in a less restrictive environment. We are now all clearer about areas for further work. We support the feelings of grief over the lost hope that things could have worked out differently, while continuing to confront the reality of the present concerns.

The Discharge Process

Discharge as a Time of Grieving

Just as children have many feelings when they enter residential treatment, they also experience a wide variety of emotions near the time of discharge. Preparation for discharge can be viewed as a modified form of grief work with the successive stages of denial, regression, bargaining, anger, and sadness, followed by reminiscing and recapitulation and culminating in constructive flight. The child is being asked to separate from staff and children whom he has learned to love and trust. He is excited and happy about leaving. He may also feel sad, angry, frightened, and anxious. It is important to give recognition and support for all the ambivalent feelings.

Beginning when the child is told he is leaving and continuing until the day he leaves, staff and child center on the separation issues. The child is likely to be flooded with many feelings and memories. For children who have had repeated losses and separations, old feelings will resurface. Helping the child to work through his feelings about the current separation can strengthen his ability to master past and future separations.

Regression is common during the pre-discharge period. Some children use their behavior rather than their mouth to express their scared, sad, or angry emotions. Staff are facilitators during these times. They help the child more appropriately express his feelings.

Many individuals have difficulty coping with sad feelings. They are more comfortable focusing on feelings of anger. At the time of separations they are likely to behave in a manner that encourages anger in others. They avoid the sadness by emotionally distancing attachment objects through the use of anger. They can then feel relief rather than the pain of loss at the time of separation. This, however, prevents a psychologically healthy resolution of the grieving process as a whole. It is the responsibility of the staff to insure that the child receives the support necessary to confront the difficult feelings that are part of the grieving process and to faciltate the resolution of this grief work.

The family needs to be prepared for the child's regression when he is told he is leaving. Parents are helped to comprehend the child's need for working through his feelings around the separation from staff and peers. Special efforts are made to help parents understand the child's anger and sadness. They need to appreciate that the child's reaction is normal rather than perceive the reaction as a sign of continuing or re-emerging behavioral problems.

Staff members also experience varied feelings about each child's discharge. Those who have the strongest relationships with the child will experience a sense of loss. Open sharing of their feelings gives the child permission to express his. At the same time modelling appropriate expression of the grief reaction is provided.

Children may also need help talking to their peers about their leaving. Some isolate themselves or try to push peers away. For many it is much easier to talk about anger toward another child than sadness about not being able to spend time together in the future. Again, acknowledgement of the full range of emotions is necessary for resolution in grief work.

Focusing on the Future

There is a need for honesty in assessing changes and areas that need continued growth. Integrating back into a family, school, and community is a difficult task. This is acknowledged along with expressions of confidence that both child and family are ready to do this work.

"You have learned to mind adults, get your school work done, and play with other kids. You and your father still have to work on getting along better. Both of you will have to make a commitment to having your relationship be closer." Statements such as this identify both the positive changes and the areas of need for continued work and growth. They identify the ongoing process as belonging to all family members, not just the youth.

When the child entered residential treatment, the parents disenfranchised their power and transferred that power to the staff to treat and care for their child. At the time of discharge we are returning the power, including the power to maintain the positive changes made, back to the parents. During visits the boy and his family have had opportunities to test different ways of relating. Ideally, by the time a child is ready to leave the Lodge visits are on a frequent basis. Parents will be trying to utilize and integrate the skills they have attained during their family work while their son was in residence. The family is working to reintegrate the child into the family system in a new, healthier role.

In some cases it is helpful for one or both parents to be at the Lodge following the child through his daily routine for a couple of days prior to discharge. This is particularly true for the younger child and for the child with organic dysfunction. In both of these instances non-verbal transfer of behavioral gains is helpful. The parents gain a better idea of staff expectations and the child's performance. The child is given permission to do as well for parents as for staff. The first day, staff usually structure the time. They take charge of insuring that the child is doing what he needs to do. They initiate activities with the parent observing and doing some interacting. The remaining time is focused on the parent setting limits and expectations, with staff observing and reinforcing parental expectations. Parents have opportunities to check out various situations and alternatives. The child sees people he cares about working together.[N]

Transferring attachment is an important component of preparing child and family for discharge. The staff members to whom the child is emotionally closest must actively give the youngster permission to separate from them and seek the same level of emotional closeness with family members. The measure of success for treatment center staff is not exclusivity of their relationships, but rather the transferability of the power of these relationships. The greatest gift that staff have to give the discharged youth is permission to go and do well, to become equally close to others, and to continue to grow and change.

The Going Away Party

The going away party is an important ritual signifying the end of our in-patient treatment process. The party takes place at a mealtime. Occasionally, but not usually, it is a combined party for two boys who are leaving at the same time. Sometimes a child's closest emotional connections are to members of one shift, as opposed to both. If this is the case, we try to have the party take place when his primary attachment objects can be present.

During the celebration there is a sequential focusing on the past, the present, and the future. The party provides an opportunity for shared reminiscing. It is a time for recapitulation about what life was like for the child and his family prior to his coming to the Lodge, followed by identifying the many changes that both have made. Adult staff and other boys both make comments. Finally, there is time for focusing on hopes for the future and wishing the resident success in his family and school setting. Shared laughter and shared tears are common. Everyone present, adults and other boys alike, makes a personal comment to the departing child. The boy who is leaving is encouraged to give personal messages to anyone whom he selects. This is a time when he is likely to identify how various staff members or peers impacted most on his change process. Although these comments may be unexpected ones, they always yield added insight into the boy's perception of his life and of the changes he has made while at the Lodge.

Preparing Family and Community for the Child's Return

No matter how or when the decision is made to discharge a child, it is anxiety provoking for the parents as well as for the child. There is always a fine balance to be achieved in preparing the community, schools, and family for the child's return. Sharing too little information is harmful. Adults need to know what to anticipate realistically. However, there is likewise a risk in too much preparation. It implies that there are magical solutions to ongoing problems and that only Lodge staff have the answers. In a way this diminishes the power of the adults who will now be part of the child's life. If adults become fearful about their ability to cope with the child's acting out, that fear is transmitted to the boy and he must behaviorally check to see if the adults can indeed provide adequate care and supervision.

Parents and son alike will have to test the changes. Parents will need to check out their son's level of control over his own behaviors. The boy will need to check out parental expectations and boundaries, seeing if they have changed as he has changed. Jointly they determine if things are going to revert to old patterns of interacting or if the changes made will be maintained in the family setting.

If a child's discharge has long been anticipated, the parents have been part of the decision making process and have had time to explore various possibilities in their home area given the child's needs. When the discharge is premature, the same things need to occur but within a shorter time frame.

Discharge planning is geared toward meshing the child's needs and the family and community resources. The extended home visit offered an opportunity for a member of the Lodge staff to identify and assess supportive services. The home visitor established communication lines with referral sources, previous therapists, school personnel, and others in the child's home community who may play a part in post-placement services. However, it is the family's responsibility, with clinical staff help, to make the final determination of a suitable school and support system. The parents' role is to advocate for their child in terms of accessing appropriate services. Again, they may ask for staff help and support in doing this, but they are resuming day to day rsponsibility for their son. This is an important part of their re-empowerment.

When the child is returning to a school that he previously attended, school personnel may need help perceiving the child in a new light. Simultaneously, the child's fears about returning to his previous school are addressed and alleviated. The student needs to be reintegrated with his current behaviors rather than focusing on past issues. It may be necessary to have teachers from the boy's home school come to the Lodge and observe him in his current classroom so that they can see the changes that he has made. Transference of expectations can be facilitated at that time. Teachers at the Lodge actively give the boy permission to perform as well in his home school as he has at the on grounds school. The teachers from the home school observe what works best in terms of supportive confrontation with this particular student. Staff can prepare school personnel for the areas where the child is likely to continue to need help.

There is value in having the child present for some of the school meetings as well as during communications with parents or the therapist who will be seeing the child after discharge. This creates an atmosphere of open communication. It alleviates the child's fears about what others will be told. It provides opportunities for actively transferring positive behavioral changes and attachments. It enhances the possibility of getting the youth to make a positive commitment for continued change and growth in the post placement setting. Child and staff alike have opportunities to learn about the expectations of the new environment.

Post-Discharge Treatment

The child's primary therapist at the Lodge will identify areas for ongoing treatment post-discharge. Usually the family has been involved in family therapy either in their home community or at the Lodge while their child has been in residence. Post-placement treatment may occur in our out-patient clinic or elsewhere. Some families have continued with the therapist who was seeing the child prior to admission. Others have sought help for their individual problems from a different source. They may select any of these individuals to do the follow up therapy.

Post-discharge problems are common and are to be expected. The family has reorganized itself in the child's absence. The reintegration process is difficult work for all. Parents and youth alike may panic when situations resemble the way things were prior to admission. They may perceive normal-for-age behaviors as a sign of severe underlying problems. Some parents and children expect that post discharge everything will be perfect. Clearly this is not reality in family life. This belief itself fosters stress.

Sometimes the amount of structure the child requires is less than residential treatment but more than family thinks it can provide. Many families expect adolescents in particular to be able to manage for long periods of time without adult supervision. This frequently is not realistic for youth who have had problems severe enough to necessitate residential treatment. Families may need ongoing help in clarifying the levels of supervision necessary for their child.

At times of stress people are likely to regress to old patterns of interacting. Sometimes, once the child is home there is a retriggering of old family dynamics. Although both parents and child will have acquired new interpersonal skills, at times of stress it is sometimes difficult to utilize recent learning without the support and encouragement of a therapist. Rather than occurring in the immediate post-placement period, times of regression may be associated with subsequent developmental stages. An example would be the child who readjusted well in grade school after discharge but who, a couple of years later, with the move to middle school, experiences a re-emerging of old behavioral symptoms.

No matter where the family lives and no matter who provides the post-discharge therapy, there is a need to acknowledge that the Lodge relationship with both child and family was important. We encourage ongoing contact throughout the years. We want families to feel free to continue to view us as a resource. Parents call to talk about incidents and how they handled the situations. Support and talking with someone who knows them well and who has confronted similar problems with their son can clear up areas of confusion or reinforce positive changes. Parents or children may call to get encouragement or to share successes. We want our boys and their families to share with us either by telephone calls, letters, or subsequent visits information about milestones such as graduation, marriages, the birth of children. Many of our boys continue contact for years. They bring their fiancees, wives, children to visit the Lodge, sharing this aspect of their past with these important family members and sharing their present with us.

Guide for Parents

As you and your child approach his discharge it is likely to be a time of mixed emotions. Hopefulness is likely to be combined with anxiety about what the future will bring. At this time you will want to know more about what support the treatment facility will provide for you both now and in the future. The following questions are meant to help you in determining this.

1. What will be the nature of your family's input into discharge planning, including the discharge criteria?

2. How does the center work toward transferring the gains made in residence to the post-placement setting?

3. How much help and support is provided in identifying and accessing post-placement services within the home community?

4. If you live close by, does the center staff provide post-discharge therapy?

5. Once your child is discharged will staff continue to be available to help you in planning or will contact essentially be terminated?

Conclusion

Successful discharge planning and post placement follow-up represent the overall goal of placement. If this final step is not achieved, all of the efforts made during the pre-placement period, in the milieu, in the school program, while working with the family, while involving the child in individual and group therapy, are devoid of meaning. From the time a child is accepted into a residential program until the day he leaves, all efforts basically are aimed toward the goal of successful discharge. While in treatment the child changes and grows toward health. It is important that he take the fruits of his labor with him when he leaves and to continue to utilize them.

As one of our boys said years after treatment, "You can leave the Lodge, but the Lodge never leaves you." We hope this is true. It typifies the essence of residential treatment.

Ken was discharged from Forest Heights Lodge seven years ago. He recently completed eleventh grade. There have been some ups and downs in his and the parents' adjustment. The family was involved with Dr. Jorgenson on a regular basis for about six months after the case was transferred back to him. During part of that time, he was seeing the parents separately around some marital issues. Then contacts ceased for a while with the understanding that they could be reinstated at any time for another bout of short term therapy.

This became necessary when Ken entered junior high. The combination of less structure at school and the normal adolescent tasks of further psychological separation from the family with its concomitant control issues had led to resurfacing of many of the old problems. However, both Ken and his parents were able to make good use of therapy to help sort out which were normal adolescent issues and which were indeed problem areas.

304   Again last year Ken asked to be involved in therapy with Dr. Jorgenson, this time on an individual basis as he reprocessed some of the old issues and looked ahead to his future.

During the first year after discharge Ken would call friends and staff at the Lodge every couple of months. His contacts then decreased in frequency, but Martha would write about his progress at least once a year. Recently the Summers stopped by en route from a family vacation They were reminiscing about how different this vacation had been from the one years before to Disneyland. During the visit, Martha commented that the two scariest days of her life were the day they had left Ken at the Lodge and the day they came to pick Ken up when he was discharged.

At this point, Ken chimed in with, "Well, do you want to know about the two scariest days in my life? They both were last year. The first was the day I tried out for the varsity swim team. I wasn't sure that I could make it, but I did. That was the same day that I flunked the history quiz and I was really scared that you wouldn't let me be on the swim team because of that. The second time was when I asked Jenny to the Prom. Now, that's really scary—the first time you ask a girl to a dance." ∎

Notes and Elaborations

pg. 286 Treatment centers vary just as much in discharge planning and staff involvement post-placement as in all other aspects of their programs. The option for parents to be involved in the milieu for several days and for our staff to provide post-placement services in the home community may be unique.

pg. 299 Children with organic dysfunction have more problems with changes in routine and transferring gains in one area of functioning to another. The transfer of both attachment and behavioral control is most easily accomplished in these cases by direct experience rather than just talking about expectations. Parental observation of the details of caregiving seems to be most important in these cases.

GLOSSARY

adolescent development conflicts;
The adolescent's primary psychological tasks center around psychological separation from the family and identity formation. Some youths' behavioral problems have their onset then and are a reflection of the struggles with these conflicts rather than a reflection of unresolved early life issues.

adolescent onset psychosis:
Psychoses are characterized by the severity of their symptoms, over which the patient has no control; there are usually associated disorders in thinking; most psychoses are now thought to be secondary to changes in the brain chemistry and are usually treated with medication. Schizophrenia, one type of psychosis may have its onset in adolescence.

Attention Deficit Disorder:
A clinical condition characterized by hyperactivity, distractibility, impulsivity, and shortened attention span. (See Note for Chapter 1 page 26 for further discussion.)

character disorder:
A personality disorder in which there is a long term history of severe problems in forming and sustaining interpersonal relationships; absent conscience development, usually as demonstrated by serious and repeated instances of breaking the law; an absence of the social emotions (empathy, sympathy, joy, pride, embarrassment, shame and guilt); and virtually no feelings of anxiety or internal discomfort about his current status.

claiming:
A way of increasing attachment that focuses on helping an individual feel that they are more like other group members as opposed to being excluded or isolated.

confidentiality:
Traditionally information shared with mental health therapists has been viewed as exclusive in nature and not to be shared with any others without the patient's (client's) express written permission.

core issues:
These represent the earlier life events or perceptions that seem to hold the central position in determining an individual's subsequent behaviors and ways of interacting.

eco-map:
A pictorial representation of a family's involvement with its environment. More completely described in Note on page 123-124 of Chapter 4.

empower:
To give permission to another to take responsibility for something or someone; in this text we are talking of emotional as opposed to legal power.

family systems theory:
Rather than viewing pathology as coming from individual vulnerabilities, family systems theory views each individual's symptoms as related to family interactions. Proponents facilitate change by focusing on, and changing, family interactions.

family therapy:
The focus of the therapeutic measures is on the needs and functioning of the family as a whole, as opposed to any one individual; the entire family may be seen together or family members may be seen in various combinations.

geno-gram:
A pictorial representation of a family's history. More completely explained in Note on page 123 of Chapter 4.

group therapy:
Non-related individuals are seen together for therapy. Meeting with others who have similar problems decreases the individual's sense of isolation and provides unique opportunities to overcome resistances to change as each individual observes the barriers to change that other members of the group erect.

"hooks":
Psychological jargon for an action that is difficult to resist; "hooks" are aimed at engaging another person into an interaction.

house staff:
Another term used for child care staff; those who live in the residence with the children being treated.

individual therapy:
The focus of the sessions is on the patient's thoughts, feelings, perceptions, and interactions. The patient may be seen one-on-one by a therapist. If others, such as parents or child care workers are involved the focus remains on this particular individual's issues, rather than on those of a group.

insight oriented therapy:
Therapy based on changing perceptions and emotional reactions to past life events thereby effecting changes in current functioning.

intra-psychic:
Inside the mind as opposed to externally observable.

line staff:
Those staff members who are in constant contact with residents, involving themselves in the process of daily activities; this term is synonymous with milieu staff and includes child care staff and teachers.

maladaptive:
Not helpful to adjustment to the environment.

milieu staff:
Another term for child care staff; those who provide their primary treatment within the milieu.

misperceptions:
Incorrect observations of reality; these can be based either on an organic basis such as occurs in a child who has difficulty perceiving the difference between a *b* and a *d,* or a child who has difficulty discriminating between similar sounds; misceptions can also be based on incorrect assumptions as to why things are happening—for example adults frequently misperceive a child's expression of his needs as a manipulative attempt to gain unhealthy attention.

organic problems:
Those difficulties, which may affect behaviors or emotions, arising from changes in body functioning. They may arise from either anatomical or chemical changes. These changes may occur on a genetic basis, due to pre-natal events, or secondary to subsequent life trauma or disease.

paradoxical therapy:
The patient is faced with comments or directions that are seemingly contradictory. For example, the long range goal for Kenny is to be able

310   to express anger in more appropriate ways; however, during holding therapy sessions he is not only given permission, but indeed is encouraged to express the anger in any way that he chooses while the adult holders insure that no one will be physically hurt.

pathogenesis:
The cause and development of disease.

perseveration:
Continuance of an activity after the stimulus that initiated it is no longer present. This is commonly seen in children with Attention Deficit Disorder; once they start an activity or way of doing something they have difficulty stopping even though it is non-productive to keep on.

pro-active:
Initiating an interaction as opposed to re-acting to what another individual is doing.

psychoanalytic:
Relating to the method of elicing from patients their perceptions of their past emotional experiences in order to discover the mechanism by which their current mental state has been produced.

psychodynamics:
The science of mental or psychological processes.

reciprocity:
The mutual giving and taking that occurs in many interactions, as opposed to power-based interactions.

re-education:
The process of providing new learning which replaces or modifies previously held perceptions.

treatment modalities or techniques:
Many different ways of understanding or explaining psychological problems are used in developing specific interventions to facilitate the change process.

"unattached" children:
These are children who never formed a close interpersonal relationship. Since healthy psychological growth is dependent upon attachment, these individuals are seriously impaired in their ability to relate to others and seem incapable of forming close interpersonal connections.

I N D E X

Index

academic skills: 48
  assessment of: 196, 203

administrative staff:
  as role models: 83, 84
  continuity of: 74, 80-81
  FHL: 74-75
  relationship to philosophy: 73-74
  relationship with board of trustees: 74, 84
  role of: 74, 76

admission:
  criteria for: 95
  day of: 110-121
  family's role in decision making: 98-99
  FHL admission criteria: 96
  procedures: 107, 116
  reaction to: see also grief process 166
  staff and resident preparation for a new admission: 119

adoption, as discharge plan: 239-40

alliance building:
  with child: 69, 92, 100, 102, 105, 114, 116, 186, 205, 211, 246, 247
      254, 267, 270, 285
  with family: see family, alliance with

arts and crafts: 68, 135

assessment: see also family, assessment of
    academic: 109, 186, 196, 203
    via extended home visit: 101-02, 105
    via psychological testing: 47, 246, 273
    via therapeutic encounters: 37, 261, 265

attachment(s):
    barriers to: 53-56, 257
    causes of disturbances in: 55, 99
    characteristics of: 56, 144
    definition: 56
    developing: 57, 116, 120, 143, 146, 151, 153, 164, 225, 228, 235, 237, 240, 248, 249, 268
    environment supportive of: 147-48
    long range effects of: 53-57
    model of treatment: 56, 143, 150
    problems in: 56, 57, 77, 98, 122, 152, 155-56
    theory: 53, 55, 146
    transfer of: 164, 169, 226, 240, 287-88, 299

Attachment Holding Therapy: 247, 249, 252-53, 269, 270, 274, 275-77

Attention Deficit Disorder: 26, 32

autonomy vs. dependency balance: 56, 58, 98-99, 292-93

bedtimes: 162, 180, 283

behavioral control: see also discipline and control and supportive
    control: 58, 59, 102, 103, 105, 113, 130, 131, 149-61, 174
    relationship to philosophy: 59, 60, 149, 172, 285
    self-control: 55, 151, 152, 153, 169, 287, 288
    transfer to parents: 164, 237-38, 240-41, 255, 261, 265, 284, 287

birthday celebrations: see rituals

Board of Directors: 12
    relationship with administrative staff: 73, 84
    role of: 84

child care staff:
    as role models for residents: 78, 154
    hiring and training of: 76-79
    role of: 59, 72, 75-76, 80, 120, 143, 144, 277
    shifts: 69, 81-82
    turnover: 80-81

claiming, as part of development of attachments: 148, 153, 240

community activities, involvement in: 189

confidentiality: 86, 145, 246, 266-67

conflict resolution: 59, 60, 213, 231, 237-38, 260

consultants: see therapist, as consultant

crisis:
    as a way to facilitate attachment: 237
    management: 78

custodial care: 35, 181

day treatment programs: 40

dependency vs. autonomy balance: 56, 58, 98-99, 292-93

Director: see Executive Director

discharge planning: 281-304
    child's participation in: 141, 290-91
    commitment to the future: 255, 282, 298-99, 301-02
    criteria for successful discharge: 261, 274-75, 286-91
    family's participation in: 224, 236, 238, 281
    relationship to philosophy: 285-86
    see also premature discharges

discipline and control: 156, 157
    see also behavioral control and supportive control

eco-map: 104, 123, 227-28

education: see school

emotions, emotional:
    child care staff as models for appropriate expression of: 78
    emotional bonds: 56
    emotional development: 55
    expression and management of: 54, 59, 60, 78, 115, 118, 121,
        136, 137, 138, 147, 152, 154, 186, 201, 215, 217, 218, 229, 247,
        251, 265, 267, 282-3, 297
    nurture: 57, 78

empowerment: 61, 115, 119, 224, 225, 226, 228, 240, 282
    of child care staff: 144-45, 222, 260, 262, 264, 267, 288

environmental manipulation to control behaviors: 159-60

Executive Director:
    as a model for staff relationships: 75
    relationship with Board of Trustees: 73, 84
    role of: 74-75, 82, 98

expectations: 121, 151, 153, 156, 163, 166, 169-70
    of self: 255

314   **family:**

alliance with (partner in treatment): 52, 60, 61, 93, 94, 97, 99, 104, 106, 109, 116, 222-24, 225, 226, 227, 228, 231, 285
assessment: 108-09, 227, 228, 233, 235
dynamics: 61, 103, 106, 108, 111, 118, 231-32, 261, 283, 285
extended: 100, 109, 227
importance of: 55, 94, 97, 99, 222, 225, 228, 233, 237, 239, 242-43, 249, 252-53
system: 227, 231, 298
therapy: 214, 217, 222, 228, 233-34, 235, 246, 250, 301-02
visits: 70, 116, 213, 219, 232, 235, 237, 253
work with: 60, 97, 119, 134, 187, 217, 218, 229, 235

funding: 31, 35, 38, 39, 40, 48, 69, 73, 207, 295

geno-gram: 102, 123, 227

gratification, importance of unconditional: 78, 142, 146, 148, 271, 274

grief process: 31, 42, 118, 119-20, 132, 228, 235, 238, 239, 240, 264, 282, 297-98

group homes: 36, 38, 39

group therapy: 121, 129, 271-73, 274

health insurance: see funding

holding:

as a disciplinary technique: 130, 131, 135, 160
as a therapeutic technique: see Attachment Holding Therapy

holiday celebrations: (see also rituals) 130, 131, 132, 136, 139

individual therapy: 72, 239, 247

as a way to increase skills: 133
child care staff involvement in: 140, 251, 255, 260, 269-70
family involvement in: 134, 269, 270
"homework" in: 254
identifying defenses: 247, 252
objectives: 259, 262, 264-66
readiness for: 262-64

isolation: see time-out

Lifebooks as a therapeutic tool: 268, 278

limits:

behavioral: 149-50, 153
programmatic: 149, 150

logical consequences: 153, 160

loyalty issues: 119, 213, 226, 228 315

mealtimes: 161-62, 173

medication: 26, 105, 112, 258

milieu: 10, 58-9, 143
    definition of: 10
    entering on admission day: 113-16
    milieu therapy (therapeutic milieu): 10, 52, 53, 58-59, 141, 145,
       181
    overall goals of: 263
    parent involvement in: 217, 218, 298-99, 304
    philosophy and milieu: 49, 55, 142

nurture:
    emotional: 57, 78, 79

One-Minute Scolding: 158-59

peer relationships: 30, 105, 179, 253, 255, 283

permanency planning: 35, 117, 238

philosophy:
    characteristics of effective: 51, 62
    FHL philosophy: 53, 55, 56, 143
    importance of: 49, 50, 51, 77, 83
    relationship to behavioral control: 143, 149
    relationship to educational program: 190-208
    relationship to family work: 222-26
    relationship to post-discharge services: 285-89
    relationship to pre-placement contracts: 93
    relationship to staffing patterns and interrelationships: 88,
       144

placement:
    alternatives: 22, 28, 31, 35, 37, 38
    decisions: 28, 29, 38, 95, 99, 105-06, 109

post-placement services: 87, 107, 238-39, 255, 281, 282, 285

premature discharges: 291-96

pre-placement contracts: 67-73, 91-110
    extended home visit: 102-10, 123, 228
    involvement of sibs and other family members: 100
    relationship to philosophy: 93

privileges:
    restriction of: 160

Professional Practices Committee: 17, 84

professional staff:
    relationship with line staff: 85, 86
    role of: 85-86

psychiatric hospitals: 37

psychotherapy: see individual therapy, group therapy and family therapy

re-admission: 296-97

recreation: 54, 58

re-education (re-learning): 53-54, 57, 58, 141, 145, 197-98, 274

referral sources: 38, 101, 105, 107, 109
    relationship with: 86-87, 285, 300

re-framing: 158, 246

relationships:
    adult-child: 49-50, 54, 55, 57
    disrupted: 49-50, 55
    family: 61
    importance of in treatment: 54-57, 59-61
    peer: see peer relationships
    problems in: 49-50, 55
    skills related to: 59
    staff interrelationships: 57
    trusting: 49-50, 55

residence:
    physical description: 71

residential treatment centers: 36
    characteristics of: 9, 16, 141

rhythms, control of: 157, 175

rituals (see also traditions, routines, holiday celebrations): 162-63, 299-300

routines, importance of: 162

rules: 113, 144, 150-51, 163, 167, 169

safety, importance of: 143, 274

school:
    academic problems: 109, 187, 190, 198
    attendance: 69, 129, 130, 148, 167, 186, 191-93, 194, 211
    behavioral expectations in: 194, 200, 201
    behavior problems in—discipline: 186, 190, 194, 196, 198
    curriculum: 203

family work around educational problems: 187, 192, 205, 217,   317
    218, 233, 235
goals (see also treatment planning): 197, 198
individualization: 203-04
physical description of FHL school: 69
public school attendance: 138, 169, 187-89, 253, 254, 255,
    284-85
relationship to philosophy: 73, 190, 201-02
relationship with milieu: 196, 198, 211
reports: 205-06
schedule: 197, 204

self-care:
    physical: 54, 58
    psychological: 54, 58

self-control: see behavioral control

self-worth: 54, 156, 271-72

separation:
    effects of: 99, 140
    minimizing trauma of: 106, 116, 122
    separation interview: 114, 116-20, 228-29

sex education: 272-73, 274

siblings: 108, 119

sitting, as a disciplinary technique: 92, 113, 153, 160, 174

skill acquisition:
    child: 55, 58, 59, 60, 168, 177, 179, 197, 254, 289-90
    family: 233, 235

social skills (see also relationship skills): 59, 271

spontaneity, importance of: 161, 162

staff:
    child care: see child care staff
    staff interrelationships: 77, 79, 82-84, 85-87, 145, 196, 218, 253,
       254, 256, 260, 261, 262, 264, 265, 266, 273, 291
    staffing patterns as a reflection of philosophy: 73-76, 81-82
    teaching: see teachers

stages of the treatment process: 58, 164-65
    early treatment: 165-66, 226-27, 259
    middle phase: 167, 233-38, 260
    final phase: 168-69, 261

structure: see also routines
    islands of: 161, 178

supportive control:
> principles (and techniques of) associated with: 151-56, 157-61, 218, 219, 235

teachers:
> relationships with other staff: 82, 196, 200, 211
> role of: 82, 198, 202

therapeutic fostercare: 35, 39

therapeutic techniques: 31, 33, 34, 267-68

therapists:
> as consultants: 263
> role of: 76, 82, 256-58, 259, 264, 267, 273

therapy: see family therapy, group therapy and individual therapy

time out: 47, 113, 152

traditions (see also rituals and holiday celebrations): 162-63

treatment planning: 106, 117, 141, 145, 197, 198, 236, 258, 286, 290, 291

visits: see family, visits

About the Authors

Forest Heights Lodge is a residential treatment facility in Evergreen, Colorado, considered to be among the most innovative and successful in the country. Because of its successes and considerable reputation, the Lodge has been called upon to supply consultation and training services throughout the world. In order to try to fill the gap in information about residential treatment and to explain how their unique program is constructed, over the course of several years the full staff of the Lodge participated in the writing of *RESIDENTIAL TREATMENT: A TAPESTRY OF MANY THERAPIES*, each contributing from the unique perspective of his or her own role in the milieu.

The manuscript was then edited by Vera Fahlberg, M.D., who wrote and interwove "Kenny's Case" to exemplify the Forest Heights Lodge approach in action. Dr. Fahlberg is a pediatrician and psychotherapist who has worked with disturbed children and their families since 1964. For thirteen years she served as Medical Director of Forest Heights Lodge. Although she relocated to the Seattle area in 1987, she continues to do training and consultation for Forest Heights.

Since 1974, much of Vera's work has been focused on attachment and separation problems with special emphasis on children in out-of-home placements. She has completed over 400 evaluations of children in placement with various public and private agencies as well as seeing numerous children in out-patient therapy and serving as an expert witness in child welfare related cases. Since 1976 she has conducted workshops in over 40 states as well as in Canada, England, Scotland, Ireland, Sweden, Greece, Israel, and Australia.

Publications include a series of four workbooks, *Fitting the Pieces Together*, composed of "Attachment and Separation;" "Helping Children When They Must Move;" "Child Development;" and "Common Behavior Problems of the Child in Placement." She has contributed to a variety of child welfare related training curricula, including written materials, films, and videotapes.

LET US INTRODUCE OURSELVES . . .

Perspectives Press is a narrowly focused publishing company. The materials we produce or distribute all speak to issues related to infertility or to child welfare issues. Our purpose is to promote understanding of these issues and to educate and sensitize those personally experiencing these life situations, professionals who work in infertility adoption and fostercare, and the public at large. Perspectives Press titles are never duplicative. We seek out and publish materials that are currently unavailable through traditional sources. Our titles include . . .

Perspectives on a Grafted Tree

An Adoptor's Advocate

Understanding: A Guide to Impaired Fertility for Family and Friends

Our Baby: A Birth and Adoption Story

The Mulberry Bird: Story of an Adoption

The Miracle Seekers: An Anthology of Infertility

Real For Sure Sister

Filling in the Blanks: A Guided Look at Growing Up Adopted

Sweet Grapes: How to Stop Being Infertile and Start Living Again

Where the Sun Kisses the Sea

Our authors have special credentials: they are people whose personal and professional lives provide an interwoven pattern for what they write. If **you** are writing about these issues, we invite you to contact us with a query letter and stamped, self addressed envelope so that we can send you our writers guidelines and help you determine whether your materials might fit into our publishing plans.

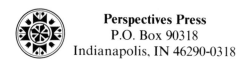

Perspectives Press
P.O. Box 90318
Indianapolis, IN 46290-0318